Why SQL? Why the Instant Guide?

SQL is the one standard language with which you can query databases. Despite the fact that most database tools offer many varying menu and wizard functions with which to query the database, they all share one common interface: the underlying SQL engine. If you talk directly to the engine, you can utilise the real power of the database.

There isn't a catch either. SQL isn't low level machine code that you need a degree in electronics to understand; it relies on simple English-like syntax, which is simple to learn and very powerful once you've mastered it. As with all of the Instant guides, this is for you if you don't want to be treated like an idiot. This book will take you step-by-step through creating a database, inserting data into a database and making complex queries of the database in SQL. By the end of the book you'll have the confidence to create and run your own independent databases in SQL.

What is Wrox Press?

Wrox Press is a computer book publisher which promotes a brand new concept - clear, jargon-free programming and database titles that fulfill your real demands. We publish for everyone, from the novice through to the experienced programmer. To ensure our books meet your needs, we carry out continuous research on all our titles. Through our dialog with you we can craft the book you really need.

We welcome suggestions and take all of them to heart - your input is paramount in creating the next great Wrox title. Use the reply card inside this book or mail us at:

feedback@wrox.demon.co.uk
or
Compuserve 100063, 2152

Wrox Press Ltd.	**Tel:** (312) 465 3559
2710 W. Touhy	**Fax:** (312) 465 4063
Chicago	
IL 60645	
USA	

Instant SQL Programming

Joe Celko

Wrox Press Ltd.®

Instant SQL
Programming

© 1995 Joe Celko

Published by Wrox Press Ltd. Unit 16, 20 James Road, Tyseley, Birmingham, B11 2BA
Printed in the USA
Library of Congress Catalog no. 95-60736

ISBN 1-874416-50-8

Trademark Acknowledgements

Wrox has endeavored to provide trademark information about all the companies and products mentioned in this book by the appropriate use of capitals. However, Wrox cannot guarantee the accuracy of this information.

Oracle is a trademark of Oracle Corporation, Sybase is a trademark of Sybase Corporation, Microsoft Access is a registered trademark of Microsoft Corporation and Watcom SQL is a trademark of Watcom International Corporation.

Credits

Author
Joe Celko

Technical Editor
Chris Ullman

Series Editors
Luke Dempsey
Adrian M. Sill

Technical Reviewers
Steven Berkovich
Sharon Dooley
Mark Gokman
John F Rogers

Managing Editor
John Franklin

Operations Manager
Gina Mance

Production Manager
Deb Somers

Design\Layout
Eddie Fisher
Greg Powell
Lee Kelly
Neil Gallagher
Graham Butler

Proof Readers
Melanie Orgee
Pam Brand
Jenny Nuttall
Emma Duncombe

Cover Design
Third Wave

For more information on Third Wave, contact Ross Alderson on 44-121 236 6616
Cover photo supplied by The Image Bank

About the Author

Mr. Celko has been a member of the ANSI X3H2 Database Standards Committee since 1987. He has had eight regular monthly or biweekly columns in the past ten years in the computer trade and academic press. His current columns are: *"SQL Explorer"* in *DBMS (M&T Publishing)*, *"Celko on Software"* in *COMPUTING (VNB Publications, UK)* and *"SQL Puzzle"* in *BOXES & ARROWS (Frank Sweet Publishing)*.

Most recently, he also wrote: *"Celko on SQL"* in *DATABASE PROGRAMMING & DESIGN (Miller-Freeman)*; *"DBMS/Report"* in *SYSTEMS INTEGRATION (Cahner-Ziff)*; *"Data Desk"* in *TECH SPECIALIST (R&D)*, *"Data Points"* in *PC TECHNIQUES (Coriolis Group)* and was editor for the puzzles & problems section of *ABACUS (Springer-Verlag)*.

He is a regular speaker and SQL instructor for Digital Consulting Inc., Norm DiNardi Enterprises, Boston University Corporate Education Center and Miller-Freeman Seminars.

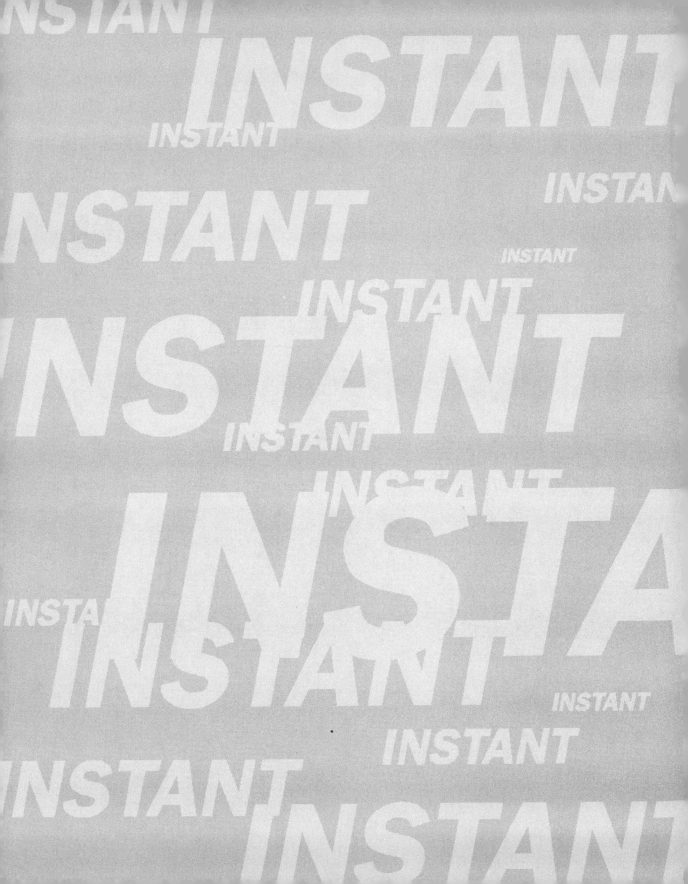

INSTANT

Summary of Contents

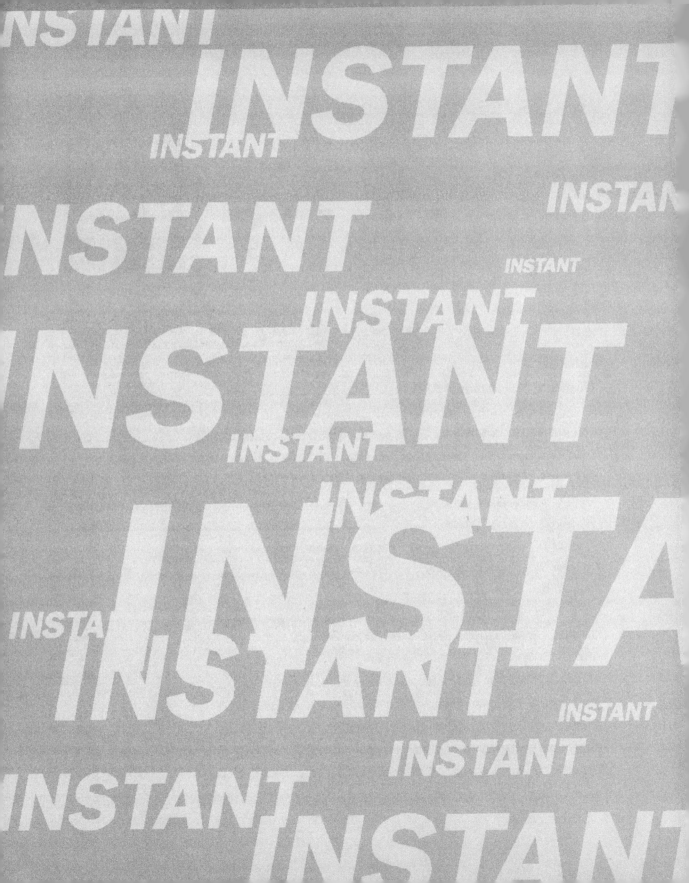

INSTANT

SQL

Table of Contents

Table of Contents

Table of Contents

Table of Contents

Table of Contents

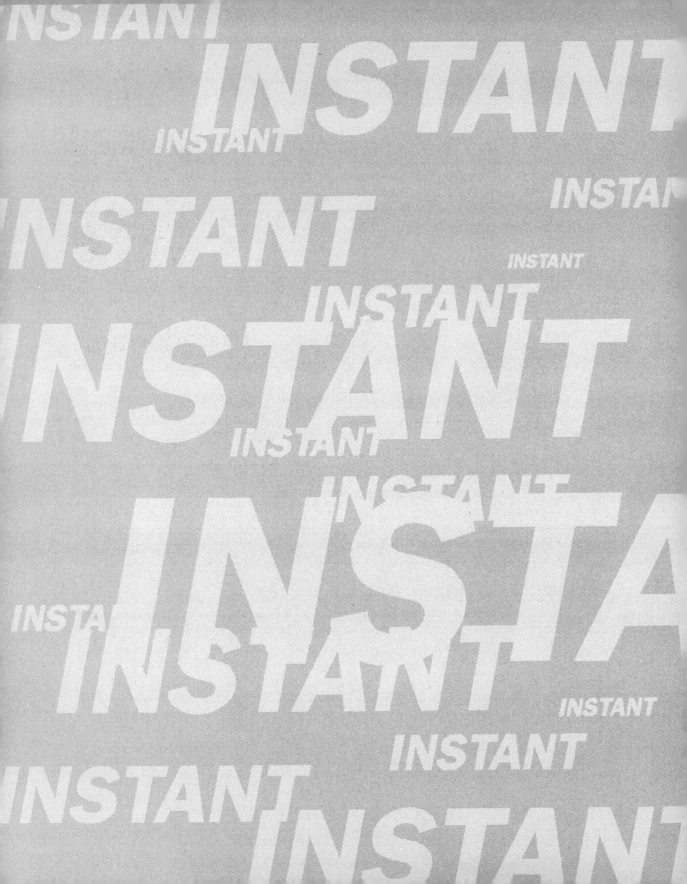

Instant

Introduction

Welcome to the latest Instant Guide from Wrox Press, Instant SQL. This book has been designed to give you, as database developer and end-user, an edge when designing and querying databases using the powerful features that SQL has to offer. What is unusual about this book is that Watcom have provided an actual SQL engine (included on the disk at the back of the book) with which to query the database.

Please return the reply card at the back of the book and tell us what you think. We are always interested in what you have to say and are more than willing to answer your questions on a variety of subjects. We are also open to constructive criticism (although we do prefer unadulterated adoration!)

What Can SQL Do for Me?

Why not just point and click? Why not just use the Query window and tools that have been provided? Many people are reluctant to use SQL without the safety net of popular front-end tools to shield them from its low level intricacies. However, in reality there are many more nastier languages masquerading under the user-friendly misnomer. There are several important points worth considering if you're thinking of learning SQL:

 SQL is the one industry standard language for querying databases.

 You can't use all of the features of your database unless you get down to conversing directly in the SQL language.

 The tools you're provided with often don't exploit the full functionality of the underlying language.

 From a client-server viewpoint you can run a SQL query in any application host language and get *exactly* the same results.

Still not convinced? Well, why should you have to learn another application from scratch each time the whims of your workplace require you to pick up another brand new cutting-edge database product, when you can learn one language and master them all?

Who Should Use This Book?

This book is aimed at programmers and developers who want to add SQL to their collection of language skills. The goal is not to make you an expert, but to give you the skills required to read SQL and to write programs of your own. We aim to take you up to a competent programming level at a pretty fast pace. While there's plenty of theory involved in designing databases, the idea is to give you only a quick outline of the theory needed, so that you can get stuck into the example code from the database at each stage along the way. With this method you don't have to wade through reams of theory before you get to the juicy and practical part.

How To Use This Book

This book will be a little unusual for an introductory language book in that we are writing in the first person, as if we were coaching you through your first attempt at writing an SQL database. Instead of just dragging you through a series of examples with notes attached to them, we want to give you the flavor and rationale of the SQL language followed by a running example as we introduce each feature.

What You Should Know

You should have at the very least some basic programming knowledge. We don't assume too much and we take you through the concepts of SQL and how it differs from the concepts of traditional procedural-based programming languages. You won't find explanations of the more fundamental aspects of programming in this book - we trust that you'll probably know why you want to program and you just want the necessary information quickly.

You need access to a SQL Server or database allowing you to directly type in SQL code and interactively return results. You should also have a working knowledge of the database application you intend to program on as well. We're giving independent variations of the code used in the Example Database for Sybase System 10, Oracle 7.1 and Microsoft Access in Appendix A, but you'll need to know how to access the SQL query window in each of these applications in order to do this.

Conventions Used

To enable you to find your way around this book easily, we have used various different styles to highlight contrasting references. Each style has been selected to enable the reader to successfully understand the content as efficiently as possible.

Program Code

All programs in the book are highlighted with a gray background so you can easily find them. Keywords appear in upper-case, whilst variables provided by the user or the author are stored in lower-case. Here is a sample selection of code:

```
SELECT orderid, custid
  FROM Orders AS O1
 WHERE 2 < (SELECT qty
             FROM OrderItems AS I1
             WHERE O1.orderid = I1.orderid
             AND I1.partid = 1007);
```

In some instances, we define parts of SQL syntax. In this case we will use the following style, where entries in angle brackets, <>, are to be replaced by the relevant entity:

```
CREATE TABLE <table name> (<table element list>);

<table element list> ::=
  <table element> | <table element>, <table element list>

<table element> ::=
  <column definition> | <table constraint definition>
```

Fonts and Styles

Throughout Instant SQL we will consistently be using the following styles and fonts for a variety of textual distinctions:

 When code or a command is mentioned in the middle of a sentence, we write it in **this_style**, so as to emphasize its origin.

 Important words and concepts are introduced in **this style**. These are significant words that we're meeting for the first time. Subsequently they will appear as normal text.

 File names are all in **THIS_STYLE**. All file names appear like this in the text, even when they're conventionally written in lower-case within a program.

Actual keys that you press will be displayed in *this style*, for example 'press the *Return* key'.

 Text that appears on your screen such as field names, menu items or headings appear in this style.

> **When an important piece of information needs to be** *really* **emphasized, we will place it in a box like this.**

Watcom SQL engine

Included with this book are two disks containing the runtime version of Watcom SQL 4.0. This is a restricted and limited edition of the Watcom SQL retail product. It also includes their interactive SQL tool, ISQLW.

Product Details

The runtime version of the database engine doesn't allow **ALTER**, **CALL**, **COMMENT**, **CREATE**, **DROP**, user-defined trigger commands or stored procedures to be performed. **GRANT** and **REVOKE** allow you to add new users and change passwords, but the runtime database engine prevents a user from changing the permissions on the tables. In addition, to simplify database administration, the runtime system has an integrated transaction log.

> **The Watcom SQL Server product has networking features which are beyond the scope of the standalone version of Watcom SQL. As a result, features such as DBWATCH, DBCLIENW and DBSERVEW are only available on the Watcom SQL Server product line and aren't included in Watcom SQL or Watcom SQL runtime.**

Requirements

Before you install the Watcom SQL runtime product, your system must adhere to the following requirements:

- A minimum of 2.5 Mbytes of hard-disk space.
- A minimum of a 386-based PC with 4Mb of RAM.
- Windows 3.1 or later, Windows NT or Windows 95.

Installation Instructions

The installation of the software is very simple: it's contained within a self-extracting archive. Firstly, we must insert Disk 1 and then we can install the software in any one of three ways:

- You can select the Run option from the File menu from the Program manager window and type in:

  `A:\ SETUP.EXE`

- You can go to the File Manager, select the `A:` drive, and then double click on `SETUP.EXE`.

- You can go to the Command Prompt DOS window and make sure that the `A:` drive is selected. Now type in `SETUP.EXE`.

This installation program will ask you to create a new directory to place all the files in and ask you for confirmation that you wish to copy the files into the new directory. You should follow the on-screen instructions from now on, and select the options appropriate for your own system. Once the installation has been completed, you will find a new Watcom SQL 4.0 program group has been created. To run the engine click on the ISQL icon. If you have any queries click on the comprehensive Watcom SQL manual icon.

Screen Display

On starting the Watcom SQL engine, you should be greeted with this startup screen:

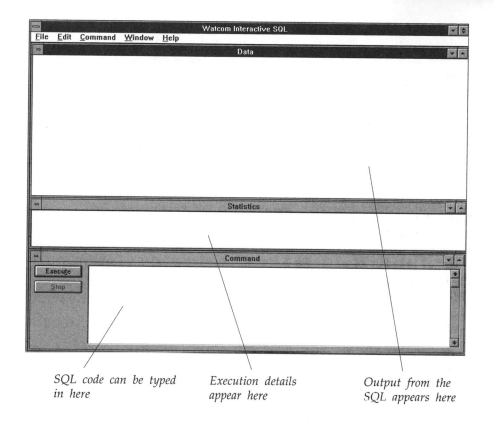

SQL code can be typed in here   Execution details appear here   Output from the SQL appears here

There are three windows visible in the Interactive tool. In the screenshots provided throughout the book you will find the following format:

- The results or output to the SQL queries will be displayed in the top Data window.

- The execution details, which don't concern us, appear in the middle Statistics window.

- The code to be typed in appears in the bottom Command window.

Whenever you encounter a screenshot, you only need to type in the code that appears in the Command window. You can press *Return* at the end of each line as this doesn't send the message to the SQL engine - it just moves you down a line. When you wish the statement to be executed, simply click on the Execute button, next to the Command window. The execution plan will appear in the Statistics window, and the output will then appear in the Data window. This should all take a matter of seconds.

Error Trapping

The code in this book has all been extensively tested on a Watcom SQL 4.0 engine, so if you encounter an error message while using the SQL engine provided, please thoroughly check that you've typed the code in correctly. A punctuation mark in the wrong place can cause an error in SQL. If you type in the code given throughout the book, you will gradually add to and update the example database as intended by the text into a full application. If you don't type in all of the examples, then you may encounter problems later when certain structures or features haven't been created.

> **For full details of how you can obtain the full Watcom SQL 4.0 retail version see the information at the back of the book.**

The runtime version of Watcom SQL 4.0 accompanying this book doesn't support the **CREATE**, **ALTER**, **DROP**, **CALL** or **COMMENT** commands. This means that you can't type in the text provided in chapters two to four. The code necessary for these chapters already exists within the example database. You can only begin to use the code in the book from Chapter 5 onwards. Happy typing!

Tell Us What You Think

One last thing. We've tried to make the book enjoyable and accurate. The programming community is what we're here to serve, so if you have any queries or suggestions, or comments about this book, let us know, we will be delighted to hear from you.

You can help us ensure that our future books are even better by simply returning the reply card at the back of the book or by contacting us direct at Wrox. For a quick response, you can also use the following e-mail addresses:

feedback@wrox.demon.co.uk
Compuserve: 100062,2152

Chapter

The Nature of SQL

This chapter will give you a brief overview of SQL and how it compares to other programming languages. We'll look at some of the basic concepts and elements of SQL databases and see how SQL handles data within them. We'll also take a look at the core elements of SQL manipulation and introduce basic terms you'll encounter throughout SQL usage.

In this chapter we will look at:

- Procedural versus declarative languages
- How SQL organizes data
- The SQL sub-languages
- An introduction to syntax

Procedural Versus Declarative Languages

Perhaps the main problem experienced programmers have with SQL is that they have to 'unlearn' their other languages. What SQL asks you to do is to change the ways you think about a programming problem.

Many programmers use **procedural** languages such as C, FORTRAN, BASIC, COBOL, Pascal, PL/1 and so on. Procedural languages are often referred to as third generation languages, or 3GLs for short. (Third generation languages can be thought of as the languages that provide the bridge between assembly language and structured English). They're characterized by statements which tell the computer exactly what to do, in a structured, step-by-step way (even when these steps are repeated in loops).

SQL, on the other hand, is a **declarative** language. Declarative means that you tell the computer what it is you want to achieve, and then let the machine decide on how to effect the correct result. You never have to see the details - all you see are the results.

SQL - the Shopper's Language

By way of analogy, imagine that you go to a supermarket with a shopping list and a detailed set of directions showing you which aisles and shelves contain the merchandise you require. You execute the procedure - the detailed set of shopping directions - and you get your order filled. This is a procedural approach to shopping. In terms of programming, the data files are the shelves, the data is the merchandise and your program is the instructions.

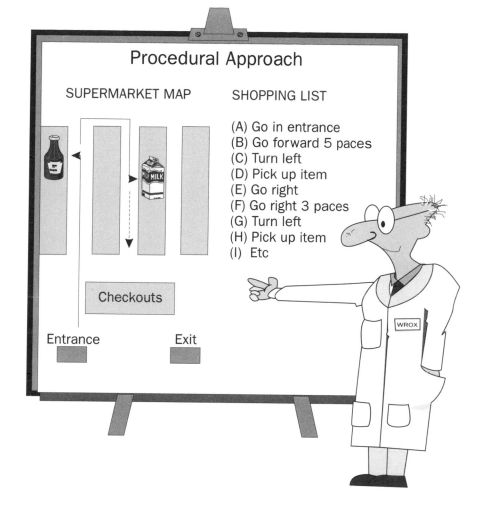

Now imagine that you go to a supply house and simply hand your shopping list over to the clerk at the order counter. While you wait, he goes to the warehouse and pulls your order. This is a declarative approach to shopping. The shopping list is declarative - 'this is what I want!' - and the clerk is your language processor who figures out how to do it, based on the information he has about the warehouse, such as a map of the current locations, the quantity on hand, and whatever else he needs to know to pull your order.

There are advantages and disadvantages to both approaches. Procedural languages usually execute much faster, but they don't easily adapt to changes in the data. For example, if you were to change the fields in a file, then all of the **READ** and **WRITE** statements in the program would have to be changed so that they matched, even if those fields were not used by the program. You might even have to re-write the entire program from scratch!

Declarative language programs don't change unless there are serious modifications to the data organization, since they reference things by names or descriptions, not by physical orderings.

To carry the store analogy further, if the management at the supermarket re-arranges the shelves, then your detailed set of shopping directions is useless. Or worse, you could follow it and bring home a year's supply of boiled buzzard eggs! However, dealing with pure commodity requests, the supply house clerk will always be aware of the new shelving arrangement, and won't get fazed when he gets your list from the order clerk.

SQL Basics

SQL is now so dominant because it has become the standard query language across the board of database systems. It acts as a bridge between the user, the database management system, the data tables and the transactions involving all three. It allows you to formulate queries in English-like syntax in order to specify exactly what is wanted from the database. The queries that you make are created in short four or five line statements, and the answers are quickly returned.

SQL also allows the system to be administrated and managed by a database administrator using the same format. There are simple commands for controlling security, setting authorizations and ids. It allows different views of the database for different levels of user, so that both the novice and the expert can utilize the same database in different ways.

For programmers, SQL can be embedded into any source code, from C to Pascal. It also allows the creation of total databases and can be used to manage the consistency of the information contained within those databases.

Vendors and the Relational Model

SQL revolves around the relational database model. This is what all the current vendor products on the market are based upon. Sybase, Oracle, SQL6, DB2 and others use the relational model for storing data. They also use SQL as the main tool for communicating with the database management system and for querying the database.

One of the original envisaged advantages of SQL was to be the portability of the language between different systems. Each vendor, however, likes their own product to be that little bit different - naturally enough, so that it stands out in the market place. Hence, each has additional features that won't be found in the other 'flavors' of the language.

> **This vendor-specificity is what makes producing a book on general SQL so difficult. Your own version of SQL is going to be fussy with some of the examples you'll be using in this book, so you're going to need your manual close at hand. Don't worry, as there are plenty of tips and comments on why a statement might not work when you first type it in!**

To talk politics for a moment, a lot of the blame for the lack of portability is laid at the door of the standards. The ANSI SQL-89 standards in particular, failed to address issues such as error codes, and failed to define popular data types like **MONEY**. This criticism isn't totally fair, as the SQL-92 standard closed many of the pre-existing loopholes. Some of the problems couldn't be dealt with by the standards as they were matters for the individual implementation. It might also be said that quite a few of the concepts specified in the SQL-92 standard have yet to be implemented in any SQL product.

This book deals heavily with the SQL-92 standard. All versions of SQL are moving towards the standard, however gradually. It's, therefore, desirable that you should learn the 'correct' way of doing things where possible. The standards are there not only to provide a uniform way of doing things, but also a method that will help prevent logical mistakes from occurring within your database. Hence, the version of SQL on the accompanying disk is the runtime version of Watcom SQL 4.0. This version of SQL, out of all vendor versions, is the most compliant with the SQL-92 standard. However, if you do choose to use your own preferred version of SQL, we won't ignore you!

Most vendor products boast 'compatibility' with the ANSI SQL-92 standards and this is what makes it possible to cover SQL as a 'general' language concept. The concepts are the same for every product, and these are what you'll need to learn to program in SQL.

Sets Versus Sequences

SQL is a set-oriented language, while many programmers are used to file-oriented languages. The term **set** is the same one you ran into in elementary school math - an unordered collection of items, all of the same type and structure.

These sets are called **tables** in SQL, and their elements are called **rows**. Rows are made up of **columns**. You can carry the comparison one stage further as SQL allows the same mathematical operations on **tables**, as you can perform on sets (union and intersect). In fairness, an SQL table isn't quite a true set, since duplicate rows *are* allowed. This is a mathematical structure called a **multi-set** or **bag** (the latter term fits our shopping analogy very nicely).

> **There is a rough correspondence between a file and a table, between a row and a record, and between a column and a field. But they are not alike! This is the first thing to be careful to *unlearn*.**

A file is a sequence of records which a procedural program navigates. The program has to open the file, fetch one record at a time, do its work on each record, and finally close the file (usually when the last record is read). The navigation is done in terms of the next record, the prior record, a record position within the file and so on. The exact methods vary from language to language, but you still have a sequence of records and a very physical model of how they are stored.

A Very Physical 'Model' Of File Storage

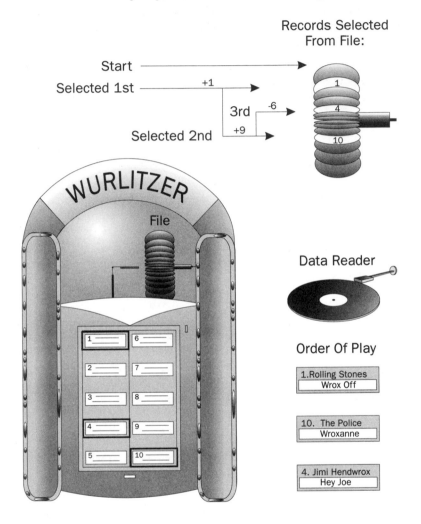

SQL connects the user to the whole database (which is made up of many tables) all at once. Some SQL products, such as Sybase, use a single file for the database and manage databases within that file. Some SQL products, such as Quadbase, use one file for each table. Other products, such as DB2, put multiple tables in a single disk storage allocation unit. Yet others keep their data in exotic data structures, such as the compressed bit vectors used by Nucleus International, which have no direct relation to the original data. No two SQL vendors have products with the same management approach.

> In short, tables are more conceptual and less physical than
> files. Files tend to be managed by the operating system while
> tables are managed by the SQL database system.

The SQL programmer never worries about opening or closing particular
tables. He or she has a subset of tables to which they are allowed access and
privileges. All the *allowed* tables are available *all at once* when they connect to
the database.

Going back to the issue of duplicates for a minute, a file treats duplicate
records as different from each other because they are in different locations
within the sequence of the file. SQL will maintain duplicate rows, but can't
easily tell one from the other.

This theme of *all at once* carries throughout SQL because of the underlying
set model. A query returns a whole result set all at once, rather than part
of the answer a little at a time. All the appropriate rows of a table are
updated, inserted or deleted, or none of the rows are - the whole set
involved in the transaction works, otherwise the whole transaction fails. And
those updates, insertions and deletions occur all at once in the table, not
one record at a time. We will discuss this in more detail later in the book.

Tables and Files

There is a key interdependence between files and tables of which you need
to be aware. While a *file* has a known ordering (that is, there is a first
record, a following record, a prior record, and a last record), a *table* has no
ordering. Therefore, navigation makes no sense at all - things are either *in
the bag*, or they're not! SQL 'knows' the positioning of records via the
flagging of data in relation to its column.

The columns of a table are like the fields in a record, except that they are
referenced by name only, never by their relative position. If you re-arrange
the columns in a table, the SQL statements are not affected. If you re-arrange
the fields in a file, all the procedural programs must be changed.

You can write almost any data you like into an open file from a procedural
program in C, FORTRAN, BASIC and so on (COBOL, Pascal and PL/1 can
require files to contain only certain record types). In SQL, you can only
insert, update and delete rows that have the same structure as the rest of
the rows in the table.

An Example of Structure Considerations

Let's have a look at an example database to clarify some ideas about their required structure:

JOB ID	JOB TITLE	JOB DESCRIPTION
1001	Fat Cat	Sit around all day
1002	Manager	Issue orders
1003	Train Spotter	Stand around all day

The following row has the correct structure, and could be inserted into the table:

1004	Guard	Wave flags,and so on

The following row, however, would be rejected as the structure differs from the original table structure. SQL would reject putting characters into a numeric column, and it would also reject putting four columns into a table of three columns. If there were other constraints specified by you, which the data in the row did not match, then the row would also be rejected:

Guard	1004	$5000	Wave flags,and so on

In short, a table is a set of rows of one particular type.

Rows

SQL can have a table with zero rows, while procedural languages, or rather programmers of procedural languages, tend to have trouble with empty files.

> To get around the problem of empty files in procedural languages, you should always make sure your program will run if the first thing it hits is the end of the file.

The empty table in SQL will still only accept properly constructed rows and can be used anywhere that a table with rows can be used. This is like the empty set, but it's empty of a particular kind of row:

Heading 1	Heading 2	Heading 3
X	1	100
Y	2	200
Z	3	300

Record/Row 1
Record/Row 2
Record/Row 3

Heading 1	Heading 2	Heading 3

Empty table has same structure as filled table.

The order of the fields in a record must match the order of the values in the **READ** and **WRITE** statements of the procedural language. In SQL, there's a default ordering of columns within a row, but columns are referenced by name and not by position. The ordering that occurs in a table can be used as a default, but ordering isn't critical since you can always use explicit column names.

> In short, a row is a set of columns.

Columns

The columns that make up a row in a table are always scalar, or atomic data types. That is, they are complete in themselves and can't be broken down into smaller parts.

> Put in terms of programming, they're not Pascal RECORD data types, C structures, PL/1 structures, COBOL records, any kind of pointer, any kind of array (C, Pascal, FORTRAN, P1) or a repeating group (COBOL occurs).

Columns can have constraints placed on them when the table is created. These constraints are not part of any program, but are part of the database itself. Conversely, files would have to depend on procedural code in application programs to enforce any such rules.

> In short, a column is a scalar or atomic value, which has a data type and possibly some constraints on it.

The Spreadsheet Analogy

Because spreadsheets present data in rows and columns, and many SQL products have tools that display data in a spreadsheet-like format, there is a tendency for people who are used to spreadsheets to think that tables are like the tool they already know.

A table is a set of rows and those rows are made up of columns. A spreadsheet is a *grid* of rows and columns which all behave in a similar way. That is, you can interchange rows and columns in a spreadsheet without changing anything important. The rules and results for doing math on rows are the same as for columns in a spreadsheet. Rows and columns behave differently in SQL. Operations on rows are easy within SQL, but operations on columns are more difficult, as you'll see in later chapters.

The cells of a spreadsheet can hold procedures as well as data. You usually only see displayed the results of the procedures. A column in a table can hold only data.

The SQL Sub-languages

We've looked at how SQL handles data and now we'll give you a brief overview of the language itself. SQL can be split into three sub-languages, each with a different function. A database is usually, by its very nature, a shared resource, and the three sub-languages are based on how the work is split among the people who work with shared data.

Data Definition Language - DDL

The Data Definition Language is used to create, drop and alter objects in a database. The DDL doesn't put any data into the database, do searches or take out any data. It's used strictly to build a framework in which programmers and end users can place their data.

As an analogy, think of a contractor builder who builds a house, but doesn't furnish it. The person who handles this part of the operation is the Database Administrator (DBA) and he/she has access to certain commands which is denied to the ordinary programmers. He/she probably works with a database designer, who would be like the architect of the aforementioned house. The database designer comes in, sets up the database, and leaves the DBA to handle the day-to-day maintenance. The DBA can arrange the furnishing of each room, but the arrangement of furniture is open to alteration, by an interior designer armed with the DDL.

Programmers and users of the database are usually restricted in their access to these design commands. You don't want someone changing the structure of the database while other people are using it - it would be like living in a house where someone could remove your bedroom floor without telling you!

> The first section of this book will deal in some detail with creating a database. you'll find that many introductory SQL books gloss over the DDL, launching straight into the SELECT statement syntax. Whilst this is a good way to get quickly into using SQL, it misses out a very important part of the language. This book is not aimed just at the programmer who wants to query existing data, but also at the administrator who has to set up a database. We're sure that programmers will find the following section useful too, as they often design or alter tables in real projects. Besides, having DBA skills makes you more promotable!

Data Manipulation Language - DML

The Data Manipulation Language (DML) can insert, delete, and update data as well as perform queries against the database. It can't be used to change the structure of the database.

The main basis for manipulating data is the querying structure, the **SELECT**... **FROM** clause. It works in a logical English manner. You specify what it is you want from the database, and from which area, and the query is returned to you in tabular form.

Let's have a look at a purely hypothetical case. Here's a jobs database, with a table for each type of job:

Railroad Jobs

Job Type	Wage
President	$1,000 per hour
Manager	$100 per hour
Driver	$20 per hour
Guard	$10 per hour
Train Spotter	$1 per hour

Tax Jobs

Job Type	Wage
Treasury Secretary	$1,000 per hour
Manager	$100 per hour
Tax Inspector	$20 per hour
Tax Collector	$10 per hour
Tax Evader	$-100 per hour

If you wanted to see the details of all the jobs working on the railroads that paid over $5 per hour, you could phrase the **SELECT** statement needed to get that output in English terminology. You'd roughly say "**SELECT** jobs paying over $5 an hour **FROM** the table of railroad job". You'd get a table looking like the following:

Results Table

Job Type	Wage
President	$1,000 per hour
Manager	$100 per hour
Driver	$20 per hour
Guard	$10 per hour

The power of SQL's DML structure is that you could format your original command to change the sequence in which the answer is displayed. You could compare the wages of the manager with the wages of managers in other industries using just a few simple statements.

SQL programmers can easily spend 90% of their SQL programming time doing queries. These days, insertions are usually handled by an input program which was built with a front-screen painter. Deletions are usually handled by a batch program or another program built with a screen painter. But it takes a programmer to design a clever query for a report or an *ad hoc* request! We will spend the bulk of this book talking about queries, but please don't think that this is all there is to SQL

Data Control Language - DCL

The Data Control Language (DCL) provides internal security to a database. This is more than just a simple password system to get you into the database. Each user is granted privileges (actions he or she can do, such as update, delete or query) against database objects such as tables. The user can also be given the power to grant privileges to other users, based on what he or she is allowed to access.

In some cases, it's the DBA who's in charge of security in a database, while in other cases it's a separate job function for a security officer. The DCL in SQL-89 was a weak language, and large companies usually add other security products to their database. SQL-92 is somewhat better, but at the cost of more complexity. No product has yet implemented all of this particular standard.

Real security buffs may want to have ways to absolutely deny certain people access to certain data, set up levels of security (public, confidential, secret, top secret), provide encryption or even set up false information.

> **Remember though, the more sophisticated the security mechanism, the more likely it is to impact on performance. It's always a good idea to keep it simple where you possibly can.**

We won't look at the Data Control Language in detail at this point because it is dealt with in Appendix C. There we offer some thoughts on how to set up different levels of authorization.

Transaction Control

A **transaction** in SQL is either completely finished or not done at all; there's no way to do only part of the work. This is the principle of working with sets again! The work can be **committed**, which means it's made a permanent part of the database, or it can be **rolled back**, which means the database is restored to the state it was in before the transaction began. Transaction control is the part of the system that makes sure that the database is in a valid state when a transaction is over - the stuff that needed updating is updated, the stuff that needed deleting is deleted, the housekeeping is all in place.

The part of transaction control that the SQL programmer needs to be aware of is **concurrency** control, or transaction **levels**. The programmer has to set these levels in his program, so it's the only part of transaction control that he sees. These levels determine how the database is shared among transactions - does one transaction get exclusive use of some objects, or can other transactions change them while the first transaction is still running?

Integrity

Integrity is where most people will start turning off. It's an obscure term which doesn't mean much, and when you see it in a book, your eyes begin to glaze. Nevertheless, it's essential to the creation of any database that's going to work. What does it mean? Well, its use is similar to the semantic meaning of the word itself. A database has to have integrity before you can trust the information inside it. Why shouldn't there be integrity in a database? Surely, the user inputting the information isn't going to deliberately or knowingly put false information into it? That's exactly the problem. They can unwittingly corrupt the database at anytime.

Consider the Jobs example we looked at earlier. Imagine now, that two people are involved in interviewing applicants for the one post. They both have the same access to the database, but from different views. One view table could be a global list of available jobs, and the other one a table of local jobs. The first manager likes his applicant, offers him the job and takes the job off the global table. However, it's still on the local table. Before he can contact the other manager to tell him to stop interviewing, the other manager sees the job is still available on the database on the local table and offers it to his applicant. Two people have the same job, down to the database not having what is known as **referential integrity**.

If the database had referential integrity, it would mean that when the job was removed from the global table, all the references to that job in other lists would also be removed. SQL has a whole host of features to deal with exactly these types of problems. These are constraints, which when properly programmed, stop the users from making these scenarios into real problems.

That's the overview of the parts of the SQL language.

Interactive SQL Tools

Every SQL vendor will provide you with an interactive SQL tool which will let you log into the database and play with the tables from a terminal. This isn't part of the standard, and every product is a little different, but they have some parts in common.

- There's a window in which you build your SQL statements and submit them to the database engine. Most products allow you to submit several statements from a single window.

- The tool has a simple text editor and you can usually read from and save to any ASCII files. Most of the products save several of your previous submissions in an internal list from which you can reuse them.

- There's a window in which you see the results of your last SQL statement, write it to a printer or file, and perhaps edit it or put it into a report format.

- There's a window in which you can look up the names of the tables and their columns. Sometimes you can also get the attributes of the columns, sometimes not.

- There's some on-line help facility.

The interactive tool is the best tool to use when you're learning SQL, fixing a database or trying to be sure that a query will work before it goes into production. They're not too hard to learn, since they're very much like other

PC-based development environments, only simpler. The reasons we say they're simpler are that SQL statements tend to be short, and you do no other compilation work once you submit the statement. You can simply push the button and away you go!

Connecting to the Example Database

Connecting to the example database provided on the complementary disk via the Watcom SQL engine, is made very easy by the interactive SQL tool. Once you've clicked on the interactive SQL icon, it just takes two steps: creating the connection and logging on to the example database. You can connect to the example database now if you wish, or you can wait until we actually make use of it in Chapter 5.

Creating the Connection

To create the connection, you must select the Command menu followed by the Connect... option. You'll be greeted with a dialog box, this will present you with seven options. At the moment we only need to fill in four of these, as follows (use **sql** as the password):

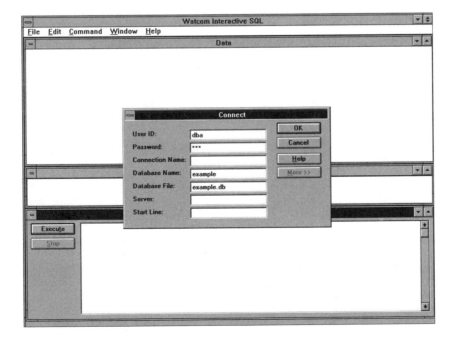

Remember not to press *Return* or select OK until you've entered all the information. If all goes well then you should be presented with a screen of blank forms awaiting your instructions.

> If you're using a 32-bit system then you might encounter a message about the 16-bit subsystem. Click on the Ignore option if this happens - don't worry this won't affect subsequent usage of the Watcom SQL engine.

Logging In to the Database

Now you should repeat the earlier steps of selecting the Commands menu and the Connect... option. This time the dialog box should only have two options: the User ID and Password. Fill them in as you did in the first dialog box, and the message Connected to the Database will appear in the Statistics window. You're now free to type any SQL code into the Command window. The results of any queries will appear in the Data window.

Logging Out of the Database

If you wish to log out at any time, simply select the File menu and the Exit option. You don't actually need to save the data beforehand since the database is updated as it's worked on, and any changes have hopefully been saved already. In fact, the Save option on the File menu only applies to any queries that you might create in the Command window.

Alternative SQL Systems

If you're using an alternative system to the Watcom SQL engine that we've provided you with, such as Oracle, Sybase or Access then you'll have to create the database as you progress through the book. There are tips on how you can do this for specific implementations in Appendix A.

> At this point, you might want to stop reading this book and try to learn the basics of your interactive SQL tool. Just scroll around and see where the buttons are located, so you can use it in the upcoming chapters.

In the next chapter we'll start writing SQL code, but first we'll give you a brief description of the example database that we'll work with throughout this book.

Introduction to the Example Database

The easiest way to learn a programming language is by example, so rather than giving you a lot of unrelated sections of code, we'll develop a complete database as we progress through the book. The database we're going to build is for a telephone sales organization. Some of the objects involved in the system will be salespersons, the inventory, customers and orders.

Some of the columns we'll need in our database are as follows:

 Customer credit rating code and name

 Employee name, salary and rank

 Order identification number, part identification code, price of part, date of sale and description of part

We could include a column for sales commission but this can be calculated from the existing columns.

This is just a brief outline of what we may want to include in our example database. A full description of the business problem could run to several pages and could include many more tables and columns.

Finally, we'll have a look at the type of syntax and grammar we'll be using throughout this book.

Syntax Awareness

> If you already know about the use of grammar in defining computer syntax then you can skip this section and move on to the summary at the end of the chapter.

Programmers of any language need to have a knowledge of computer syntax. This is because syntax defines simply and succinctly the rules of the language - it acts as a road-map. It defines all the possible routes you can take with your code. If your destination isn't on the map you can't get there! The same goes for the syntax - if you can't derive your example code from the syntax, then that code is incorrect.

This is one of the easiest concepts in computer programming, and syntax is useful to you not just in SQL, but in every programming language. More than that, it's essential to good programming practice. Syntax defines in a few lines what is and what isn't legal code. SQL syntax presented throughout the book is outlined in this computer grammar form. You need to know this first so that when you're presented with the syntax definitions, you're going to be able to create your own legal SQL code from them. You also need to be able to learn what *isn't* possible from the syntax.

Grammar is made from just two parts: **terminals** and **non-terminals**. Think of it as being like a subway system. Imagine you want to get from the center of town to the end of the line. Each station you go through is a non-terminal, because you can go beyond it to the next station. Each station is just a point on your journey. You want to get to the terminal at the end of your route, and this corresponds to the keyword. You don't give a hoot for the stations you're passing through - the same goes for the non-terminals. You only need to know the code you're going to type in 'at the end of the day'.

The whole structure we're creating is termed a **construct**. Let's have a look at the different styles and objects you'll encounter in the syntax.

Terminal

KEYWORD

A keyword is what you can type in directly to the SQL engine. Terminals can also be punctuation, such as commas, which is a vital part of syntax. Missed commas and semi-colons can prevent an otherwise correct query from functioning.

Non-Terminal

`<expression name>`

A non-terminal is an expression that can be decomposed (further expanded) into expressions and/or keywords. The aim is to get a final set of keywords which you can type in SQL.

OR

The '|' character is used to divide text up and it represents the English word **or**. It represents the different options open to the SQL engine from one specific point. You can only take one of these paths.

```
<do this>                        means  <do this>
| <do this instead>              OR <do this instead>
| <maybe you should do this>     OR <maybe you should do this>
```

Optional Section

An optional extra to the construct is surrounded by square brackets. It can contain any number of keywords and/or expressions. You only use this if you have a part of the language that can be used *but doesn't have to be*. In the English language an example might be a noun and a noun with an adjective. A noun could be **THE CAT**, a noun with an adjective, **THE BIG CAT**. The noun doesn't have to take an adjective, it just adds to the description. The adjective in this case would be an optional extra encased by the brackets:

`[<adjective>]  <noun>`

In SQL you can test data that goes into the database but you don't have to - the test is optional. You decide whether you want to use it. If you come across this in the SQL syntax, you know that you can add this code to a definition but you don't have to. We might advise that you do it, but the code will function just fine without it.

Definition

::=

A :: = B, means that an expression A is defined in an expanded form as B. Here, expanded doesn't mean there are any more or any less terms, but that the expressions are closer to their terminals or keywords.

Example of Syntax

Instead of computer syntax we'll use an English language example. It's much easier to relate to, and it functions in the same way in SQL, as SQL has an 'English-like' feel. But beware, we're going to create our own definition of the English language, so we can relate it to computer syntax. It's going to be vastly simplified. In our version of the English language, every sentence can be created from a noun, followed by a verb, followed by a noun. We will decide that **A** and **THE** (the indefinite and definite articles) are going to be included in our description of a noun. Therefore, a noun might be **THE CAT** or **A DOG**. We're also going to allow adjectives in this expression, but only as optional extras. The whole kitten caboodle now reads **A [<adjective>] <noun>** or **THE [<adjective>]** noun shall be known as a **<noun expression>**. A verb can be made only from a verb word (there are no modifying prepositions or the like). This is the only way to cut down on the sheer volume of sentences that could be created by the syntax.

Our own definition of a language will be as follows. A sentence can be made up from these three expressions:

```
<sentence>::= <noun expression> <verb expression> <noun
expression>
```

A noun can be made from these expressions and keywords:

```
<noun expression>::= A [<adjective>] <noun>
                   | THE [<adjective>] <noun>
```

A verb can be made from these expressions and keywords:

```
<verb expression>::= <verb>
```

The possible words are:

```
<noun>::= MAN | DOG
<verb>::= BIT
<adjective>::= BIG | SMALL | STUPID
```

In this example we'll now try to discover if **A DOG BIT THE STUPID MAN** is a legal English sentence, according to our definition of syntax. Each **<expression>** could be further decomposed. If you reach a keyword, this is where you end. You then backtrack to the last **<expression>** you looked at. You would then check to see if you had finished all of it, or if there were any more expressions to expand to keywords. Otherwise you would move on to the next expression.

Let's start with a sentence structure - **A DOG BIT THE STUPID MAN** is your final target. Look up the first rule, which is that a **<sentence>** is made up from **<noun expression>** followed by a **<verb expression>**, followed by a **<noun expression>**. Break it up into a tree-like structure as you go along.

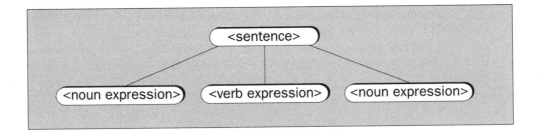

Start with the leftmost expression, the first one in the list. **<noun expression>** can be expanded to one of two things:
A [<adjective>]<noun> or **THE [<adjective>]<noun>**. The sentence starts with **A** so you use the former breakdown of **<noun expression>**.

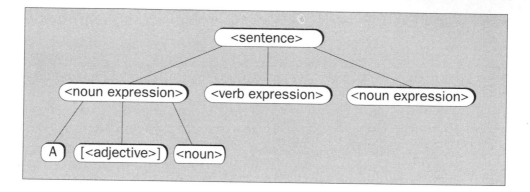

A is left on one side as this is now a keyword, however you still need to expand the rest of the expression. You are left with `[<adjective>]<noun>`. Intuition tells you immediately that the next word **DOG** is a noun. As the adjective is only optional, you can ignore it and jump straight to the noun. (The SQL engine is able to do the equivalent.) If you were to throw in two command keywords, the equivalent of putting two verbs together say, the engine would recognize this as incorrect syntax. What it wouldn't be able to do is tell you whether the way the language is used is illogical. A sentence such as **THE SKY BIT THE DOG** makes no sense if you take the words literally but it is 'grammatically' correct. However, this doesn't interest you because all you want to know is whether or not your statement will be accepted by the SQL engine.

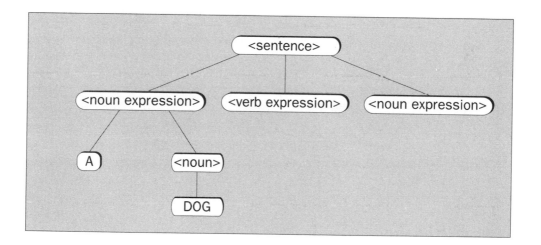

Your sentence so far reads **A DOG <verb expression> <noun expression>**. Move on to the next construct which is **<verb expression>**. According to the rules, **<verb expression>** can be expanded to **<verb>**. There is only one word that can be a verb so we have our next word **BIT**.

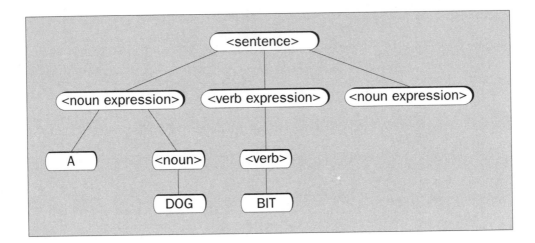

We have finished expanding out the **<verb expression>** expression. All that's left is the final **<noun expression>** expression. This time we choose the latter option and use **THE [<adjective>] <noun>** as this is what fits our statement. We look at the next word in our sentence, **STUPID**. We know that this is an adjective. The SQL engine would also be able to determine the type of expression in a sentence. We, therefore, utilize the optional extra part, so we can accept the adjective **STUPID** as correct. (The general rule is that if it's possible via the syntax, then it will be possible in the language.)

We're left finally with the **<noun>** part to expand. This is expanded to the word **MAN** to fit our statement. This has completed the syntax definition of a statement and also completed our statement. Therefore, the statement has been successfully **parsed**.

> **Parsing is the method of 'walking' through the syntax to obtain our sentence.**

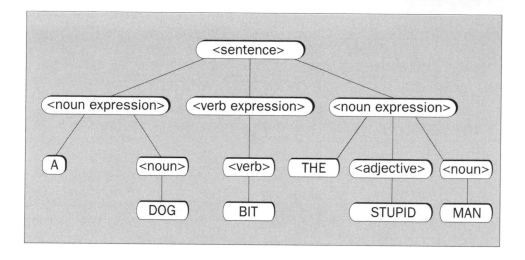

We have now proved via our syntax that this is a legal statement. Fine, but what has this to do with SQL? This is what the SQL engine will do (more or less) when presented with an SQL statement such as **SELECT thingamajigs FROM wherever**. Each statement in SQL has its own syntax for determining whether the statement is or isn't valid. The **CREATE TABLE** statement will have one syntax, the **SELECT** statement will have another. This is equivalent to the **<noun expression>** having its own syntax, and the **<verb expression>** having another. Everything goes back to the **<sentence>**. This is equivalent to what you type in at the command line. SQL will break down the syntax and label the different parts of the code. You have just broken down the different parts of the sentence and labeled them.

OK, now you might still wonder why this is relevant to the book. Why can't you just get some example code and type it in? Well, you can, but in this way with the syntax you can create your own example code and know that it's syntactically correct. Instead of giving you 10 million examples of what is right and what is wrong, you'll get a working knowledge of SQL with the syntax and a couple of examples. SQL is quite different across the different vendor products. What doesn't differ much is the syntax. It's of much more use to you to learn SQL generally so that your knowledge is transferable across vendor products. We could give you example code for only one product, and you may find you'll type it in on your product and when it doesn't work you'll be none the wiser. With the syntax you'll be able to create general SQL code, so if your product has a different keyword or slightly different way of doing things, you'll be able to just change the 'wording' of things rather than the whole structure. For example, a function for converting one data type to another is **CAST()** in one language but **CONVERTTO()** in another yet the working is the same.

You're probably wondering what would happen in the case of an illegal statement. The answer is that you can't create the whole tree for the statement. You'll get stuck somewhere along the line. We'll demonstrate this for you now.

If we were to use the sentence **THE DOG BIT MAN**, then it would have a different effect upon our syntax. You would create the tree structure up to the point where you have just expanded the verb to the word **BIT**:

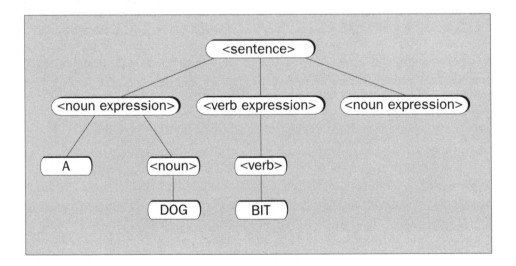

Then there would be a difference. You would have a choice of **THE [<adjective>] <noun>** or **A [<adjective>] <noun**. However, you have the word **MAN** to match up. The syntax is looking next for either the word **THE** or **A**. As the next word in our statement is **MAN**, then it doesn't match up to either **THE** or **A**, which you need to have to continue to the **<noun>** construct, so the parse would fail here and the sentence would be rejected.

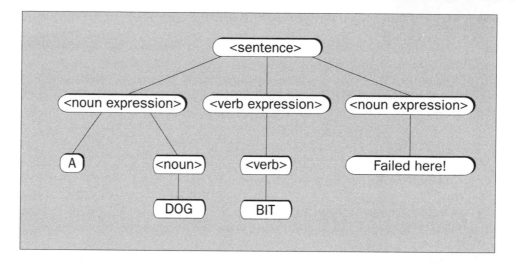

In SQL, if a statement can't be parsed, then the appropriate error message is output, mentioning approximately where in the statement the error was found. There isn't much else to using the syntax that appears in this book. If there are any small differences, we'll introduce them first. To get used to the idea of defining languages with a syntax it would be a good idea to try these exercises.

Exercises

1 Would the following sentence **A MAN BIT THE MAN** be legal in our first syntax?

2 Would the sentence **A MAN BIT THE DOG STUPID** be legal in our first syntax?

3 Amend the definition of the previous example sentence to include a full stop at the end.

4 Amend the definition of a **<noun expression>** to allow two adjectives, both of them optional, separated by a comma.

5 Extend the definition of **<noun expression>** to allow the word **AN** as well, using the same format as **A** and **THE** and using also your answer to exercise **4**.

Summary

We've covered most of the basic structure of SQL in this chapter.

We looked at the differences between procedural and declarative languages and some of the issues you'll need to address if you are coming to SQL from another programming discipline.

We've introduced you to the standards and mentioned how they affect SQL in general, and how they affect this book.

We looked at the differences in terminology such as row and record and settled upon which we should commonly use throughout the book.

We looked at how SQL can be logically subdivided into the three SQL 'sub-languages': DDL, DML and DCL. We've also skimmed very quickly over transaction control and integrity both of which we deal with in far greater detail in later chapters.

Finally, we gave you a quick primer to computer syntax and the style of syntax we will be using throughout this book.

In the next chapter we'll see how you set up a database using SQL code.

Chapter

Defining a Database

The creation of databases is one of the most powerful uses of SQL. It isn't as simple, however, as merely setting up a table with the relevant column and row names. There are many different things you will need to think about. You will need to get to grips with thinking in 'sets' and agreeing with SQL's constraints and data types. You may be familiar with setup routines in SQL Access or dBase, whereas we will outline the basis for safely distributing your data universally. This will also ensure a secure interrogation path in the future.

In this chapter we will look at the following topics:

- The underlying model upon which SQL is based
- Table terminology
- Creation of schema and tables
- Data types and constraints
- Other table manipulation commands

Languages and Their Underlying Model

One of the initial problems with learning SQL is that programmers are used to thinking in terms of files rather than tables. Programming languages are usually based on some underlying model and, if you understand the model, then the language makes more sense. For example, FORTRAN is based on algebra. This doesn't mean that FORTRAN is exactly like algebra, or vice versa. But if you know algebra, then FORTRAN doesn't look that strange to you. You can write an expression in an assignment statement or make a good guess as to the names of library functions you have never seen before.

The Set Model

The model for SQL is 'data kept in sets', and not physical files. Programmers are used to working with files in almost every other language and they have to unlearn that mindset.

Let's start with the basics. Returned sequential files consist of records that are ordered sequentially within the file. There is a first record when you open a file, a series of next records as you use the data and a last record to raise the end of file condition. You navigate these records and perform actions one record at a time. These files model how people would handle real-world paper forms.

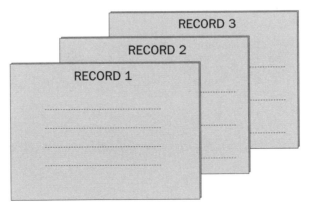

On the other hand, sets are those mathematical abstractions you studied in school. Sets are not ordered and their members are all of the same type. When you do an operation on a set, the action happens 'all at once' and to the entire membership. That is, if you ask for the subset of odd numbers from the set of positive integers, you get all of them back as a set. I don't build the set of odd numbers one element at a time. You define odd numbers with a rule: 'if remainder is one when you divide the number by two, it's odd'. This could test any integer and classify it.

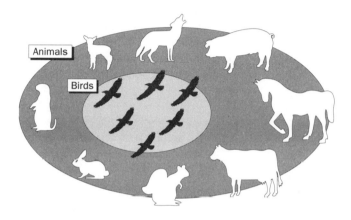

SQL isn't a perfect set language any more than FORTRAN is a perfect algebraic language, as we'll see, but when in doubt about something in SQL, ask yourself how you would specify it in terms of sets and you'll probably get the right answer.

Schema and Table

A schema is the data, the operators and the rules of a database you have defined. The only data structure the programmer handles is the table. Tables can be permanent (base tables) or virtual (views). Any operation you do in SQL will return a **result table**.

The advantage of having only one data structure is that the results of all operations are also tables - you never have to convert structures, write special operators or deal with any irregularity in the language.

SQL-92 is more orthogonal than the old SQL-89 standard. (That is, the language allows you to nest expressions inside each other, but you should always try to do so carefully so as to avoid undue complexity.) You can use a result table with one value where you use a scalar value, a result table with one row where you use a row literal and a result table with one column where you could use a column expression.

> **Scalar values - A scalar value is a value that isn't an array. Any data type can be a scalar value, as long as it has only one dimension. For example, 1 is a scalar value but (1,2) isn't.**
>
> **Literals - A literal is a constant that is referred to by its value. A literal 3 would be 'the integer data type having the value 3.'**
>
> **Column Expression - A column expression is a calculation that will eturn a value for any data item within that column.**

Conceptually, a table is a set of zero or more rows, and a row is a set of one or more columns.

TABLE	Column 1	Column 2	Column 3	Column 4
Row 1 Row 2				

Each column has a specific data type. How a table is physically implemented doesn't matter, because you access it only with SQL. The database engine handles all the details of the physical implementation for you. This is one of the great advantages of SQL, to a new programmer. When you create a table, you don't have to worry about where it's going to be stored within the murky depths of the filing system. You don't have to worry about specifying how many disks you're going to take up with the database, or how the input/output operations are going to work, because SQL's looking after that for you.

If, of course, you're one of those people who take delight in the internal particulars of how things are stored and organized, then it's possible to specify some of the storage characteristics. Really that isn't what SQL is used for and defeats a lot of its purpose. The ways things are stored is individual to each package; use the manual for your own vendor product. This is really only of use to a DBA (Database Administrator).

Common Conceptual Errors

There are two common conceptual errors made by programmers who are accustomed to file systems or personal computers. The first is thinking that a table is a file, and the second is thinking that a table is a spreadsheet. Tables don't behave like either files or spreadsheets.

It is easy to imagine that a table is a file, a row is a record and a column is a field, because this model works almost all the time. The big difference between working with a file system and working with SQL is in how SQL fits into a host program. Using a file system, your programs must open and close files individually. Using SQL, the whole schema is connected or disconnected to the program in one step and brings all the authorized tables with it.

Fields within a file are defined by the program, while SQL defines its columns in the schema. If you are a FORTRAN programmer, you use the **FORTRAN FORMAT** statement, a COBOL programmer uses a Data Division and a C programmer uses the order that the variable names appear in the list of a **Read** statement.

You can reference the same data by a different name in each program. If the file layout changes, you must rewrite all the programs which use that file. When a file is empty, it looks exactly like all other empty files. When you try to read an empty file, the **EOF** flag pops up and the program takes some action.

Column names and data types in a table are defined within the database schema. Within reasonable limits, the tables can be changed without the knowledge of the host programs. The host program only worries about transferring the values to its own variables from the database. Remember, the empty set from your high school math class? It is still a valid set. When a table is empty, it still has columns, but zero rows. There is no **EOF** flag to signal an exception.

A table isn't a spreadsheet, even though they look alike when you view them on a screen or in a printout. You can access a row, a column, a cell or collection of cells in a spreadsheet by navigating with a cursor. Also, in terms of a spreadsheet, the position of a cell matters, whereas a table has no concept of navigation.

Cells in a spreadsheet can also store instructions and not just data. There is no real difference between a row and column in a spreadsheet, as you could flip them around completely and still get valid results. In SQL, rows and columns are different things.

Table Terminology

SQL tables have their own terminology, but there isn't very much to learn and what there is, is quite simple to understand. We will use the following table to explain some of the terminology:

TABLE	Column 1	Column 2	Column 3	Column 4
Row 1 Row 2				

Cardinality of a Table

This is simply the number of rows in a table and can be zero or greater. The example table has a cardinality of 2.

Degree of a Table

This is the number of columns in a table and must be one or greater. The example table has a degree of 4.

Domain Compatible Data Types

If two data types are **domain compatible** they can be converted into one common data type. There are not too many surprises here and you can reference the table of legal conversions.

> The legal conversions table specifies which data types can be converted from one to another found. It can be found in Appendix E.

The rules of this table are that you can convert numerics to numerics of higher precision and character strings to longer character strings. Also, character strings which are made up of numeric characters and legal punctuation can be converted into numerics. Likewise, character strings which hold an ISO (International Standards Organization) display date or time string can be converted into temporal (time/date) data types.

Union Compatible Rows

Two rows are said to be **union compatible** if they have the same degree, and their columns have domain compatible data type in corresponding positions. The following rows from different tables are union compatible:

TABLE 1 ROW	Character String	Numeric	Character String	Numeric

TABLE 2 ROW	Character String	Numeric	Character String	Numeric

Essentially, they have the same structure and could have come from the same table.

Manipulating Tables

The three basic table statements in the SQL Data Definition Language (DDL) are **CREATE TABLE**, **DROP TABLE** and **ALTER TABLE**. They pretty much do what you would think they do from their names.

Guidelines for Defining Schema and Tables

Before we cover the syntax of these let's look at some guidelines to defining schema and tables.

1 The table name must be unique in the schema and the columns' names must be unique within a table. The names in SQL can consist of letters, underscores and numbers, and they can have other characters or space in them if you enclose them in double quote marks. A table must have at least one column.

2 SQL can handle a table and column with the same name, but it is a good practice to give tables plural or collective nouns for names and use singular attribute names for columns. This helps you think of tables as sets and columns as parts of a row. For example, don't name a table 'Employee' and then have a column for the employee identifier also called 'employee'. Instead, use something like 'Personnel' or even 'Employees' for the table name.

3 It is also a good idea to use the same name for the same attribute or thing in different tables. That is, don't name a column 'sex' in one table and 'gender' in another when they refer to the same attribute.

4 While not mandatory, it is also a good idea to place related columns in their natural order in the table. By default, the columns will print out in the order in which they appear in the table. That is, put name, street address, city, state and postal code in that order, so you can read them easily in a display. (If you're going to use abbreviations make sure you work out a standard set prior to the design.)

Making Rules for Data

You can put a lot of rules about your data into the SQL schema. In fact, the more you can declare in the schema, the easier the programming will be. This is a major advantage of a database over a file system. If one of hundreds or thousands of application programs forgets to enforce a single rule, then the database is corrupted. If a rule changes, then all the application programs have to be changed. For example, if the age for a liquor serving license goes from 18 to 21 years, all your hiring rules must change.

But if that rule is enforced in the database, then none of the applications need to repeat the validation in their code. A change at the database level will find all the data that doesn't meet the new rule and none of the application programs will have to change.

Another advantage is that if the rules are in the schema, then the database system can use them to decide how to allocate storage and optimize queries. Many of these rules are stated as SQL search conditions and can be used directly in the query processor.

Create Table Statement

The **CREATE TABLE** statement does all the hard work. The basic syntax looks like this:

```
<table definition> ::=
 CREATE TABLE <table name> (<table element list>);

<table element list> ::=
 <table element> | <table element>, <table element list>

<table element> ::=
 <column definition> | <table constraint definition>
```

We'll start with a piece of SQL code that you can type straight in. The code creates a table called **Example** which has three columns. The structure is empty and can't be viewed as such. However you need to know how we got there via the syntax, so we'll walk you through how to create the code from the basic syntax. To define a table we need the first clause in the command definition above.

Actual Code	Syntax Version (i)
CREATE TABLE Example	CREATE TABLE <tablename>
(Column 1 INTEGER NOT NULL,	(<table element list>);
Column 2 INTEGER NOT NULL,	
Column 3 INTEGER NOT NULL);	

A **<table element>** is a column by any other word. A **<table element list>** is made up of two objects, a table element and the rest of the table element list. For each element or column in the table, either it is the last column or there is another one after it. Unless you are at the last table element in the list, you take the latter option which is **<table element>** comma **<table element list>**, as there must be more table elements to come. Commas are used to divide each element within the list. Each statement must always end with a semi-colon. All of the items within the list are enclosed by one set of parentheses.

Each table element can be reduced, according to the syntax above, to the following:

Syntax Version (ii)	Syntax Version (iii)
CREATE TABLE <table name>	*CREATE TABLE Example*
(<table element>,	*(<column definition>,*
<table element>,	*<column definition>,*
<table element>);	*<column definition>);*

Any time you see a name in an expression such as **<table name>**, that means you can name the object yourself. As we're creating an example table, it's best to call the table 'Example'. We wish to have three columns, so we need three elements in the table which correspond to the columns.

Syntax Version (iii)	Syntax Version (iv)
CREATE TABLE Example	*CREATE TABLE Example*
(<column definition>,	*(<column name> <table constraint definition>,*
<column definition>,	*<column name> <table constraint definition>,*
<column definition>);	*<column name> <table constraint definition>);*

Each table element is reduced to the column definition (whether the column contains integers or characters or dates) and rules for all data that goes into the table. The rules for handling that data might typically be 'only allow a row to be inserted into the table if the phone number and fax number of that row are not the same number'. These rules are known as table constraint definitions. They are methods of checking whether data that's going into a table is correct or valid. This means that a table acts more like an object (with its data and methods) than just a simple, passive file.

Column Definitions

Beginners to SQL programming often fail to take full advantage of the options available to them, and they pay for it with errors or extra work in their applications. Saving yourself time and trouble begins with column definitions. The syntax is as follows:

```
<column definition> ::=
 <column name> <datatype>
 [<default clause>]
 [<column constraint>...]
```

The first important thing to notice here is that each column must have a data type. There are also no array, pointers or data structure declarations in SQL; everything is a simple scalar or atomic value. This means that a column definition must be at least made up from a **<column name>** and the **<data type>** of the that column. Optionally you can add a default and a constraint to the column, but they aren't essential to the working of the table structure. In its simplest form you could use this definition, where you need only a column name and the data type of that column.

Actual Code	Syntax Version
CREATE TABLE Example2	CREATE TABLE Example2
(Column 1 INTEGER,	(<column name> <data type>,
Column 2 INTEGER,	<column name> <data type>,
Column 3 INTEGER);	<column name> <data type>);

We'll look at default clauses and column constraints in detail a little later in the chapter, but an example using them would look like this:

Actual Code	Syntax Version
CREATE TABLE Example2	*CREATE TABLE Example2*
(Column 1 INTEGER DEFAULT 1 NOT NULL,	*(<column name><data type><default clause><column constraint>,*
Column 2 INTEGER DEFAULT 1 NOT NULL,	* <column name><data type><default clause><column constraint>,*
Column 3 INTEGER DEFAULT 1 NOT NULL);	* <column name><data type><default clause> <column constraint>);*

You can mix columns freely whereby some will have constraints and defaults and others won't have anything at all, apart from the basics. There are several different types of column constraint, all which require their own syntax. We will worry about those later. First, we must define the different possible data types.

SQL Data Types

There are 3 main data types in SQL:

 NUMERIC

CHARACTER

TEMPORAL

There are also vendor data types - the most common is **MONEY**. This is really a **DECIMAL** or **NUMERIC** data type which also accepts and displays currency symbols in input and output. Another one is **BLOBS** (those cursed picture files), which are replaced in the SQL-92 standard with the **BIT** and **BIT VARYING** data types. Products that have **BLOBS** usually have functions that can use them, while the standard is silent on what to do with them.

Numeric Types

The SQL standard has a very wide range of numeric types. The idea is that any host language can find an SQL numeric type which matches one of its own.

> Numbers in SQL are classified as either exact or approximate numerics.

Exact Numerics

An exact numeric value has a precision **P** and a scale **S**. The precision is a positive integer that determines the number of significant digits in a particular **radix** or base (you know from school, binary is base 2 and so on). The standard says the radix can be either binary or decimal, so you need to know what your implementation provides. The scale is a non-negative integer which tells you how many decimal places the number has. An integer has a scale of zero. The data types **NUMERIC**, **DECIMAL**, **INTEGER** and **SMALLINT** are exact numeric types. **DECIMAL(P, S)** can also be written **DEC (P, S)** and **INTEGER** can be abbreviated **INT**. For example, **DECIMAL (8,2)** could be used to hold the number 123456.78, which has eight significant digits and two decimal places.

The difference between **NUMERIC** and **DECIMAL** is subtle:

 NUMERIC specifies the exact precision and scale to be used.

 DECIMAL specifies the exact scale, but the precision is implementation-defined to be equal to, or greater than, the specified value.

COBOL programmers can think of the **NUMERIC** as a COBOL picture numeric type, while **DECIMAL** is like a BCD or COMPUTATIONAL type. Personal computer programmers these days probably have not seen anything like this. You may find that many small machine SQLs don't support **NUMERIC** or **DECIMAL**. This is because they don't want to have COBOL style math routines that operate on character strings or an internal decimal representation.

Approximate Numerics

An approximate numeric value consists of a mantissa and an exponent. The mantissa is a signed numeric value, and the exponent is a signed integer that specifies the magnitude of the mantissa. An approximate numeric value has a precision. The precision is a positive integer which specifies the number of significant binary digits in the mantissa. The value of an approximate numeric value is the mantissa multiplied by 10 to the exponent. **FLOAT (P)**, **REAL** and **DOUBLE PRECISION** are the approximate numeric types. There is a subtle difference between **FLOAT (P)**, which has a binary precision equal to or greater than the value given, and **REAL**, which has an implementation defined precision.

The Three Parts of an Approximate Numeric Value

Sign	Excess + Exponent	Mantissa

In recent years, the IEEE (Institute of Electrical and Electronic Engineers) introduced a floating point standard which can work well with SQL. As more vendors adopt it, query results will become more uniform across platforms. The IEEE floating point standard also has certain bit configurations called NaNs (Not a Number) to represent overflow, underflow, errors and missing values which provide a way to implement **NULL**s as well as to capture errors.

Character Types

SQL-89 defined a **CHARACTER(n)** or **CHAR(n)** data type, which represented a fixed length string of **(n)** printable characters, where **(n)** is always greater than one - you can't declare a column to have an empty string. Some implementations allow the string to contain control characters, but this is a rare case. The characters which are allowed are usually drawn from **ASCII** or **EBCDIC** character sets and most often use the order defined by these standards for sorting.

> **ASCII** - The American Standard Code for Information Interchange is a simple assignment of numeric codes to printable characters and device control codes.
>
> **EBCDIC** - The Extended Binary Coded Decimal Interchange Code is an assignment of eight bit numeric codes to printable characters and device control codes. It differs from the ASCII code in that if you added one to the numeric code for 'R' you wouldn't get 'S'.
>
> They're available in many manuals or computing dictionaries.

SQL-92 added the **VARYING CHARACTER(n)** or **VARCHAR(n)** which was already present in many implementations. A **VARCHAR(n)** represents a string which varies in length from one to **(n)** printable characters. This is important; SQL-92 doesn't allow you to store a string of length zero in a table.

SQL-92 also added **NATIONAL CHARACTER(n)** and **NATIONAL VARYING CHARACTER(n)** data types which are made up of printable characters drawn from ISO defined foreign language character sets. SQL-92 also allows the database administrator to define collation sequences (a sort order is a collation sequence - a,b,c,d would be a collation sequence) and do other things with the character sets. Most products have not implemented these features yet, so they won't be covered in this book - we will assume you are using ASCII or EBCDIC.

Temporal Data Types

SQL-92 has a very complete description of **DATE**, **TIME**, **DATETIME** and **TIMESTAMP** data types. There are rules for converting from numeric and character strings into these types, and there is a schema table for time zone information which is used for conversions. It is so complete and elaborate that nobody has yet implemented it. It will take them years to do so.

The standard is silent on *how* dates and times are stored internally in the database, so products do it very differently. Some use a character string, some use a large number which represents fractional seconds from a starting date and there are variations on those approaches. The important thing is that the programmer doesn't care, as he or she never handles the internal date format in SQL.

All SQL implementations have a **DATE** data type and most have a **TIME** and a **TIMESTAMP** data type.

> Beware, Sybase users, your product doesn't provide separate **DATE** and **TIME** data types, only a **DATETIME** data type. Also your **TIMESTAMP** data type has nothing to do with real world time - it is used for running transaction control.

These values are drawn from the system clock and are therefore local to the host machine, which betrays the more global approach of SQL-92. They are based on what is now called the 'Common Era' calendar, also called the

Gregorian or Christian calendar. Technically, 'AD' and 'BC' are replaced by 'CE' and 'BCE' respectively.

The SQL-92 standard is based on the Gregorian calendar and UTC (Universal Coordinated Time, formerly GMT or Greenwich Mean Time) and standard time zones. These are ISO standards in common usage as well. The data schema tables have to include a table for the time zones which gives their displacement from the UTC. It is so elaborate that only a multi-national corporation would worry about it!

The SQL-92 standard also has a full set of operators for temporal data types. The full syntax and functionality has not been implemented in any SQL product yet, but you can use some of the vendor extensions to get around a lot of problems in most existing SQL implementations today.

Back to the column definition, the next clause after a data-type in the `<table definition>` construct is the default clause.

The Default Clause

The default clause is an under-used feature. Here's its syntax:

```
<default clause> ::= DEFAULT <default option>

<default option> ::= <literal> | <system value> | NULL
```

Whenever the system doesn't have an explicit value to put into a column, it will look for its `DEFAULT` clause and insert that value. An example of use of a default value would be in a table of employees with credit limits. Those, who hadn't had their credit limits extended and didn't know their credit limit, would have a minimum rating of $500. The default value would therefore be 500. The `<default option>` can be a literal value of the appropriate data type, such as `1` or `999` or `John`, or something provided by the system, such as the current timestamp, the current user identifier, and so on. If you don't provide a `DEFAULT` clause, then the definition acts as if you had declared it `DEFAULT NULL` and the value `NULL` would be assigned to that column. This is because the `NULL` value is the default value of `DEFAULT`.

Actual Code	Syntax Version
CREATE TABLE Example4	*CREATE TABLE Example 4*
(Column 1 INTEGER DEFAULT 1,	*(<column name><data type>* *<default clause>,*
Column 2 INTEGER,	*<column name><data type>,*
Column 3 CHAR(15)DEFAULT 'ACME');	*<column name><data type>* *<default clause>);*

This would assign a default of one to **Column 1**, there would be no default assigned to **Column 2** and a default of **ACME** assigned to **Column 3**. Remember the default that you assign must be appropriate to the data type, such as not assigning a character default to an integer data type, because the SQL you use might not always pick it up until you come to insert data into it.

This is a good way to make the database do a lot of work that you would otherwise have to code into all the application programs. The most common tricks are to use a zero in numeric columns, a string to encode a missing value ('unknown') or true default ('same address') in character columns, and the system timestamp to mark transactions.

Column Constraints

There are four different types of column constraints that can be applied. You can use any single one, or all of them independently in conjunction with the **NOT NULL** constraint.

```
<column constraint> ::= NOT NULL
  | <check constraint definition>
  | <unique specification>
  | <references specification>
```

Column constraints are rules attached to a table. All the rows in the table are validated against them. File systems have nothing like this, since validation is done in the application programs. They're also one of the most under-used features of SQL, so you can look like a real wizard if you can master them.

In fact, it's not that difficult to master them. Not only is it better practice to do as much validation at application level, but it makes it easier for you. If your application rejects the data that's input, it'll tell you from which column the item was rejected and you should be able to figure out which row as well and, therefore, which item was the offending one. The alternative is having to trawl the error code from the database which doesn't always refer to the point the error occurred and will typically be in computeresque jargon such as 'Error Code 25987'.

In the short term this is more work for you, but in the long term it will save you effort. The database shouldn't have to do all your work. If possible work out the rules on paper beforehand. Look at the columns. Can you find a way of preventing erroneous data going in?

For example, if you were storing data about credit cards for accountancy purposes, and you had a column of expiry dates, you could prevent incorrect data being entered into this column by stopping dates earlier than the current date and later than five years on from the current date (as most cards are only valid for five years) from being input.

Imagine at the same time, the flipside. What happens if you let an incorrect date go in for 1986 instead of 1996? Now, say you have an automatic aging system which checks by today's date and says this card is invalid as from today. How can it pick up one from 1986? It can't.

Not Null Constraint

The most important column constraint is the **NOT NULL** which will forbid the use of **NULL**s in a column. The **NULL** is a missing or unknown value; it isn't the same as an empty string or zero value. The **NOT NULL** constraint prevents the user from failing to enter a value into a column. Confused? Well, maybe that's because you haven't yet come across the actual inputting of data into a table. This occurs in conjunction with the **INSERT** command which we'll cover in Chapter 5. For now, imagine a table with three columns:

	custname	custaddr	phone
Row 1 Row 2			

The table requires an entry for each column: one for the customer name, one for the address and one for a phone number. You can enter the customer's name into the **custname** column, the customer's address into customer address, but if you didn't know the phone number, you could leave that blank. The database would automatically insert a **NULL** value into that column, as it doesn't mean that there isn't a phone number, just that it isn't yet known:

custname	custaddr	phone
John Doe Richard Roe	New York Washington	9999-9999 (null)

Some sales organizations, however, with a database of potential customers, would be useless without their phone numbers. The management might prefer that the person wasn't entered into the database at all. Therefore, to prevent a customer being entered into the table without a phone number, a **NOT NULL** constraint is applied to the phone column. To create this Customer in a database you would use this code:

Actual Code	Syntax Version
```CREATE TABLE Customer```	*CREATE TABLE Customer*
```(custname CHAR(15),```	*(<column name> <data type>,*
```custaddr CHAR(30),```	*<column name> <data type>,*
```phone INTEGER NOT NULL);```	*<column name> <data type>* *<column constraint>);*

> Use the NOT NULL constraint automatically, on all columns, and
> remove it only when you have good reason. From now on
> we'll use this constraint as a matter of course.

The NOT NULL constraint will help you avoid the complications of NULL
values when you make queries against the data. We will look at some of
the implications of the dreaded NULL in the next chapter.

Check() Constraint

The CHECK() constraint is under-used, even by experienced SQL
programmers. It tests the rows of the table against a logical expression, which
SQL calls a **search condition**, and rejects rows that don't pass the test. Here
is its syntax:

```
<check constraint definition> ::=
  CHECK (<search condition>)
```

There is an important point to remember here - if the **<search condition>** is
FALSE, then the constraint rejects the data; if the **<search condition>** is
TRUE or UNKNOWN, then the constraint accepts the data. A NULL gets the
benefit of the doubt!

Actual Code	Syntax Version
CREATE TABLE Customer2 (custname CHAR(15) NOT NULL,	CREATE TABLE Customer2 (<column name> <data type> <column constraint>,
custaddr CHAR(15) NOT NULL,	<column name> <data type> <column constraint>,
creditlim INTEGER NOT NULL CHECK (creditlim<5000));	<column name> <data type> <NOT NULL <check constraint>);

The CHECK above would simply stop a value above **5000** being entered in
the creditlim column. The usual technique is to do simple range checking
such as CHECK (rating BETWEEN 1 AND 10) or verify that a column's value
is in an enumerated set such as CHECK sex IN ('M', 'F') with this
constraint.

> We will look at the BETWEEN and IN predicates in Chapter 6.

The real power comes when writing complex expressions, which verify relationships with other rows, other tables or with system values. For example, you can use a single check clause to enforce the rule that we don't hire anyone under 21 years of age for a job that requires a liquor serving license by checking their birth date, the current system date and the job requirements table.

Unique and Primary Key Constraints

The UNIQUE constraint says that no duplicate values are allowed in a column. The SQL-92 syntax for this is as follows:

```
<unique specification> ::= UNIQUE | PRIMARY KEY
```

File system programmers will understand the concept of a PRIMARY KEY, but unfortunately for the wrong reasons. They are used to a file which can have only one key because that key is used to determine the physical order of the records within the file. However, in SQL there is no sequential order in a table; the term PRIMARY KEY has to do with distinguishing rows in a table and making sure they are not repeated elsewhere.

> There are some subtle differences between UNIQUE and PRIMARY KEY. There can be only one PRIMARY KEY per table, but many UNIQUE columns.

custid	custname	custaddr
1	John Doe	New York
2	John Doe	Boston

The PRIMARY key might be the customer identifier (custid), which would uniquely identify all the different customers who had the same names.

A PRIMARY KEY is automatically declared to have a NOT NULL constraint on it, whereas a UNIQUE column can have one and only one NULL in a row, unless you explicitly add a **NOT NULL** constraint. Adding the **NOT NULL** *whenever possible* is a good idea.

Actual Code	Syntax Version
`CREATE TABLE Customer3`	`CREATE TABLE Customer3`
`(custid INTEGER NOT NULL PRIMARY KEY,`	`(<column name> <datatype> NOT NULL <unique specification>,`
`custname CHAR(15) NOT NULL,`	`<column name> <data type> <column constraint>,`
`custaddr CHAR(30) NOT NULL);`	`<column name> <data type> <column constraint>);`

There is also a multiple column form of the **<unique specification>** which is usually written at the end of the column declarations. It is a list of columns in parentheses after the proper keyword; it means that the combination of those columns is unique. For example, we might declare **PRIMARY KEY (city, department)**, so that we can be sure that while there are offices in many cities and many identical departments in those offices, there is only one personnel department in Chicago.

The truth is that not many implementations of SQL follow the ANSI syntax for **<unique specification>** yet. Instead, you first create the table, then have to use a separate statement which also varies from product to product, but probably looks like **CREATE UNIQUE INDEX <index name> ON <table>(<column list>)**. File system programmers don't tend to mind this separate structure, since it is how they have always done it.

> We will look in more depth at **UNIQUE** and **PRIMARY** keys in Chapter 4.

References

The references specification is the simplest version of a referential constraint definition - it can be quite tricky. For now, let's consider the simplest case:

```
<references specification> ::=
REFERENCES <referenced table name> [(<reference column>)]
```

This relates two tables together, so it's different from the other clauses we have discussed so far. What this says is that if the value is in the column of the referencing table, call it table B, then it must either be **NULL** or that same value must appear somewhere in the table A's (the referenced table) column named in the constraint. So table A must match logically to table B.

TABLE A : Customer Address Book

custid	custname	custaddress
1001	John Doe	New York
1002	Richard Roe	Boston

TABLE B : Customer Credit Limits

credit limit	interest	custid
$500	2	1001
$1000	4	1002

This means that the customer identification number 1001 in TABLE A, must match the customer identification number in TABLE B, and that the John Doe who lives in New York must be the same guy who has a credit limit of $500. Furthermore, the referenced column must have a **<unique specification>** on it. Accepting the **NULL** is another example of the 'benefit of doubt' principle in SQL.

For our example code we're going to create these two tables so that one references the other. The first table is a list of customers with their details, the second is a list of credit limits. For each credit limit there could be a number of customers who have that credit limit. If we put a value into the table **CreditLimit1** under **custid** then we must ensure that there is already a customer with that id number. This is why we will use the **REFERENCES** constraint, it enforces this. The credit limit is the unique item in this table. The table that does the referencing (TABLE B in this example) must always be created second as you can't make a reference to a table (TABLE A) that doesn't yet exist.

Actual Code for Table A	Syntax Version for Table A

CREATE TABLE Customer4
 	
(custid INTEGER NOT NULL PRIMARY KEY,
 	
  custname CHAR(15) NOT NULL,
 	
  custaddr CHAR(30) NOT NULL);
	CREATE TABLE Customer4
	
	(<column name> <datatype>NOT NULL <unique specification>,
	
	  <column name> <data type> <column constraint>,
	
	  <column name> <data type> <column constraint>);

Actual Code for Table B	Syntax Version for Table B

CREATE TABLE CreditLimit1
 	
(creditlim INTEGER NOT NULL
  PRIMARY KEY,
 	
  interest INTEGER NOT NULL,
 	
  custid INTEGER NOT NULL
REFERENCES Customer4(custid));
	CREATE TABLE CreditLimit1
	
	(<column name> <data type>NOT NULL <unique specification>,
	
	  <column name> <data type> <column constraint>,
	
	  <column name> <data type> NOT NULL <references specification>);

> We will get back to the question of referential integrity in Chapter 4 and show how you can use it to cause the database to change itself automatically. We will also discuss how some of these column constraints are related to multi-column constraints. In short, the database can do a lot to maintain itself without any external programming.

Comments

Some versions of SQL also have ways of attaching a comment to each column of a table. This is often done with a special COMMENT statement, as in DB2. What's actually happening is that the comments are placed in a special schema table where users can get to them as a form of on-line documentation. Commenting isn't standard, but it's a good way to document your database and you should do it if your product has the facility to do so.

A typical statement in Watcom SQL using a comment feature would be as follows:

```
COMMENT ON TABLE Customer IS 'This is an example table';
```

It might be that your version of SQL supports comments on other features such as indexes and primary keys as well. To remove such a comment, it is usual to set it to **NULL**.

You will also see some SQL products which use the C language convention of '**/***' and '***/**', the pairs of comment brackets. The actual comment convention in SQL is taken from the ADA programming language; you put comment text between a double dash and a new line. These comments are like the comments you would see in a program - they are part of the source code and are not available to the user.

```
-- This is a comment line example --
```

> One tip when programming in SQL is to write one column declaration per line and put the name of the table on a single line, so that you have room for a comment beside each data item name.

The Example Database

We said in Chapter 1 that we are going to build a database for a telephone sales organization. Some of the objects involved in the system are salespersons, the inventory, our customers and the orders that the customers place with us.

The information we need about our salespersons includes their names, the rank they hold (junior salesman, senior salesman, manager), their salaries and their commissions. The choice of data types for some of these attributes is obvious - a person's name is going to be **CHAR** and salaries are going to be **DECIMAL**.

But how big should we make them? The answer is that it depends on the project itself. The United States Postal Service and most label manufacturers say that the name line in an address should be 30 characters long. But if we're only storing their last name, this is probably a bit much.

Likewise, if we're recording weekly salary then **DECIMAL(6,2)** will probably be fine, but if w'are recording annual salary then we probably need **DECIMAL (8,2)**.

The salespersons rank can be a numeric code or a character string. If there's some industry standard code for an attribute, then you should probably use it. You can usually obtain such standard codes in machine readable format. They are complete, and they allow you to exchange data with other systems which use them. (Designing codes is a whole book in itself!)

Commissions are going to be computed from the sales that each salesperson makes. If you put a column in the salespersons table for their commission, then you'll have to change that value every time they make a sale and every time merchandise is returned. Does the column hold the total commissions earned, or just this month's commissions? How do I compare one month's commissions against another when I have only one column?

As you can see, we shouldn't have a column for commissions in the table at all. It's a calculated value, which can have a lot of definitions. We'll have to construct it as needed, using whatever definition applies.

Some of the columns we'll need in the database are as follows:

Customer related:

 `customer credit rating code = CHAR(1)`

`customer name = CHAR(15)`

Employee related:

`employee name = CHAR(15)`

`employee salary = DECIMAL(5,2)`

`employee's sales staff rank = INTEGER`

Order related:

- order identification number = **INTEGER**
- part identification code = **INTEGER**
- price of a part = **DECIMAL(7,2)**
- date a sale was made = **DATE**
- description of the parts we are selling = **CHAR(10)**

This isn't even close to a complete description of the business problem or the database, but it does get us started. We wouldn't advise using those long phrases for column names in the final database, but these data items should be documented somewhere, along with any information you have on them and the rules for maintaining them.

Let's have a first crack at the tables for the sale support database.

> Each version of SQL is going to have slight variations on the same definitions. Appendix A deals with the major differences and gives you alternative code definitions for Sybase and Oracle. The example text here has been created in Watcom SQL, which is included on the disk in the back of the book. So, if you read through and understand these examples, then you can try one of two things:
>
> Type in the equivalent version from Appendix A
>
> OR type in the code directly from here and try to figure out the differences yourself
>
> Sybase is quite different from Watcom SQL, and so are some of the smaller machine SQLs such as Access, but most are going to be almost identical.

So let's not type it in straight away but firstly consider what a **CREATE TABLE** definition might look like. Starting with a table for the salespersons, we might declare that table to be as follows:

```
CREATE TABLE Salespersons
(empid INTEGER NOT NULL,
 ename CHAR(15) NOT NULL,
 rank INTEGER NOT NULL,
 salary DECIMAL(7, 2) NOT NULL);
```

We decided that their rank will be a number instead of a character string. But we also decided to use an employee identification number, just in case we have two salesmen with the same name.

This would effectively create a table with four columns. The table can't be viewed, as it doesn't yet contain anything. All that exists are the column headings along with their legal data types and constraints:

	empid	ename	rank	salary
Row 1 Row 2				

Now inspect each column declaration. Is there any good reason for removing the **NOT NULL** constraints from a column? No, probably not. Should we add some defaults to any column? The lowest salary we pay anyone is $100 per week and the lowest rank they can hold is class one salesman. Let's add those:

```
CREATE TABLE Salespersons
(empid INTEGER NOT NULL,
 ename CHAR(15) NOT NULL,
 rank INTEGER NOT NULL DEFAULT 1,
 salary DECIMAL(7, 2) NOT NULL DEFAULT 100.00);
```

Should we add some check constraints to any column? The salary has to be a positive amount and we only use three ranks. Let's add those:

```
CREATE TABLE Salespersons
(empid INTEGER NOT NULL,
 ename CHAR(15) NOT NULL,
 rank INTEGER NOT NULL DEFAULT 1 CHECK (rank IN (1,2,3)),
 salary DECIMAL(7, 2) NOT NULL
     DEFAULT 1000.00 CHECK (salary >= 1000.00));
```

Notice that the **CHECK()** clause doesn't automatically imply that there can't be **NULL** - remember the rule that lets a **TRUE** or **UNKNOWN** result pass the test.

Do we have a primary key? Yes, that's why we created the **empid** column, to be sure we can find each individual employee. So here is the final declaration:

```
CREATE TABLE Salespersons
(empid INTEGER NOT NULL PRIMARY KEY,
 ename CHAR(15) NOT NULL,
 rank INTEGER NOT NULL DEFAULT 1 CHECK (rank IN (1,2,3)),
 salary DECIMAL(7, 2) NOT NULL
    DEFAULT 1000.00 CHECK (salary >= 1000.00));
```

Technically, we could remove the **NOT NULL** constraint from the **empid** column since it is redundant. But we prefer to leave it so that it will still be there if we alter the table and change the primary key. Now it's ready to type in.

> If you typed the table declaration earlier, then this one won't work. Once a table has been declared, it can't be re-declared. If you have entered it all correctly, then you should get no response from the compiler. Hence, each of our examples has been numbered progressively. We'll learn how to remove excess or old tables at the end of this chapter.

Some SQLs will let you know that the query has been processed, but some will give no indication whatsoever. You can't actually view the table, as it is empty. However, you are able to view the table headings and this should reassure you that the table exists! The command you will need to do this has not been covered yet, and it won't be until Chapter 6. It will simply display the whole contents of the table.

```
SELECT * FROM Salespersons;
```

Use this at any time to display any table simply by substituting the name of the relevant table you wish to look at for **Salespersons**. In this case, the column headings **empid**, **ename**, **rank** and **salary** should be all that are displayed.

If you got an error message when you typed in the **CREATE TABLE** definition (and you typed the code in correctly), then this will have been caused by your specific vendor project. The problem might be that your version of SQL doesn't support **DECIMAL** data types. Oracle has its own **NUMBER** data type, as it uses its own internal storage mechanism. If you have problems with **DECIMAL** then refer to your manual. At a push you could substitute it for **INTEGER**, but this isn't very satisfactory.

Also, if you are using your interactive SQL tool, then it may not support **DEFAULT** values. If this is so, then you will have to remove them. Some versions of SQL support **DEFAULT** values, but only for specific data types, which means you can't assign them to a number. In these versions, the defaults for any one data type will be assigned automatically to one value. For example, the default value of the **INTEGER** data type would always be zero and the **CHAR** would be the empty string.

Assuming that **Salespersons** table has now been created successfully, using the same line of reasoning, let's construct the other tables in the schema:

```
CREATE TABLE Customers
(custid INTEGER NOT NULL PRIMARY KEY,
 cname CHAR(15) NOT NULL,
 credit CHAR(1) NOT NULL CHECK (credit IN ('A', 'B', 'C')));
```

The **custid** column is an arbitrary customer number. Yes, we probably should have more columns here for his address, phone number and so forth, but let's keep things simple for now. Let's create a table for the inventory next:

```
CREATE TABLE Inventory
(partid INTEGER NOT NULL PRIMARY KEY,
 description CHAR(10) NOT NULL,
 stockqty INTEGER NOT NULL,
 reorderpnt INTEGER,
 price DECIMAL(7, 2) NOT NULL);
```

The **partid** is an arbitrary number used to identify the parts. The **stockqty** is the number of units we have in stock right now - if it is negative, that means we have backordered parts. The **reorderpnt** is the reorder point - when the inventory level drops to this number or less, we place an order for more of that part. Notice that we have let it go **NULL**. This will handle the case where we don't want to reorder a particular part, and so it is no longer possible to obtain it. Can you see why zero or some dummy value wouldn't work? (Hint - what value would you use if you had run out of a particular part and did want to reorder it?)

Now to declare a table for orders:

```
CREATE TABLE Orders
(orderid INTEGER NOT NULL PRIMARY KEY,
 empid INTEGER NOT NULL REFERENCES Salespersons(empid),
 custid INTEGER NOT NULL REFERENCES Customers(custid),
 salesdate DATE NOT NULL DEFAULT CURRENT DATE,
 item1 INTEGER REFERENCES Inventory(partid),
 qty1 INTEGER,
 item2 INTEGER REFERENCES Inventory(partid),
 qty2 INTEGER,
 item3 INTEGER REFERENCES Inventory(partid),
 qty3 INTEGER,
 item4 INTEGER REFERENCES Inventory(partid),
 qty4 INTEGER,
 item5 INTEGER REFERENCES Inventory(partid),
 qty5 INTEGER);
```

Again, **orderid** is an arbitrary number used to identify the orders. We need to be sure that the **empid** of the salesperson who took the order is a current employee, so we use the **REFERENCES** clause. We need to be sure that the **custid** of the customer who placed the order is a current customer, so we use the **REFERENCES** clause again. We could put a **CHECK()** clause on the salesdate to ensure that no salesman tries to backdate an order, but let's not do so at the moment - instead, just default to the current date.

We are allowing the customer to order up to five items and make sure that the **partid** is something in inventory. This is a copy of a paper or video terminal order form. The first columns in the table are the header at the top of the page, and items and quantity fields are the last ten columns.

Other Table Manipulation Commands

SQL-92 defines a number of new options in the creation of a table, which are not yet available in vendor products. These options allow you create temporary tables with local or global access. There are also further options on how the rows in these tables are handled after the end of a session (preserved or deleted).

Vendors will often have other commands or clauses which relate to the physical storage of tables in the database. There is no general advice as to how to use them, you need to take a vendor training course for that.

However, there are two other actions you can perform on a table in any SQL product. You can drop a table from the database and alter the structure of the table. Let's go into the details.

Drop Table

The **DROP TABLE** statement gets rid of a table. This is primarily used for removing old or unwanted tables. There is no method of recovery of a table once it has been dropped. It is important to remember that this is *not* the same as making the table an empty table. When a schema object is dropped it is gone forever, together with any data belonging to it. According to the SQL-92 standard, the syntax of the statement is as follows:

```
<drop table statement> ::=
        DROP TABLE <table name> <drop behavior>
```

The **<drop behavior>** is new to SQL-92. It is a difficult concept to grasp immediately. This part is required so as to determine what happens to the various related database objects when a table is dropped. We haven't looked at related database objects yet so the **<drop behavior>** clause doesn't affect us, at the moment. It is important to be aware of it, as it will affect us later.

Most SQL products will accept the following non-standard/SQL-89 standard syntax:

```
<drop table statement> ::=
        DROP TABLE <table name>
```

To a drop a table you simply specify it by name.

```
DROP TABLE Customer;
```

This would remove the table **Customer**. Don't type it in, unless you want to re-create the table from scratch! However, if you are typing in the examples from the example database and you wish to type each one in as it is amended, simply type **DROP TABLE <table name>** to get rid of the old version of the table and then you can use the **CREATE TABLE** command to redefine the new amendment of that table. As we said earlier, you can't re-declare a table once it has been created, you can only **ALTER TABLE** or **DROP TABLE**.

> Once you are using tables that are related, it is essential to use the `<drop behavior>` clause. The reasons behind this, along with a comprehensive look at the `<drop behavior>` clause are examined in depth in Chapter 4.

The SQL-89 standard was silent concerning what happened when you dropped a table. Either the particular SQL product would post an error message and deal with the problem, or you would find out about any references to the offending table by having your database blow up when it ran into constructs which needed the missing table.

The **DROP** keyword and `<drop behavior>` clause are also used in other statements which remove schema objects, such as **DROP VIEW**, **DROP SCHEMA**, **DROP CONSTRAINT** and so on.

Alter Table

The **ALTER TABLE** command adds, removes or changes columns in a particular table. It gives you a chance to re-do your schema after you already have a database. This wasn't part of the SQL-89 standard, but most SQL products had some form of it, with slightly varying power and syntax. In SQL-92, the syntax is as follows:

```
ALTER TABLE <table name> <alter table action>

<alter table action> ::=
 <add column definition>
   | <alter column definition>
   | <drop column definition>
   | <add table constraint definition>
   | <drop table constraint definition>
```

Let's explain the sub-clauses by starting with the `<add column definition>` clause. This is probably going to be used more than the others because you always forget something when you design a database. This clause will add a column to a table using the following syntax:

`ADD [ COLUMN ] <column definition>`

The column defined by the `<column definition>` is added to the table in the position just after the last existing column. It comes into existence with all its values set to `NULL` (unknown value, covered in detail in Chapter 3) or to whatever the default value is given in the definition.

The column has to follow all of the rules for a column that would apply if it had been created with the schema. This means there can be no duplicate column names in the same table, and so on. Likewise, the `SELECT`, `UPDATE`, `INSERT` or `REFERENCES` privileges that were in effect apply to the new column name:

	empid	ename	rank	salary
Row 1 Row 2				

This is the table created by the example database. We will now add an extra column to it for phone numbers:

`ALTER TABLE Salespersons ADD phone INTEGER NOT NULL;`

> **The added column can only have a NOT NULL constraint, if there is nothing in the database, and only if your implementation allows it. Consider if you have data in the database for ename, rank and salary. The column is added to the end, and has to have a value. As a value has not yet been specified, it must be unknown and hence a NULL value.**

The extra column is always added onto the end of the existing table. As before, you can't view the effect of this statement as the table is empty. Theoretically it would be like this:

	empid	ename	rank	salary	phone
Row 1 Row 2					

You can get rid of this column with **DROP**. The **<drop column definition>** clause will destroy a column in the table. The syntax for this clause is as follows:

DROP [COLUMN] <column name> <drop behavior>

The same rules apply on this **DROP [COLUMN]** as with **DROP TABLE**. The syntax below is accepted by some SQL products.

DROP [COLUMN] <column name>

It has all the same pitfalls that the **DROP TABLE** syntax minus the **<drop behavior>** clause had. Using this syntax then, a typical **ALTER TABLE** statement would look like this:

ALTER TABLE Salespersons DROP Phone;

This will simply remove the column created by the **ALTER TABLE ADD [COLUMN]** which was performed earlier, returning the table to its original form.

The following functions are supported under different names by some SQL products, such as **MODIFY** in Watcom SQL rather than **ALTER**. The **<alter column definition>** clause will change the default of a column. The syntax is as follows:

ALTER [COLUMN] <column name> <alter column action>

<alter column action> ::=
 <set column default clause> | <drop column default clause>

The **<set column default clause>** sub-clause uses this syntax to change the default value for the column:

SET <default clause>

The **<drop column default clause>** will drop the default. This is its syntax:

DROP DEFAULT

The `<add table constraint definition>` clause will add a constraint to the table:

`ADD <table constraint definition>`

Likewise, the `<drop table constraint definition>` will destroy a constraint on a table. The syntax is this:

`DROP CONSTRAINT <constraint name> <drop behavior>`

This clause requires that the constraint has a name. This is why it is a good idea to always name constraints, otherwise you can't easily change them.

The problem comes when you try to drop a **PRIMARY KEY** or **UNIQUE** table constraint and there exists a referential constraint in another table which references this table. Again, we will have to look at how this is dealt with when we look at drop behavior.

Summary

We have covered a lot of ground in this chapter and have made a start on our example database. Working through the creation of this database will help you get used to the different requirements SQL demands of you as a programmer.

In this chapter we looked at a wide range of issues in SQL. We began by looking at SQL and how it differs conceptually from other language models and then moved on to some of its particular terminologies.

We created our first table using the **CREATE** statement and looked at how data types differ in SQL from other languages. We looked at all the different aspects available under the **CREATE TABLE** statement such as column constraints and commenting.

We began our work on the example database by writing some SQL code to create the headings and structure of the tables and columns.

Finally, we briefly covered how to **DROP** and **ALTER** table and non-standard commands involved in their usage.

In the next chapter we'll move on to some theory behind some of the features we have used, such as the **NULL** clause, making sure you understand properly how and why they are used. But first we'll look at how SQL handles the data types we've already used in the database such as **INTEGER**s, **CHAR**s and **NUMERIC**s and what rules are applied when using these data types.

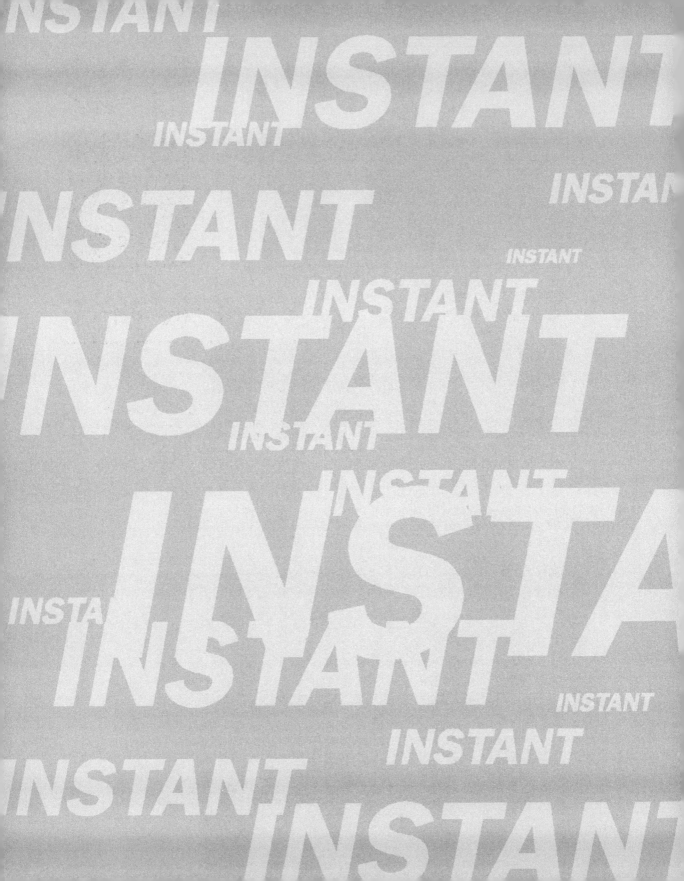

SQL Arithmetic, Logic and the NULL

SQL is strictly a database language and not a language of calculation or algorithm, so its arithmetic capability is weaker than any programming language you may have used. Much of the arithmetic and the functions are implementation-defined, so you should experiment with your particular product and make notes on the defaults, precision and tools in the math library of your SQL.

In this chapter we'll look at the following topics:

- The use of some of SQL's numeric and string functions
- How SQL handles arithmetic
- The peculiarity of SQL's three-valued logic
- The importance of the **NULL**

Numeric Type Conversion

We're back into theory now for this chapter. You know now how to define a database, but you need to know more about the actual data types you are using within your definitions. We'll start off with how to go about changing from one data type to another, and particularly the problems caused for the numeric types. There are a few surprises in converting from one numeric type to another. The SQL standard left it up to the implementation to answer a lot of basic questions, so the programmer has to know the package with which they are working.

Rounding and Truncation

When an exact or approximate numeric value is assigned to an exact numeric column, there is a chance that it might not fit. SQL says that the database engine will use an approximation which preserves leading significant digits of the original number after rounding or truncating. The choice of whether to truncate or round is implementation defined, however. This can lead to some surprises when you have to shift data among SQL implementations, or storage values from a host language program into an SQL table. Therefore, it's probably a good idea to create the columns with more decimal places than you think you need.

Rounding

SQL leaves rounding to the implementation. There are two major types of rounding in programming:

The Scientific Method

The 'scientific method' looks at the digit to be removed. If that digit is 0, 1, 2, 3 or 4, you drop it and leave the higher order digit to its left unchanged. If that digit is 5, 6, 7, 8 or 9, it is dropped and the digit to its left is incremented. For example, 3.141592653 rounds to 3.142 because the fourth decimal place is a five. This method works with a small set of numbers and was popular with FORTRAN programmers because it is how engineers are used to operating.

The Commercial Method

The 'commercial method' looks at the digit to be removed. If that digit is 0, 1, 2, 3 or 4, it is dropped and the digit to its left remains unchanged. If that digit is 6, 7, 8 or 9, it is dropped and the digit to its left is incremented. However, when the digit is 5, you want to have a rule which will round up in about half of all cases. One rule is to look at the digit to the left; if it is odd, then leave it unchanged, if it is even increment it. There are other versions of the decision rule, but they all try to make the *total* rounding error in a summation as small as possible. For example, 3.141592653 rounds to 3.141 because the fourth decimal place is a five, so we have to look at the fifth decimal place. Nine is odd, so we truncate instead of increment. This method works with a large set of numbers and was popular with COBOL programmers and bankers because they need accurate totals. Bankers especially, needless to say.

Truncation

Truncation is defined as truncation towards zero. This means that 1.5 would truncate to 1, and -1.5 would truncate to -1. This isn't true for all programming languages - everyone agrees on truncation towards zero for the positive numbers, but you will find that negative numbers may truncate away from zero (for example, -1.5 would truncate to -2) in some products.

CAST() or CONVERT() Function

The `CAST()` function converts one data type to another. (In some SQLs such as Sybase, the `CONVERT` function provides the same purpose.) SQL-92 defines the general `CAST(<cast operand> AS <data type>)` function for all data type conversions, but most implementations use several specific functions of their own for the conversions they support. The usual convention is to make the target data type the name of the conversion function. For example, `MONTH(DATE)` would take a date and convert it to a numerical month number.

> The SQL-92 CAST() function isn't only more general but it also allows the <cast operand> to be either a <column name>, <value expression> or a NULL. You should expect to see it replace vendor functions in the next few years.

However, some SQL implementations will also have formatting options in their conversion functions which are not part of the standard. These functions turn the internal numeric format into a string using either a template string, like COBOL's PICTURE clause or C's print functions, or else they return the result in a format set in an environment variable. This is very implementation-dependent.

Four Function Math

SQL has less calculation abilities than a pocket calculator. The dyadic arithmetic operators +, -, *, and / stand for addition, subtraction, multiplication, and division, respectively. The multiplication and division operators are of equal precedence and are performed before the dyadic plus and minus operators.

In algebra, and in some programming languages, the precedence of arithmetic operators is more restricted. They use the 'My Dear Aunt Sally' rule, that is: multiplication is done before division, which is done before addition, which is done before subtraction. This can lead to subtle errors, for example, (largenum + largenum - largenum), where largenum is the maximum value that can be represented in its numeric data type. If you group the expression from left to right, you get ((largenum + largenum) - largenum) = overflow error! However, if you group the expression from right to left, you get (largenum + (largenum - largenum)) = largenum.

Because of these differences, an expression which worked one way in the host language might get different results in SQL, and vice versa. SQL could re-order the expressions to optimize them, but in practice, you will find that many implementations will simply parse the expressions from left to right. The best way to be safe is to always make extensive use of parentheses in all expressions, whether they are in the host language, or your SQL.

The monadic plus and minus signs are allowed, and you can string as many of them as you like in front of a numeric value of variables. The bad news about this is that SQL also uses the double dash ADA-style comments, so the parser has to figure out if '--' is two minus signs or the start of a comment. Of course, you can use parentheses to make it clear.

> Most versions of SQL support C-style comment brackets (/* comment text */), and they have been proposed as the general comment style in the SQL3 standards discussion papers, because some international data transmission standards don't recognize a 'newline' convention and view text as a single string of characters.

If both operands are exact numeric, then the data type of the result is exact numeric, as you would expect. Likewise, an approximate numeric in a calculation will cast the results to approximate numeric. The tricky part is in how the results are assigned precision and scale.

Let's work through a brief example to sort this out. Let S1 and S2 be the scale of the first and second operands, respectively. The precision of the result of addition and subtraction is implementation-defined and the scale is the maximum of S1 and S2. The precision of the result of multiplication is implementation defined and the scale is (S1 + S2). The precision and scale of the result of division is implementation-defined and so are some decisions about rounding or truncating results.

The ANSI X3H2 committee debated about requiring precision and scales in the standard, and finally gave up. This means we can start losing high order digits, especially with a division operation, where it is perfectly legal to make all results single digit integers. No vendor does anything that stupid in their product. Some products will allow you to adjust the number of decimal places as a system parameter, some default to a few decimal places, and some display as many decimal places as they can, so that you can round off to what you want. You will simply have to learn what your implementation does by experimenting with it.

Most vendors have extended this set of operators with other common mathematical functions. The most common additional functions are modulus, absolute value, power and square root. But it is also possible to find logarithms to different bases, exponential, trigonometry and other scientific, statistical and mathematical functions. Precision and scale is implementation-defined for these functions, naturally, but they will tend to follow the same design decisions as the arithmetic did. The reason is obvious - they are using the same library routines under the covers as the math package in the database engine.

Vendor Math Functions

All other math functions are vendor extensions, but you can plan on several common ones in most SQL implementations. They are implemented under assorted names and often with slightly different functionality:

- **(x MOD y)** = modulo or remainder arithmetic. This is tricky when the values of x and y are not both positive, non-zero integers. Experiment and find out how your package handles negative numbers and decimal places.

- **ABS(x)** = return the absolute value of x.

- **COUNTER()** = returns a new incremented value each time it is used in an expression. This is a way to generate unique identifiers.

- **POWER(x, n)** = raise number x to the nth power.

- **ROUND(x, p)** = round number x to p decimal places.

- **SQRT(x)** = return the square root of x.

- **TRUNCATE(x, p)** = Truncate number x to p decimal places.

Many implementations also allow for the use of external functions written in other programming languages.

Problems of String Equality

In SQL, character strings are printable characters enclosed in single quotation marks. The SQL-92 standard introduced the convention that double quotation marks are used to enclose names which have embedded spaces or which are also reserved SQL keywords. Look at these various occurrences of the same word as different types:

 INTEGER is an SQL keyword.

 'INTEGER' is a character string.

 "INTEGER" is a name of a program variable.

> **Beware - some SQLs allow " " to delimit character strings as well as variables.**

No two languages agree on how to compare character strings as equal unless they are identical in length and match position for position, exact character for character.

The first problem is whether the upper and lower case versions of a letter will be treated as equal to each other. Many programming languages treat them in that way within the program text, including all proper SQL implementations. While the standard says that the two cases are different, it is very implementation-dependent. Some implementations, such as Sybase, allow case-sensitivity or lack thereof to be specified when the system is installed.

The SQL-92 standard has two functions which change the case of a string. **LOWER (<string expression>)** shifts all letters in the parameter string to corresponding lower-case letters. **UPPER (<string expression>)** shifts all letters to upper-case. Most implementations have had these functions (perhaps with different names) as vendor library functions.

Equality between strings of unequal length is done by first padding out the shortest string with blanks on the right hand side, until the strings are of the same length. They are then matched, position for position, for identical values. If one position fails to match, the whole equality fails.

In contrast, the XBase languages (FoxPro, dBASE, Clipper, and so on) truncate the longer string to the length of the shorter string and then match them position for position.

String Functions

SQL-92 defines a set of string functions which have been in most products, but with vendor specific syntax. You will probably find that products will continue to support their own syntax, but also add the SQL-92 syntax in new releases.

String concatenation is shown with the '||' operator taken from PL/1 (the programming language of the 60's and 70's that was intended to complement third generation computer systems). There are some special rules that govern what happens if you concatenate a string with a missing/ unknown or **NULL** value, but we will cover those when we cover the **NULL** value, later this chapter.

The Substring Function

The syntax for the **SUBSTRING** function is as follows (it can be **SUBSTR** in some versions):

```
SUBSTRING (<string> FROM <start> [FOR <length>])
```

It uses three arguments: the source string, the starting position of the substring and the length of the substring to be extracted. Truncation occurs when neither the implied starting nor the ending positions are within the given string.

If any of the three parameters are **NULL**, this function returns a **NULL**. If the **<start>** position is greater than the length of the **<string>**, or if the **<string>** is empty, then the result is the empty string. If you leave off the **FOR <length>** clause or give a value that is too long, it defaults to the rest of the string.

The Fold Functions

The fold functions is a name given to a pair of functions for converting all the lower case characters in a given string to upper case or all the upper case ones to lower case. The syntax is very simple for either function:

UPPER(<string>) to convert all the characters to upper case.

LOWER(<string>) to convert all the characters to lower case.

When you perform either one of these functions it is known as a 'fold'.

The Trim Function

The **TRIM** function is used to remove an unwanted character from the beginning or end of a specified string. The **TRIM** syntax looks like this:

```
TRIM ([[<trim specification>] [<trim character>] FROM] <trim source>)
```

This produces a result string that is the source string with an unwanted character, removed from the start or the end of the string. The **<trim source>** is the original character value expression. The **<trim specification>** is either '**LEADING**' or '**TRAILING**' or '**BOTH**' and the **<trim character>** is the single character that is to be removed. The SQL-92 function is very general, but you will find most SQL implementations have a version which works only with leading blanks.

Length and Position

The **LENGTH(<string>)** gives the length of a given character string as an integer, in characters or bits according to the choice of function.

The **POSITION (<search string> IN <source string>)** determines the first position, if any, at which the **<search string>** occurs within the **<source string>**. If the **<search string>** is of length zero, then it occurs at position one for any value of the **<source string>**. If the **<search string>** doesn't occur in the **<source string>**, then zero is returned. In some SQLs **LOCATE** is used.

Vendor String Functions

The most common extension to pattern matching predicates is a version of **grep()**, the 'General Regular Expression Parser' from the UNIX operating system. A version of **grep()**, **<string expression> SIMILAR TO <pattern>**, has been proposed for SQL3 which follows the POSIX model.

> Since there are several versions of **grep()** and it isn't common in SQL implementations, we won't discuss it in this book. Look in your product manual to see if you have it.

As we already mentioned, many vendors also have functions which will format data for display by converting the internal format to a text string. A vendor whose SQL is tied to a 4GL is much more likely to have these extensions simply because the 4GL can use them. The most common one is something to convert a date and time to a national format.

Vendor extensions are varied, but there are some which are worth mention. The names will be different in different products, but the functionality will be the same.

Reverse

REVERSE(<string expression>) will reverse the order of the characters in a string to make it easier to search. This function is impossible to write with the standard string operators since it requires either iteration or recursion.

Flip

FLIP(<string expression>, <pivot>) will locate the pivot character in the string, then concatenate all the letters to the left of the pivot onto the end of the string and finally erase the pivot character. This is used to change the order of names from 'military format' to 'civilian format'. Therefore, if you used the command **FLIP ('Smith, John', ',')** it would become 'John Smith'. This function can be written with the standard string functions, however.

Numtowords

NUMTOWORDS (<numeric expression>) will write out the numeric value as English words to use on checks or other documents which require both numerals and text versions of the same value. This was replaced by the CAST function in the SQL-92 standard.

Displaying Dates

Everybody likes a different date display format, so most databases will give you several options. The usual ones are a mixture of a two or four digit year, a three letter or two digit month and a two digit day within the particular month. The three fields can be separated by slashes, dashes or spaces. SQL-92 can't use abbreviations for month names and still be international (that is, language independent), so the format in the standard is a four digit year, a dash, a two digit month (01-12), a dash and a two digit day within the month (01-31). This 'yyyy-mm-dd' is called the **calendar date format**. It is a string that gets converted into an unspecified internal format in the database.

Timestamps

The TIMESTAMP(n) data type is defined as a timestamp to (n) decimal places (for example, TIMESTAMP(9) is nanosecond precision), where the precision is hardware-dependent. You can expect to get at least four to five decimal places after the second.

Timestamps usually serve two purposes. They can be used as a true timestamp to mark an event connected to the row in which they appear, or they can be used as a sequential number for building a unique key which isn't temporal in nature.

> **The latter option isn't recommended practice as it is very hard to display or search on this type of key.**

For example, the date and time a payment is made on an account is important and requires a true timestamp for legal reasons. The account number has to be different from all other account numbers, so we need a unique number and the timestamp is a quick way of getting one.

Remember that a timestamp will read the system clock once and use that same time on all the items involved in a transaction. It doesn't matter if the actual time to complete the transaction is days; a transaction in SQL is done as a whole unit or not done at all. Most of the time this isn't a problem for small transactions, but it can be in large batched ones where very complex updates have to be done.

Times

Most databases live and work in one time zone. If you have a database which goes over time zones, you might consider storing time in UTC (Universal Time Coordinate, formerly GMT, Greenwich Mean Time) and adding a numeric column to hold the local time zone offset. The time zones start at UTC, which has an offset of zero. This is how the system level time zone table in SQL-92 is defined. There are also ISO standard three letter codes for the time zones of the world, such as EST for 'Eastern Standard Time' in the United States. The offset is usually a positive or negative number of hours, but there are some odd zones which differ by 15 minutes from the expected pattern.

You should use a twenty-four hour time format. Twenty-four hour time display format is less prone to errors than twelve hour (AM/PM) time. It is less likely to be misread or miswritten. This format manually sorts more easily and is less prone to computational errors. Americans use a colon as a field separator between hours, minutes and seconds, while Europeans use a period. Most databases will give you these display options.

Intervals

One of the major problems with time is that there are three kinds: fixed events ('he arrives at 13:00 hours'), duration ('the trip takes three hours') and intervals ('the train leaves at 10:00 hours and arrives at 13:00 hours') and all three are inter-related.

SQL-92 introduces an **INTERVAL** data type which doesn't exist in most current implementations. There are two classes of intervals. One class, called year-month intervals, has an express or implied datetime precision that includes no fields other than **YEAR** and **MONTH**, though not both are required. The other class, called day-time intervals, has an express or implied interval precision that can include any fields other than **YEAR** or **MONTH**.

Date Arithmetic

You may assume that your SQL implementation has simple date arithmetic functions. The syntax will vary from product to product, but the basic operations every product has are:

1 A date, plus or minus a number of days, yields a new date.

2 A date, minus a second date, yields an integer number of days.

Here is a list of the valid combinations of datetime and interval data types in the SQL-92 standard:

- `Datetime - Datetime = Interval`
- `Datetime ± Interval = Datetime`
- `Interval (* or /) Numeric = Interval`
- `Interval + Datetime = Datetime`
- `Interval ± Interval = Interval`
- `Numeric * Interval = Interval`

There are other rules that deal with time zones and the relative precision of the two operands which are intuitively obvious.

There should also be a function which returns the current date from the system clock. This function has a different name with each vendor: `TODAY`, `SYSDATE` and `getdate()` are some examples. There may also be a function to return the day of the week from a date which is sometimes called `DOW()` or `WEEKDAY()`. The SQL-92 standard provides for `CURRENT_DATE`, `CURRENT_TIME [(<time precision>)]` and `CURRENT_TIMESTAMP [(<timestamp precision>)]`, functions which explain themselves.

DATE and TIME Functions

No two SQL products agree on the functions that should be available for use with `DATETIME` data types. The SQL-92 proposal has a function for extracting components from a datetime or interval value. The syntax looks like this:

```
<extract expression>::=
 EXTRACT (<extract field> FROM <extract source>)

<extract field>::= <datetime field> | <time zone field>

<time zone field>::= TIMEZONE_HOUR | TIMEZONE_MINUTE

<extract source>::= <datetime value expression>
       | <interval value expression>
```

The interesting feature is that this function always returns a numeric value. For example, **EXTRACT (MONTH FROM birthday)** will be an **INTEGER** between 1 and 12. No vendor has implemented this function yet, so you should look for many separate functions like **YEAR(<date>)**, **MONTH(<date>)** and **DAY(<date>)** which extract particular components from a datetime data type.

Week Functions

Another common set of functions, which are not represented in standard SQL, deal with weeks. For example, Watcom SQL has a **DOW(<date>)** which returns a number between one and seven to represent the day of the week (1 = Sunday, 2 = Monday,... 7 = Saturday, following an ISO Standard convention). You can also find functions which add or subtract weeks from a date, give the number of the date within the year, and so on.

> DB2 and XDB SQL have an **AGE(<date1>, <date2>)** function which returns the difference in years between **<date1>** and **<date2>**.

Most versions of SQL also have a library function something like **MAKEDATE(<year>, <month>, <day>)**, **DATE(<year>, <month>, <day>)** or the equivalent which will construct a date from three numbers representing a year, month and day. Standard SQL can use the **CAST** function, but the details are not pretty, since it involves assembling a string, then converting that string to a date.

> The best advice we can give you is to read your SQL product manual and see what you can do.

Comparison Operators in SQL

The large number of data types in SQL makes doing comparisons a little harder than in other programming languages. Values of one data type have to be promoted to values of the other data type before the comparison can be done. The available data types are implementation- and hardware-dependent, so read the manuals for your product.

The comparison operators in SQL are **overloaded**, which means that the same symbol will work for numeric, character and datetime data types. The meaning of, and symbols for, comparison operators are as follows:

	numeric	character	temporal
<	less than	(collates before)	(earlier than)
=	equal	(collates equal to)	(coincident)
>	greater than	(collates after)	(later than)
<=	at most	(collates before or equal)	(no earlier than)
<>	not equal	(not the same as)	(not coincident)
>=	at least	(collates after or equal)	(no later than)

> You will also see '!=' or '~=' for 'not equal to' in SQL implementation. These symbols are borrowed from C and PL/1 programming languages respectively and have never been part of standard SQL.

Beginners to SQL programming have no trouble using comparison operators with numeric data types, since they are used with numerics in all their old programming languages. They have a little trouble using the operators with character data, but not much. However, initially everyone has a hard time seeing that comparison operators work with temporal data types. We don't know why - perhaps it's because SQL is the first programming language they have used which has temporal data types!

Converting Data Types

Numeric data types are all mutually comparable and mutually assignable. If an assignment would result in a loss of the most significant digits, an exception condition is raised. If least significant digits are lost, the implementation defines what rounding or truncating occurs and doesn't report an exception condition.

Most often, one value is converted to the same data type as the other and then the comparison is done in the usual way. The chosen data type is the 'higher' of the two, using the ordering from least to highest is **SMALLINT**, **INTEGER**, **DECIMAL**, **NUMERIC**, **REAL**, **FLOAT** and **DOUBLEPRECISION**.

Floating point implementations in both software and hardware will often affect comparisons for **REAL**, **FLOAT** and **DOUBLEPRECISION** numbers. Two floating numbers are rarely **EXACTLY** equal, so the system allows for ignoring a small difference (this is called an **epsilon**). There is no good way to avoid this, since it isn't always reasonable to use **DECIMAL** or **NUMERIC** in their place. A host language will probably use the same floating point hardware, so at least errors are constant across the application.

CHARACTER and **CHARACTER VARYING** data types are comparable if, *and only if*, they are taken from the same character repertoire. That means that ASCII characters can't compare to graphics characters, English can't compare to Arabic, and so on. In most implementations, this isn't a problem since the database has only one repertoire. The comparison takes the shorter of the two strings and pads it with spaces. The strings are compared position by position from left to right, using the collating sequence for the repertoire (ASCII or EBCDIC in most cases).

DATETIME data types are mutually assignable only if the source and target of the assignment have the same **DATETIME** fields. That is, you can't compare a date and a time.

The **CAST(<value expression> AS <data type>)** operator can do explicit type conversions before you do a comparison.

> The table of the valid combinations of source and target data types in SQL-92, which are also referred to as the table of legal conversions, can be found in Appendix E.

Logic and SQL

SQL databases search for and control data using logical expressions, which are called **search conditions** in SQL, or sometimes **predicates**. The logic that most programming languages use was developed by George Boole in his book *The Laws of Thought* over a hundred years ago, and it attached his name to Boolean algebra forever. It's based on the two values, **TRUE** and **FALSE**, and the operators **AND**, **OR** and **NOT**. ' is also the logic embedded in virtually every programming language you have ever used. It's the basis for the digital computer, whose two states (ON and OFF) make binary calculations very easy. Computer people really like Boolean logic!

But Boolean algebra isn't the only possible system of logic and SQL doesn't use it. SQL has a three valued logic based on the values **TRUE**, **FALSE** and **UNKNOWN**. The SQL standard still refers to Boolean operators, but they have slightly different rules. This linguistic confusion and the strangeness of thinking in *three* values is hard for beginners to SQL programming. The first problem is realizing that **UNKNOWN** is a logical value (this isn't the same as the data value **NULL** which is also a missing or unknown character).

Notice that SQL-89 doesn't have a **BOOLEAN** or **LOGICAL** data type. If there *were* such a data type, then you could store **TRUE**, **FALSE**, **UNKNOWN** and **NULL** in columns with that declaration. Ouch - that gives us four logical values and would make all kinds of problems which we don't want to even think about in an introductory book!

If you need to store a logic value in a column, then use flags in some other data type. The most common choices are **CHAR(1)** with allowed values of 'Y' for 'yes' and 'N' for 'no', or 'T' for 'true' and 'F' for 'false'. You will also see a **SMALLINT** declaration used with allowed values of one and zero. The **SMALLINT** declaration has the advantage that the column can be added to tell you how many **TRUE**s were in it and other logical operations can be done with arithmetic.

Boolean Operators for Three Values

Here are the truth tables for the three basic Boolean operators in SQL:

The **AND** table:

AND	TRUE	UNKNOWN	FALSE
TRUE	TRUE	UNKNOWN	FALSE
UNKNOWN	UNKNOWN	UNKNOWN	FALSE
FALSE	FALSE	FALSE	FALSE

The **OR** table:

OR	TRUE	UNKNOWN	FALSE
TRUE	TRUE	TRUE	TRUE
UNKNOWN	TRUE	UNKNOWN	UNKNOWN
FALSE	TRUE	UNKNOWN	FALSE

The **NOT** table:

<EXP>	NOT
TRUE	FALSE
UNKNOWN	UNKNOWN
FALSE	TRUE

> Notice that if you removed the **UNKNOWNS** from the table, these would be the normal Boolean operators you have seen in every other programming language.

The operands for these operators are simple comparisons (or other operators) which are *shorthands,* which expand into chains of comparisons - (comparison operators are also called **theta** operators in relational database theory). Let's start with the simple comparison operators.

Unknown Logical Values

Where do **UNKNOWN** logical values come from? From trying to compare **NULL**s to other values! Since you don't know what the **NULL** stands for, you can't say if the comparison is **TRUE** or **FALSE**.

A subtle point that newcomers to SQL programming miss is that a **NULL** can't even be compared to another **NULL**. This makes sense if you think about it. But how do you find out whether or not something is **NULL**? You need to use a special operator **<expression> IS [NOT] NULL** instead of the expected **<expression> = NULL** which people first write when learning SQL.

> **Most programmers don't easily think in three values. If you
> ask for all rows where some column is equal to 2, and then
> execute a query to ask for all rows where the same column
> isn't equal to 2, you expect to see all the rows of that table
> between these two queries. It is a basic law of arithmetic! But
> only if you don't have NULLs.**

SQL-92 has solved this problem by adding a new search condition of the form **<search condition> IS [NOT] TRUE | FALSE | UNKNOWN**, which will let you map any combination of three-valued logic to two values. It applies only to search conditions and works in the following way:

IS	TRUE	FALSE	UNKNOWN
TRUE	TRUE	FALSE	FALSE
FALSE	FALSE	TRUE	FALSE
UNKNOWN	FALSE	FALSE	TRUE

The **ISN'T** form of the operator is the same as putting a **NOT** outside the whole expression. For example, the expression **((age < 18) AND (gender = 'Female')) ISN'T FALSE,** is the same as **NOT ((age < 18) AND (gender = 'Female') IS FALSE)**. This expression will return **TRUE** if **(age IS NULL)** or **(gender IS NULL)** and the remaining condition isn't **NULL**. This is a **MAYBE** operator.

The Dreaded NULL

There is no concept of zero in Roman numerals. It was centuries before Hindu-Arabic numerals became popular in Europe. In fact, many early Renaissance accounting firms advertised that they did not use the fancy, new-fangled notation and kept records instead in well understood Roman numerals. The argument against the zero was that if there is no quantity or magnitude there, how can you count or measure it? What does it mean to multiply or divide a number by zero?

Likewise, it was a long time before the idea of an empty set found its way into mathematics. The argument was that if there are no elements, how can you have a set of it? Is the empty set a subset of itself? Is the empty set a subset of all other sets? Is there only one empty set or one for each type of set?

The **NULL** is how SQL handles missing data. It is a major stumbling block for experienced as well as new programmers, so we are going to spend quite a lot of time discussing it to make sure that you have a feel for what it does and how it works.

Arithmetic and Nulls

Missing values are probably one of the most formidable concepts for the beginner to database usage. We'll give a detailed discussion of how **NULL**s work in SQL in another chapter, but this section is concerned with just how they act in arithmetic expressions.

The **NULL** is how SQL handles missing values. The **NULL** is a global creature, not belonging to any particular data type, but able to replace any of their values. So what exactly is a **NULL**?

Programmers coming from Pascal and the like might be tempted to think it is similar to the **NULL** string, which is treated like an empty string. Get rid of that idea immediately. A **NULL** is a missing value in the sense that it could be replaced with an actual value. It is *as yet* unknown. It is incorrect to say that a student who has taken an exam has got zero marks, just because they don't yet know their results. So, don't be tempted to think it is equivalent to nothing.

The basic rule for math with **NULL**s is that they **propagate**. What this means is that an arithmetic operation with a **NULL** will return a **NULL**. That *does* makes sense - if a **NULL** is a missing value, then you can't determine the results of a calculation with it.

However, the expression **(NULL / 0)** isn't consistent in SQL implementations. The first thought is that a division by zero should return an error - if **NULL** is a true missing value, then there is no value to which it can resolve and make that expression valid. However, almost all SQL implementations propagate the **NULL** and don't even issue a warning about division by zero - even when it appears as a constant in an expression. A non-**NULL** value divided by zero, however, will cause an error just as in any other programming language.

We have already discussed how **NULL**s work in arithmetic and character string expressions: they propagate. If you have a **NULL** in an expression, then the result will be **NULL**.

Instead of just going for a theoretical approach, let's start with examples that a programmer can understand and try to build a consistent model from them.

Missing Values

It's not the beginner's fault that missing values are such a difficult concept - there are a lot of reasons why values can be missing. Each kind of missing value is a little different, with a slightly different meaning, but they are all folded into the **NULL** in SQL. SQL doesn't care about semantics, only the syntax matters. Some of the ways to use a **NULL** are as follows:

1 Presently unknown values, which will later be replaced with real values when we *do* know something. For example, you just got to the hospital and they don't yet have a diagnosis for your condition. The tests are at the lab and we are awaiting the results.

2 The value is permanently missing from the attribute and won't come back. The hair color of a bald man is an example that comes to mind (see author's photograph). This kind of situation is often shown with the code 'N/A' for 'not applicable' on paper forms and in computer spreadsheet programs.

How could an attribute not belonging to an entity show up in a table? Consider a report in which you consolidate medical records and put everyone together for statistical purposes. You shouldn't find any male pregnancies in the result table. The programmer has a choice as to how to handle male pregnancies. He can have a column in the consolidated table for 'number of pregnancies' and put a zero or a **NULL** in the rows where **(sex = 'male')**. But if you use a zero, then all men and virgins are treated alike. One idea might be to introduce a code value for special cases, so you can differentiate between the separate cases.

3 The value can be a miscellaneous class of many values treated as if they were a single value. The common abbreviation for this situation is 'misc.' on paper forms. This is really a bad way to use a **NULL**, since we know that a value actually exists. You will see many older programs designed to fill a field with all 9's as a code for this situation.

4 The attribute itself doesn't apply, so it can't have a value. For example, the color of the feathers on a pig's wings can only make sense when pigs have wings. This situation also might be shown with the code 'N/A' as in situation 2 (but it is actually different).

5 The value can be un-defined in some way. A division by zero is un-defined and will cause an error message to appear in SQL when the dividend is a known numeric value. Yet, the expression **(NULL/0)** will evaluate to **NULL** and not produce an error message, in spite of the fact that there is no known numeric value that could ever be put in place of the **NULL**.

6 The value can be partly known, but not confirmed. You create a table with a column called 'Tricolor' which is limited to the values 'red', 'white' and 'blue' and put a constraint on it that says each color can appear only once.

If my table has a 'red' and two **NULL** values in that column, then I have some information about the two **NULL**s. I know they are either 'white' and 'blue' or 'blue' and 'white'. This is what is termed by one author, Chris Date, a 'distinguished **NULL**', which means we have some information in it. If my table has a 'red', 'white' and **NULL** value in that column, can I change the last **NULL** to 'blue' because it can only be 'blue' under the rule? Or do I have to wait until I see an actual value for that row?

This idea can be carried further with 'marked' **NULL** values. For example, we are given a table of hotel rooms which has columns for check-in date and check-out date. We know the check-in date for each visitor, but we don't know their check-out dates. Instead we know relationships among the **NULL**s. We can put them into groups; for example Mr and Mrs X will check out on the same day, Tour Group Y will check out on the same day, and so on. We can also add conditions - nobody checks out before his check-in date, Tour Group Y will leave after 1993 Jan 07, and so on.

7 The value can be known, but not within the range of the computer which holds it. The obvious examples would be numeric overflow and underflow in calculations, which will produce a run-time error message in SQL. However, trying to put a string into a column which is too short might also qualify, or trying to put a numeric value into a string without converting it into characters first. The inability of some computer spreadsheets to handle leap year day in the year 2000 is perhaps the most frightening and unforgivable example of such a situation.

8 The value can be wrong. Hopefully, detectable errors such as a date of 1994-Feb-31 will be rejected by SQL. Spreadsheets will often put an **ERR** symbol in the cells where the problem occurred. However, it is up to the database designer to enforce other rules. For example, there is no such metric unit as a 'QQ', but there is nothing inherent in a **CHAR(2)** column declaration to detect this before it gets into the database. Checking can be done with a **CHECK()** clause which we will discuss later.

9 We just don't care about the value because the result is the same no matter what the value is. Programmers who have used **decision** tables are familiar with this concept. A decision table is a grid of conditions and rules made up of 'Yes', 'No' and "Don't care" (shown as 'Y', 'N' and '-' respectively) to the conditions. If a rule is true, then its action is taken. The meaning of "Don't care" is that the action is taken for either a **TRUE** or **FALSE** answer to that condition.

NULLs in SQL are used for purposes **1** through **5**, since the others can't be represented in SQL. Among all these possible missing values, which is the correct way to read a **NULL**? The answer is that there is no *one* correct way to read a **NULL**. It depends simply on the context in which a **NULL** is used. Again, SQL is a language which works on syntax, not semantics. It is up to the programmer to assign meaning to the **NULL**s - it isn't up to SQL. The best approach is to avoid them unless you really need to use them.

What NULLS Are Not!

A **NULL** isn't a zero. Zero is a numeric value. If your gas tank is empty, your gas gauge is on zero. If you don't own a car or it has been stolen or destroyed, your gas gauge is on **NULL**.

A **NULL** isn't a blank string. A strings of blanks has a length greater than zero. This is one reason that SQL requires all **CHAR** columns in a table to be declared at least one character wide.

A **NULL** isn't a string of length zero. If you concatenate a zero length string to another string, that string stays the same; if you concatenate a **NULL** to a string, that string becomes a **NULL**. This is another example of the rule that **NULL**s propagate.

Comparing NULLS

If you compare a non-**NULL** value to a **NULL** with a comparison operator (equal, not equal, less than, greater than, and so on), you get an **UNKNOWN** result. In fact, a **NULL** compared to another **NULL** will return an **UNKNOWN** result. Think again about the example of awaiting a diagnosis at a hospital. The results for your condition are not always the same as the results for my condition, but they both are presently unknown.

This rule breaks down in some cases, however. There are grouping operations in SQL which will place all the **NULL**s together, as if they were equal. According to the SQL-89 standard, the implementor gives to decide how **NULL**s sort with actual data values. The rule is that you first sort all of the data values, either into ascending or descending order, then always attach the **NULL**s at the top or the bottom of the result.

Converting Values to and from NULL

Since **NULL**s 'mess up' operations on data types and host languages don't support **NULL**s, you the programmer will often have to convert **NULL**s into some value which is usable in the context of the problem. SQL has functions for just such conversions.

NULLIF() Function

SQL-92 specified two functions, **NULLIF()** and the related **COALESCE()**, which can be used to convert expressions to and from **NULL**. These functions are not yet in most SQL implementations, but you will often find something like them.

The **NULLIF(V1, V2)** function has two parameters. It is equivalent to the following pseudo-code expression:

```
NULLIF(V1, V2):= IF (V1 = V2)
        THEN NULL
        ELSE V1;
```

That is, when the first parameter is equal to the second, the function returns a **NULL**, otherwise it returns the first parameter's value. The properties of this function allow you to use it for many purposes. The important properties are as follows:

1 **NULLIF(x, x)** will convert all values of x into **NULL**. This includes **NULL** since **(NULL = NULL)** is **UNKNOWN**, not **TRUE**.

2 **NULLIF(0, (x-x))** will convert all non-**NULL** values of x into **NULL**. But it will convert a **NULL** into a zero since **(NULL - NULL)** is **NULL**, and the equality test will be **UNKNOWN** and fail.

3 **NULLIF(1, (x-x+1))** will convert all non-**NULL** values of x into **NULL**. However it will convert a **NULL** into a one. This can be generalized for all numeric data types and values.

COALESCE() Function

The `COALESCE(<value expression>,..., <value expression>)` function scans the list of `<value expression>`s from left to right and returns the first non-`NULL` value in the list. If all the `<value expression>`s are `NULL`, then the result is `NULL`.

> This is the same function under a new name as the `VALUE` (`<value expression>,..., <value expression>`) in DB2 and other SQL implementations based on DB2.

The most common use of this function is in a calculation on columns in the same row where you want a total, but where one can be a `NULL`. For example, to create a report of the total pay for each employee, you would write the expression `(salary + commission)`.

But salesmen might work on commission only or on a mix of salary and commission! The office staff are on salary only. This means an employee could have `NULL`s in their salary or commission columns, which would propagate in the addition. A better solution would be the following:

```
(COALESCE(salary, 0) + COALESCE(commission, 0))
```

Concatenating NULLs

Watch out for the difference between a `NULL` and a string of length zero when you concatenate strings! The rule is that `NULL`s propagate. This holds for strings, so a string concatenated with the empty string is unchanged, but a string concatenated with a `NULL` is a `NULL`.

Advice Time

You can't completely avoid `NULL`s in SQL, since some functions and operators will produce them. However, it is a good idea to try as hard as you can to avoid them whenever possible.

Encoded values can have special codes for missing data. For example, the ISO sex codes are as follows:

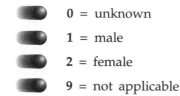 0 = unknown

1 = male

2 = female

9 = not applicable

The **0** code is for an unknown sex, while the **9** is for legal individuals, such as corporations.

Likewise with names, you are probably better off using a special dummy string for unknown values rather than the general **NULL**. In particular, you can build a list of 'John Doe #1', 'John Doe #2', and so on, to differentiate between them, and you can't do that with a **NULL**.

Quantities have to use a **NULL** in some cases. There is a difference between an unknown quantity and a zero quantity. Using negative numbers also doesn't work as it messes up calculations.

Dates and times have to use a **NULL** in some cases. Unfortunately, you often know relative times and have no way of expressing this in a database. For example, a pay raise occurs sometime after you have been hired, not before. A convict serving life might expect a release date of Eternity. The usual trick is to insert the maximum possible date for Eternity, but the problem is that it will show up in averages and other summary statistics.

Row Comparisons in SQL-92

Row comparisons could be done in SQL-89, but translating the predicates is messy. Consider this SQL-92 expression, take the row constants:

```
(a,b,c) < (x,y,z)
```

which became the following:

```
((a < x)
OR ((a = x) AND (b < y))
OR ((a = x) AND (b = y) AND (c < z)))
```

SQL-92 generalized the theta operators so they would work on row expressions and not just on non-array values. This isn't a popular feature yet, but if you have got it, it is very handy for situations where you want to collectively compare the values of more than one column. This makes SQL more orthogonal (allowing you to nest expressions inside one another) and it has an intuitive feel to it.

The SQL-92 standard decided that the theta predicates would work as laid out in a set of rules. The rules are as follows:

1 $x = y$ is **TRUE** if and only if $x[i] = y[i]$ for all i.

2 $x <> y$ is **TRUE** if and only if $x[i] <> y[i]$ for some i.

3 $x < y$ is **TRUE** if and only if $x[i] = y[i]$ for all $i < n$ and $x[n] < y[n]$ for some n.

4 $x > y$ is **TRUE** if and only if $x[i] = y[i]$ for all $i < n$ and $x[n] > y[n]$ for some n.

5 $x <= y$ is **TRUE** if and only if $x = y$ or $x < y$.

6 $x >= y$ is **TRUE** if and only if $x = y$ or $x > y$.

7 $x = y$ is **FALSE** if and only if $x <> y$ is **TRUE**.

8 $x <> y$ is **FALSE** if and only if $x = y$ is **TRUE**.

9 $x < y$ is **FALSE** if and only if $x >= y$ is **TRUE**.

10 $x > y$ is **FALSE** if and only if $x <= y$ is **TRUE**.

11 $x <= y$ is **FALSE** if and only if $x > y$ is **TRUE**.

12 $x >= y$ is **FALSE** if and only if $x < y$ is **TRUE**.

13 x **<comp op>** y is unknown if and only if x **<comp op>** y is neither **TRUE** nor **FALSE**.

The expression **X** **<comparison operator>** **Y** is a shorthand for a row X compared to a row Y and likewise X[i] means the *i*th column in the row X. The results are still either **TRUE**, **FALSE** or **UNKNOWN**, if there is no error in type matching. The rules favor solid tests for **TRUE** or **FALSE**, using **UNKNOWN** as a last resort.

The idea of the greater than and less than operators is that the values in one row are always greater than (or less than) those in the other row as you go from left to right after a certain column. This is how it would work if you were alphabetizing a word. The negations are defined so that the **NOT** operator will still have its usual properties.

> Notice that a **NULL** in a row will give an **UNKNOWN** result in a comparison.

Other Logical Operators

SQL actually has a lot of other logical operators and functions which are used to search the database. They will be discussed later in this book, since you need a little more background to understand them. However, they will all resolve back to the three Boolean operators and comparison predicates. Get these basics down and you will have much less trouble with more complex operators.

Summary

In this chapter we have covered a lot of heavy-duty math, and you should try to nail a lot of it down before you learn more about SQL. Time spent familiarizing yourself with math as it hits on SQL will be time well spent.

We looked at the numeric functions and how SQL dealt with various aspects of rounding and truncating. We looked at this in conjunction with how you can convert one numeric type to another.

We looked at string functions and different methods of pruning strings and altering them. We also looked at how SQL can compare various strings and what criteria it uses for matching strings.

Next, there were temporal data types which is where we discussed how SQL stores the date and time and how you can use these basic data types to do simple arithmetic.

We looked at comparison operators and then Boolean operators. We introduced the concept of SQL's Three Valued Logic and the **UNKNOWN** value.

Then we were ready for the **NULL**. We talked about what a **NULL** is, how it is used in SQL. Also, we took great pains to talk about what a **NULL** isn't. We covered many aspects of its usage that may arise in SQL.

Finally we looked at some rules for Row comparison operators, for which you need to understand Three Valued Logic.

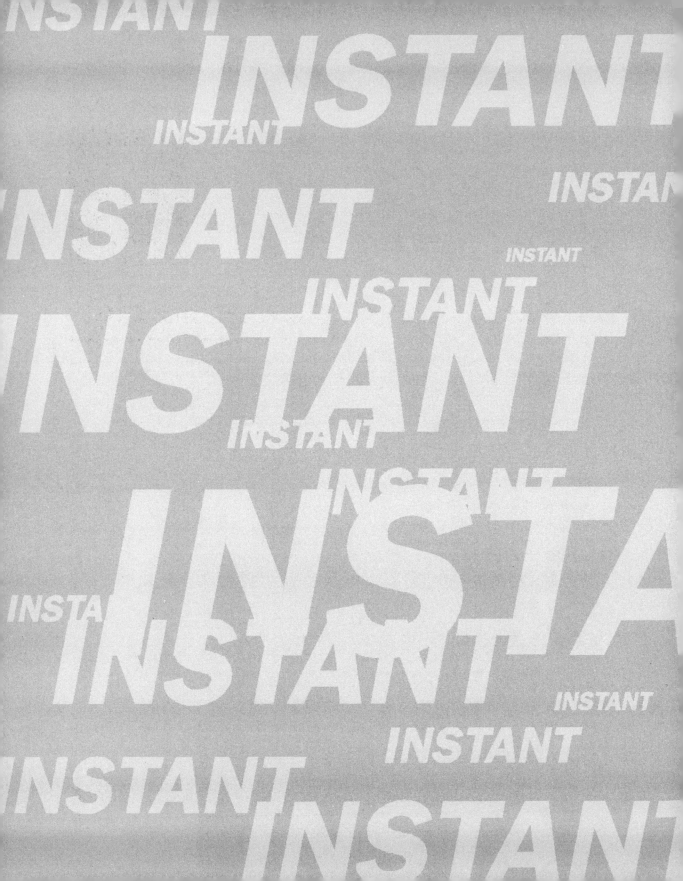

Keys and Referential Integrity

It is important when designing a database to make sure that each item in the database is uniquely identified. The way you do this is to use keys. Keys are also used to help safeguard referential integrity. We'll look at keys and the concepts behind them. We will also introduce referential integrity constraints and see how to program them into the example database.

In this chapter we will cover:

   Types of keys

   An introduction to normalization and normal forms

   Keys and the example database

   Referential integrity and other constraints

Definition of a Key

A key is a column or a set of columns in a table which uniquely identify each row within that table.

KEY	NAME
1001	John Doe
1002	John Doe
1003	John Doe
1004	John Doe

1002 identifies only this occurence of John Doe

Every time there are an identical set of entries within a table, and each item is actually completely separate and individual, you need a key to uniquely identify it. As this could possibly occur in every table, it's a very good idea to have a key within every table. Keys can have more than one column. If it's impossible to uniquely identify each entry with just one column, then you may have to use more.

PART NUMBER	ITEM NUMBER	ITEM
1000	1	Oojit
1000	2	Oojit
1000	3	Oojit
1000	4	Oojit

A Key is usually numeric, (as this makes it easy to sort) but it can quite possibly be a character, a word or even an alpha-numeric. Think about what you'd like to be able to do with that key. Does the key actually specify some sort of numerical order within the table, such as positions within a league table? (Excluding the possibility that two teams could have the same position!) If so, you might want a numeric key so you could flip the table over and have all the teams doing the worst displayed at the top of the list. So, before you make a key you can't sort easily or that can't describe every item in the table, think about what the key should actually need to do (if you used a single letter of the alphabet for every item as a key and you had 27 items, that would be pretty stupid.)

Keys are important for normalization, indexing, sorting and searching for data. Keys come in many flavors, which we will discuss in a moment. The idea of a key is that if you know the key, then you can find the rest of the data in the table. If I know the part number in an inventory, then I can look up the part and find its weight, color and price. If I know an employee identification number, then I can look up the employee's records.

In SQL, a table doesn't have to have a key, but it's still a good idea to have one. One possible exception to this is a table which holds the data from a supermarket cash register tape. Each purchase consists of one line per item, and many of those items are repeated. One can of Brand X tuna fish is like any other can of Brand X tuna fish, so we don't give them individual part numbers. (You might well give different brands of tuna fish different identifiers, however). If it were automobiles, then we would worry about telling them apart. The problem is that without a key, we will have to handle the subset of 'can of Brand X tuna fish' as a unit; that is, in SQL when we delete and search on 'can of Brand X tuna fish', we will delete or find *all* of them without a key to uniquely identify them.

Types of Keys

A **candidate key** is one of the possible keys in a table. (Yes, this does mean a table can have more than one key!) For example, a candidate key arises when there could be two likely possibilities for a primary key. Consider a car: it has a number plate, which is unique in the country. It also has a license tag which is unique in Pennsylvania. So the candidate keys are number plate and state + tag number. Either one uniquely identifies the car, while the fact that the car is a green 1995 Mazda doesn't.

A **surrogate key** is a key which has no meaning in itself. These keys are usually constructed by the database system using a sequential or random number generator. Very often, these surrogate keys are never shown to the user.

In contrast, **intelligent keys** do have some meaning in themselves. An intelligent key might be longitude and latitude. The longitude and latitude of a building uniquely identifies the building and it tells you its location. The name of the building or a property code number would uniquely identify the building, but wouldn't give you any extra information.

A **super key** is basically a key with too many columns in it. That is, you could remove some of the columns and still have a key. While this sounds like a bad thing, in practice it can be handy or even necessary. For example, if we converted our inventory system from one encoding system to another, we would probably keep the old part numbers and the new part numbers in the inventory table so that we could take orders from both the old and the new catalog.

A **primary key** is a candidate key which we pick for special treatment. As we have already said, in theory a key is a set of columns which uniquely identify each row, but in SQL a primary key has certain special properties which have to do with referential integrity and indexing. We will get to those details later.

A **foreign key** is a set of columns in one table which is a key in a second table. For example, a table of sales orders will have part numbers. Those part numbers are values of the key of the inventory table, since we don't want to sell parts that we don't have in stock. We say that the orders table part number column references the inventory table part number. In SQL, if you don't say explicitly which columns to use in the referenced table, then the default is to use the primary key of the referenced table.

Sales Orders Table   Inventory Table

Order No.	Part No.		Part No.	Amount in Stock
X0001	Thingy 002	References	Thingy 001	17
X0002	Oojit 007		Thingy 002	3
X0003	Dibdob 009		Thingy 003	0

An Example of a Foreign Key

The foreign key in this example is in the Sales Order Table (Part No.). A foreign key may or may not be a key in its own table. In the example here, Part No. isn't a key, Order No. is.

A foreign key can also reference its own table. For example, we could have a table of employees which has a column for the employee identification number of each employee's boss. Since the boss is also an employee, he or she will also have a row in the table. We have to make the owner of the company report to himself for this to work.

Employee Id	Boss Id
Lackey001	Bossman001
Lackey002	Bossman001
Bossman001	Bossman001

A Brief Look at Normalization

The relational model and normal forms of the relational model were first defined by Dr. E. F. Codd in *The Relational Model for Large Shared Data Banks (1970)*, then extended by other writers after him. He invented the term 'normalized relations' by borrowing from the political jargon of the day.

Normal forms are an attempt to make sure that you don't destroy true data or create false data in your database. One of the ways of avoiding errors is to represent a fact only once in the database, since if a fact appears more than once, one of the instances of it is likely to be an error. A man with two watches can never be sure what the correct time is.

This process of table design is called **normalization**. It isn't mysterious, but it can get complex. It involves making sure that the same facts don't appear twice in the same database. This is the concept of **redundant information**, that is, information which appears more than once in the same database. There are three stages in normalization, which are all necessary for ensuring the complete absence of redundant information in your database. You can buy CASE tools to help you do it, but you should know a bit about the theory before you use such a tool.

First Normal Form (1nf)

The first stage in designing a database has nothing to do with programming. Good software programming practice dictates you should write your original specification on paper. It's the same with databases. We've plunged straight into the programming so you could get an idea of how the physical database will actually look and a feeling for its structure. You should, however, first take pen to paper or word processor to printer for your first stage.

You should make a list of the separate physical items that will go to constitute your database. You need to know what information you will be storing, and you need to put on your list the definitions of what you want to store. For example, in the specimen database, you would need a table for Salespersons. You'd want to decide what information to store on each salesperson. A name column would be one of the first requirements, so you would have a definition reading something like **employee name** - a column containing the first and last name of each person who works in sales for this organization. Next, you would decide what other details you want on each salesperson. Their salary, perhaps; so now you need to have a heading related to employee name that would be defined as the weekly salary for each salesperson within the organization. This would become a column within the table.

Group each set of related items into a separate list (some will overlap, but this is a first draft so it doesn't matter too much where you put them, you can always rearrange later). These will form the basis of your tables. Each item in the list will become a separate column. Make sure that each 'table' has a key, that is, a key with which to identify each individual. This key will be the main way for picking out each item of data that will go into the table. You could use the employee name as a key, but what happens if two names are identical? For a key, you might want a separate identifying number for each salesperson, which would be their **id** number.

There! You've just created a database that is already in first normal form. Not too hard, was it? Here is a summary of what needs to be done for first normal form.

> **First normal form requires a separate table being made for each set of related columns. Each separate table should have a primary key.**

Now let's start from scratch and create a database about class schedules. We are required to keep the course, courseid, department, time, professor, student, major and grade. Suppose that we initially set up a Pascal file with records which look like this:

```
Classes = RECORD
    course: ARRAY [1:7] OF CHAR;
  courseid: INTEGER;
      room: ARRAY [1:5] OF CHAR;
  roomsize: INTEGER;
professor: ARRAY [1:25] OF CHAR;
Students: ARRAY [1:classsize]
        OF RECORD
                student ARRAY [1:25] OF CHAR;
                studentid INTEGER;
                major ARRAY [1:10] OF CHAR;
                grade CHAR;
                enrolmentdate DATE;
        END;
    END;
```

This table currently isn't in the most basic (first) normal form of relational databases. First normal form (1nf) also means that the table has no repeating groups. That is, every column only contains scalar or atomic values. The table can't contain an array or list or anything with its own structure. This Pascal file has several arrays.

In SQL, it's impossible to use anything other than scalar or atomic values, unless the vendor has added arrays or other extensions to the language. The Pascal record could be 'flattened out' in SQL to look like this:

```
CREATE TABLE Classes
(course CHAR(7) NOT NULL,
 courseid INTEGER NOT NULL,
 room CHAR(5) NOT NULL,
 roomsize INTEGER NOT NULL,
 professor CHAR(25) NOT NULL,
 student CHAR(25) NOT NULL,
 studentid INTEGER,
 enrolmentdate DATE NOT NULL,
 major CHAR (10) NOT NULL,
 grade CHAR(1) NOT NULL);
```

This table is acceptable to SQL. But notice that the course, and professor values, would have to be repeated for each student.

Deletion Update and Insertion Anomalies

If Professor Jones of the Math Department dies, we will have to delete all his rows from the **Classes** table. This also deletes the information that all his students were taking a Math class. This is called a **deletion anomaly**.

If student Wilson decides to change one of his Math classes taught by Professor Jones to English, we will show Professor Jones as an instructor in both the Math and the English departments. This creates false information and is called an **update anomaly**.

If the school decides to start a new department, which as yet has no students, we can't insert the data about the professors we just hired until we have location and student data to fill out a row. This is called an **insertion anomaly**.

There are some ways around these problems without changing the tables. We could permit **NULL**s in the table. We could write routines to check the table for false data. These are tricks which we will be less able to implement as the data and the relationships become more complex.

The solution is to break the table up into other tables, each of which represents one relationship or one simple fact:

```
CREATE TABLE Classes
(course CHAR(7) NOT NULL,
 courseid INTEGER NOT NULL,
 room CHAR(5) NOT NULL,
 roomsize INTEGER NOT NULL,
 professor CHAR(25) NOT NULL);
```

```
CREATE TABLE Students
(studentid INTEGER NOT NULL,
 student CHAR(25) NOT NULL,
 course CHAR(7) NOT NULL,
 major CHAR(10) NOT NULL,
 enrolmentdate DATE NOT NULL);
```

Second Normal Form (2nf)

Sometimes a table requires a key that is formed from more than one column. This is termed a **multi-value key**. Think about a database that stores information about cars such as color, make and owner, and which identifies each one via a 'number' on the number plate. Each of these is unique. Now assume that this database has every car number plate in the world. They're unique in each country, but can you be sure that a plate in the US doesn't match up with one in the UK? Probably not, so you'll have to use both the country and the car serial number to be sure, in other words, a multi-valued key.

This impacts on normalization, however. We want to use this database to help with the environment and exhaust emissions. So now we add a column for whether each car uses unleaded or regular fuel.

> For this example, we're excluding the fact that people might *choose* to use unleaded fuel, we're assuming that they are only doing so because the law says they have to!

Therefore, it's up to the administration of each individual country. Imagine that the UK government introduces a rule saying everyone has to use unleaded fuel by the end of a certain week. Previously, everyone had used regular. Whether or not a car is running on unleaded fuel depends directly on the rule of the country. It doesn't matter what car number plate you have, if you live in the UK you have to use unleaded as of next week.

You're the DBA and yes, you've guessed it, you have to change the entries for each car in the fuel column for the UK to unleaded. That's roughly twenty million entries. Can you be sure that you update every single entry? Clearly not. If you miss one out, that means the database is holding incorrect, outdated information. Wouldn't it be so much easier if there was a separate table for each country? That's second normal form.

> If a column depends on only one, or only some parts of a multi-valued key, then it should be removed to a separate table.

A table is in Second Normal Form (2nf) if it has no 'partial key' dependencies. This is where normalization can get a bit sticky. Let's return to the classroom analogy and imagine you want to create a table for enrolments. This table might include columns for **student, courseid, course** and **enrolment date**.

However, we have to use two keys to identify an enrolment. This is because a student may enroll in several courses. A course might have several enrolment dates; for example, students with names between A-L on one day and names between M-Z on another. Therefore, we need to use both

studentid and **courseid** to identify uniquely the enrolment. The enrolment date is dependent on both the **courseid** and the **studentid**. The course is only dependent on the **courseid**. Courseid '119' identifies the History of Train Spotting. It will occur every time that **courseid** comes up. This is a **partial key dependency**.

Multi Value Key   Partial Key Dependency

Student id	Course id	Course	Enrolment Date
B 101	119	History of Train spotting	8/9/95
R 102	120	Philosophy	10/9/95
S 103	119	History of Train spotting	9/9/95

Full Dependency

> You can summarize the rule as follows: if X and Y are columns and X is a key, then for any Z which is a proper subset of X, it can't be the case that Z determines Y.

This means that the table has to be in 1nf and has to have a key. So if the table is nothing but a key, then the table is in 2nf. For example, a list of classrooms on its own would be a 2nf table.

In the class schedule table, knowing the **studentid** and **course** is sufficient to determine his or her **courseid**, since students can't sign up for more than one version of the same course. We also know that a student can have only one **enrolment date** in a particular course. This is the same as saying that (**studentid**, **course**) determines (**courseid**, **enrolment date**). Looking more closely we can also see that knowing the student's name determines his major, as students can only have one major. This leads us to the following tables:

```
CREATE TABLE Classes
(course CHAR(7) NOT NULL,
 courseid INTEGER NOT NULL,
 room CHAR(5) NOT NULL,
 roomsize INTEGER NOT NULL,
 professor CHAR (25) NOT NULL,
 PRIMARY KEY (course, courseid));
```

```
CREATE TABLE Enrollment
(studentid CHAR(25) NOT NULL,
 courseid INTEGER NOT NULL,
 enrolmentdate DATE NOT NULL,
 PRIMARY KEY (studentid, courseid));
```

```
CREATE TABLE Students
(student CHAR(25) NOT NULL,
 studentid INTEGER NOT NULL,
 major CHAR (10) NOT NULL,
 PRIMARY KEY (student, studentid));
```

At this point, we are in 2nf. In every table, each non-key column is determined by the entire key. Now, if a student changes major, this can be done in one place, without affecting any of his professors. Furthermore, a student can't sign up for different versions of the same class because we changed the key of the **Enrolment** table. Unfortunately, we've still got problems.

Third Normal Form (3nf)

These problems occur if you have **transitive dependencies** within your database. How did they get there? They occur if a column relates to another column which itself relates to the key. A transitive dependency is a situation where A determines B and B determines C, therefore A also determines C. A typical transitive dependency would be Mr. Jones is older than Mr. Smith. Mr. Smith is older than Mr. Wilson. It therefore follows that Mr. Jones is older than Mr. Wilson. So, why would this be a problem?

Take a look the **Classes** table as it now stands. The (**course, courseid**) column determines the room where the class will be held. But if you know the room number, then you can find how many students it will hold, and this is a transitive dependency!

The reason they are trouble is that you might update only one of the relationships involved. For example, if I decide to move a course to another classroom, I have to also update the roomsize column. What we need to do is split the **Classes** table into the following:

```
CREATE TABLE Classes
(course CHAR(7) NOT NULL,
 courseid CHAR(1) NOT NULL,
 room CHAR(5) NOT NULL,
 professor CHAR (25) NOT NULL,
 PRIMARY KEY (course, courseid));
```

```
CREATE TABLE Rooms
(room CHAR(5) NOT NULL,
 roomsize INTEGER NOT NULL,
 PRIMARY KEY (room));
```

This is known as third normal form.

For a table to be converted to third normal form (3nf), it must first be in 2nf. Next, you must make sure that for any two columns, X and Y, of the same table, when column X determines column Y, then column X must be a key or column Y must be part of a **candidate** key (a key which isn't necessarily the primary key, but which describes some part of the primary key).

If this idea is difficult to grasp, the following might be a simpler way to think about it:

> **If columns don't contribute to a description of a key, then they should be removed to a separate table.**

The class size doesn't describe any part of the **course** or **courseid**, so therefore it should be removed. This is the same method as eliminating transitive dependencies, but taken from a different perspective.

Other Normal Forms

There are a lot of other normal forms which we are not going to discuss in this short book. In fact, we've skimmed over the first three normal forms, but you don't need to know them in too much detail, although don't confuse this with not needing to know them at all!

> We would suggest that you use a CASE tool to design real databases and let them provide a normalized schema for you. All of the current products will get to at least 3nf which is as much as you need to know.

The Example Database

Let's take a quick look over the final table declaration and see if there are any problems. Sure enough, the **Orders** table needs work.

```
CREATE TABLE Orders
(orderid INTEGER NOT NULL PRIMARY KEY,
 empid INTEGER NOT NULL REFERENCES Salespersons(empid),
 custid INTEGER NOT NULL REFERENCES Customers(custid),
 salesdate DATE NOT NULL DEFAULT CURRENT DATE,
 item1 INTEGER REFERENCES Inventory(partid),
 qty1 INTEGER,
 item2 INTEGER REFERENCES Inventory(partid),
 qty2 INTEGER,
 item3 INTEGER REFERENCES Inventory(partid),
 qty3 INTEGER,
 item4 INTEGER REFERENCES Inventory(partid),
 qty4 INTEGER,
 item5 INTEGER REFERENCES Inventory(partid),
 qty5 INTEGER);
```

Why should we restrict a customer to only five items? What happens if a salesperson puts the same part in two different item slots? Let's split this table into two new tables, one to represent the header section of an order form:

```
CREATE TABLE Orders
(orderid INTEGER NOT NULL PRIMARY KEY,
 empid INTEGER NOT NULL REFERENCES Salespersons(empid),
 custid INTEGER NOT NULL REFERENCES Customers(custid),
 salesdate DATE NOT NULL DEFAULT CURRENT DATE);
```

and one to represent the body or detail lines of the order form:

```
CREATE TABLE OrderItems
(orderid INTEGER NOT NULL REFERENCES Orders(orderid),
 detail INTEGER NOT NULL,
 partid INTEGER NOT NULL REFERENCES Inventory(partid),
 qty INTEGER NOT NULL,
 PRIMARY KEY (orderid, detail));
```

Notice that there are a lot of **NOT NULL** constraints, which is a good sign that your schema is normalized. The detail will probably be a line number taken from the screen or paper order form, but its purpose is to identify the separate items within an order.

This is the first multi-column primary key we have seen. It's the combination of (**orderid**, **detail**) which is unique - individually they are not unique.

This primary key to multi-column foreign key pattern is a typical database design. We will look at them in more detail later in this chapter. Later, you'll see how we can use what are called **JOIN** operators to associate the order and its detail lines into a single result table to answer questions. This design lets us have any number of detail lines we wish.

Referential Integrity and Other Constraints

Referential integrity constraints are rules that are part of the tables in a database schema. When you finish doing a transaction against the database, all these rules must be true. However, they can be violated during the intermediate steps of the transaction. There are a number of advantages to putting such rules into the database instead of the application programs:

1 It saves programming effort. Otherwise, every program would have to have the same code to perform the same rule checking.

2 It prevents programming errors. You could never be sure, in fact, that every program had the same code to perform the checking. Even if you put the rules in a library routine, you could never be sure that every application program got re-compiled when the library routine was updated.

3 Since the constraints are logical expressions, putting them in the database lets the optimizer use these rules to speed up performance.

The constraint name is a qualified identifier in the schema, just like a column would be, and it has to be unique within its table. In SQL-92, constraints can be given names by putting a clause in front of them that looks like the following:

CONSTRAINT <constraint name> <constraint> [<constraint attributes>]

Constraints without names can't be easily referenced by the **ALTER TABLE** statement and are therefore very hard to change. The system will give them a name, but it will be one of those horrible computer code things that mean nothing to a human being. Error and warning messages about constraint violations will use the constraint name in their text. So you can see that it is a good idea to name all constraints, if you ever intend to use them.

Actual Code	Syntax Version
CREATE TABLE ConExample1	CREATE TABLE ConExample1
(custid INTEGER NOT NULL,	(<column name> <data type> <column constraint>,
custname CHAR(15) NOT NULL,	<column name> <data type> <column constraint>,
salary INTEGER NOT NULL,	<column name> <data type> <column constraint>,
CONSTRAINT too-low CHECK (salary > 1000));	CONSTRAINT <constraint name> <constraint>);

CONSTRAINT commands are placed at the end of the list of table elements, rather than after the column definition like column constraints are, and there can be as many as you need.

Check Constraint

The **CHECK (<search condition>)** constraint is like the **CHECK** clauses that are attached to rows in a table declaration. The difference is that they appear as separate declarations in a **CREATE TABLE** statement. By disassociating the constraint from a particular column, you can use the **ALTER** statement on it separately from the columns with which it is involved.

The search condition can be anything that you could also write in a query, but it must apply only to the column in its table. The way around that is to use sub-queries which reference other tables in the schema. In theory, you can write almost all the other constraints as **CHECK** clauses, but you would have some really elaborate code to maintain.

An important characteristic of the **CHECK** constraint is that if the search condition returns a **FALSE** value, then whatever action violated the constraint (such as trying to put a figure lower than $100 under salary in the example database) is disallowed and you get an error message. However, if the search condition returns a **TRUE** or an **UNKNOWN** value, then the constraint is satisfied and the action is allowed. SQL programmers, even experienced ones, forget about the possibility of an **UNKNOWN** result getting the benefit of the doubt, so watch out for it.

> A **CREATE ASSERTION** **<assertionname>** **<constraint>**[**<constraint attributes>**] statement is another useful statement, it does exactly the same as a **CHECK** constraint, but over the whole database.

The UNIQUE Constraint

The **UNIQUE** constraint is like the **UNIQUE** clause on a single column declaration, but it has a column list in parentheses after it. This constraint means that the combination of all the columns - **not** each individual column - has to be unique within the table.

```
UNIQUE (<column list>)
```

In the old SQL-89 standard, **UNIQUE** also automatically implied that all the columns being tested were all **NOT NULL**. Now, in the SQL-92 standard, the columns get the benefit of the doubt and matching is done for equality of all the non-**NULL** values in the column(s). Trust me, it works better with the **CHECK()** constraints and other features of SQL-92. You can't have a column name appear more than once in the **<column list>**, however two or more **UNIQUE** constraint's **<column list>**s can overlap.

When you use a **UNIQUE** constraint on multiple columns, it's the combination of values in those columns that must be unique. This makes sense when both values are needed to ensure uniqueness. Consider a scheme where a

Company is divided into departments numbered 1 - n. Departments are divided into divisions. Divisions are numbered 1 - n within each department. This means that there are as many Division 1's as there are departments, and you need to know the department number in order to know which division you're talking about. In this case **UNIQUE (Department, Division)** will give you exactly what you need.

However, it is easy to get confused and think that you can use unique constraints to enforce all kinds of business rules. For example, consider this table for a school's class schedule:

```
CREATE TABLE Schedule
(teacher CHAR(15) NOT NULL,
 class CHAR(8) NOT NULL,
 period INTEGER NOT NULL);
```

We want to use **UNIQUE** constraints to enforce rules about teachers, classes taught and the time periods used. Our possible options are as follows:

1 **UNIQUE (teacher, class)**

Each teacher teaches one and only one class (we have a specialization of faculty!) By itself, this constraint would prevent the two rows (**'Jones'**, **'Engl 101'**, **2**) and (**'Jones'**, **'Engl 101'**, **3**) from appearing in the table. However, (**'Jones'**, **'Engl 101'**, **2**) and (**'Jones'**, **'Engl 102'**, **3**) would be fine, as would (**'Jones'**, **'Engl 101'**, **2**) and (**'Jones'**, **'Engl 102'**, **2**). This last pair implies that Jones is in two places at once, but our present constraint doesn't worry about that.

2 **UNIQUE (teacher, period)**

Each teacher is assigned to one period (this is a little strange, considering that we want to get more use out of them). Again, by itself this constraint would prevent the two rows (**'Jones'**, **'Engl101'**, **2**) and (**'Jones'**, **'Engl 102'**, **2**) from appearing in the table. However, (**'Jones'**, **'Engl 101'**, **2**) and (**'Jones'**, **'Engl 102'**, **3**) would be just fine, as would (**'Jones'**, **'Engl 101'**, **2**) and (**'Smith'**, **'Engl 101'**, **2**). Once more the **UNIQUE** constraint doesn't produce the result we want.

3 **UNIQUE (class, period)**

A class is taught in only one time period. At this point, you can figure out what is allowed or disallowed by the constraint, so let's move on.

4 `UNIQUE (teacher, class, period)`

You might think that this enforces the other three constraints in a single rule, but it doesn't! Consider a table with rows:

`('Smith', 'Math 101', 1) ('Smith', 'Math 101', 2)`

This would fail the first uniqueness constraint and pass the three others. Be careful and test your logic with some data. We could use any or all of these constraints on the Schedule table. The allowable rows would be different in each case; as an exercise, you might want to set up a dummy table and try all the combinations.

The PRIMARY KEY Constraint

The **PRIMARY KEY** constraint is classified as another form of the **UNIQUE** constraint. We have already seen the single column declaration. The **PRIMARY KEY** constraint does more than just use a column list in parentheses in place of a single column.

This constraint says that the column(s) involved are all **NOT NULL** and that they are also **UNIQUE**. Furthermore, a table can have only one **PRIMARY KEY** because the primary key is the default column set for foreign key references, which we will discuss shortly.

> You can't have a column name appear more than once in the **PRIMARY KEY** constraint column list. However, it can overlap with other **UNIQUE** constraint column lists in the table declaration.

Foreign Key Constraints

Yes, this constraint is a multi-column version of a clause we have seen before - the **REFERENCES** clause on a single column. But there are some differences and other features. In fact, many SQL implementations don't have the single column **REFERENCES** clause, in favor of the constraint version, as the constraint version is more powerful.

The idea of a foreign key is that we have one or more columns in one table which reference matching columns in a second table. Strictly speaking, relational database theory says that they have to reference the primary key of the other table, but SQL lets you pick the columns to use by name as long as they are part of a UNIQUE constraint. In fact, SQL will even let you use the same table as the referenced table.

This multiple column version needs to know which columns in the referencing table are being used as a foreign key, so it has an extra sub-clause:

```
FOREIGN KEY (<column list>)
 REFERENCES <referenced table> [ (<column list>) ]
```

Again, the two column lists have to be union comparable to each other. That means that they have the same number of columns and that the columns match up in position by data type. A row in this table matches a row in the other table, but if a row in this table has a NULL, you give the match the benefit of the doubt.

We'll go back to the example we used in Chapter 2 using the two tables A and B. We'll assume now that custid isn't enough as a primary key for Table A, so now we'll add another column custid2. Together custid and custid2 can uniquely identify every customer within the table. For example, before the first customer identifier might only have been enough to identify a family and second identifier might identify each individual family member. Apart from that the function of the two tables is identical to that in Chapter 2, in which table B references table A.

Actual Code for Table A	Syntax Version for Table A
```CREATE TABLE Customer5 (custid INTEGER NOT NULL, custid2 INTEGER NOT NULL, custname CHAR(15) NOT NULL, custaddr CHAR(30) NOT NULL, PRIMARY KEY (custid,custid2));```	```CREATE TABLE Customer5 (<column name> <data type>, <column name> <data type> <column constraint>, <column name> <data type> <column constraint>, <column name> <data type> <column constraint>, <unique specification>);```

Actual Code for Table B	Syntax Version for Table B
CREATE TABLE CreditLimit2	*CREATE TABLE CreditLimit2*
(creditlim INTEGER NOT NULL PRIMARY KEY,	*(<column name> <data type> NOT NULL <unique specification>,*
interest INTEGER NOT NULL,	*<column name> <data type> <column constraint>,*
custid INTEGER NOT NULL,	*<column name> <data type> <column constraint>,*
custid2 INTEGER NOT NULL,	*<column name> <data type> <column constraint>,*
CONSTRAINT reference	*CONSTRAINT <constraint name>*
FOREIGN KEY (custid,custid2)	*FOREIGN KEY (<column list>)*
REFERENCES	*REFERENCES <referenced table>*
Customer5(custid,custid2));	*(<column list>));*

Restricts and Cascades

Now cast your mind back to Chapter 2 when we looked at the **<drop behavior>** clause. At the time, how it worked wasn't explained to you as you only needed to know about the referencing of inter related tables. Now we need to know how SQL maintains referential integrity when you drop a table or drop a column within a table. The definition of a drop behavior clause is as follows:

<drop behavior>::= RESTRICT | CASCADE

When you drop a table, you have to make sure that consistent action is taken for other tables in the database, which in turn name the table you have just got rid of. You can't have references from one of your current tables to a table that no longer exists. Hence, the addition of the **<drop behavior>** clause to the **DROP TABLE**, **DROP COLUMN** and **DROP CONSTRAINT** commands. There are two methods to go about doing this, **RESTRICT** and **CASCADE**.

Firstly, for tables:

```
<drop table statement>::=
        DROP TABLE <table name> <drop behavior>
```

If **RESTRICT** is specified, then the table can't be deleted unless every table referenced in the definition of the table or the search condition of any constraint is also deleted. If the table is referencing other tables, then you will just receive an error message preventing you from doing that.

```
DROP TABLE Example RESTRICT;
```

It is good practice to add a **RESTRICT** to all of your drop commands from now on. Even if you know it isn't necessary for a particular table, it is a good habit to get into as it helps protect the database from gaining invalid references.

If **CASCADE** is specified, then all such objects (tables) that reference the table to be dropped will also be dropped/deleted along with the table.

Secondly, for columns:

```
DROP [ COLUMN ] <column name> <drop behavior>
```

If **RESTRICT** is specified, then the new column can't be referenced in a **VIEW** or **<search condition>** outside of the table. However, it will be referenced in its own constraints; so the rule is that as long as it is the *only* column in its own constraints, then it can be dropped. Not all SQL's will allow you to drop a column once you've added it. However, if your SQL does support it then it will look like this:

```
DROP COLUMN Column1 RESTRICT;
```

> A **<drop column definition>** that doesn't specify **CASCADE** will fail and post an error message if there are any references to that column resulting from the use of **CORRESPONDING**, **NATURAL** and **SELECT** * commands (except where contained in an **EXISTS** predicate), or **REFERENCES** without a **<reference column list>** in its **<referenced table and columns>**.

If **CASCADE** is specified, then any such dependent object will be dropped along with the column. Be careful! You could be doing more damage than you thought.

Thirdly, for constraints:

DROP CONSTRAINT <constraint name> <drop behavior>

If the drop behavior is set to **RESTRICT**, then no table constraint is allowed to be dependent on another, otherwise you can't delete that constraint. Assuming you were using table **ConExample1,** an example statement would look like this:

```
DROP CONSTRAINT too-low RESTRICT;
```

If **CASCADE** is specified, then any such dependent constraint will be dropped along with this constraint.

> **Summary of the two types of <drop behavior>:**
>
> **RESTRICT** - This will only work if you haven't got outside references to the table, column or constraint you are dropping. If there are outside references then you will get an error message.
>
> **CASCADE** - This will drop *all* tables, columns or constraints that reference the table, column or constraint you are dropping. Think of it like a domino effect. It is dangerous as you could, in theory, wipe a whole database which referenced itself in such a way that everything was interconnected. That's why you haven't been provided with any examples of this in action.

Referential Actions

In SQL-89, violations were reported by the system and the transaction was disallowed. In SQL-92, the programmer gets a lot more power! There is even a **MATCH** sub-clause which defines exactly how multiple columns are matched between both tables.

However, many implementations do have referential actions. These are code that causes an action to happen in the database when a table event occurs.

> The term 'table event' means something changes the table and that means one of four things: rows are inserted, deleted, updated or the table is altered. SQL-92 allows referential actions only on updates and deletes, but some products will also allow actions on insertions.

If someone attempts to insert a row which violates the foreign key constraint, there is only one action; the attempt is rejected. Since this is automatic, we only have sub-clauses for updates and deletions. The syntax is as follows:

```
<referential action>::=
ON { UPDATE | DELETE } <action>

<action>::= CASCADE | SET { NULL | DEFAULT } | NO ACTION
```

Let's do this on a case-by-case basis.

The **ON UPDATE CASCADE** will move the changes made to the matching foreign key columns over to the referenced table. This allows us to make a rule that when the part numbers are changed in the **Inventory** table, they are automatically changed in the **Orders** table, too. The **ON UPDATE SET { NULL | DEFAULT }** will move a **NULL** or a **DEFAULT** value in the matching foreign key columns in the referenced table. This allows us to make a rule that when the part number is changed in the **Inventory** table, we effectively 'blank out' the referenced values with either an explicit **DEFAULT** value, such as 'Discontinued item', or a **NULL**.

The **NO ACTION** option is the default and it means no referential actions are taken, but do make sure the constraint isn't violated.

The **ON DELETE CASCADE** will delete the row with matching foreign key columns over to the referenced table - this means the whole row and not just the columns! This allows us to make a rule that when an item is dropped from the **Inventory** table, it is automatically dropped from the **Orders** table, too. The **ON DELETE SET { NULL | DEFAULT }** will move a **NULL** or a **DEFAULT** value in the matching foreign key columns in the referenced table.

This allows us to make a rule that when the part number is out of stock, we would put either an explicit **DEFAULT** value, such as 'Out of Stock', or a **NULL** in the **Orders** table.

Again, the **NO ACTION** option is the default and it means take no referential actions but do make sure the constraint isn't violated.

Be careful with these actions! They can be written so as to give you a 'domino' effect that might not be what you wanted. When you implement an action from table A to table B, the changes in table B can affect table C, and so on. You can also write circular constraints that come back and change the original table itself.

We will hold back from giving you any example code until we look at these options within the database here, as it is very difficult to give a small example without having to create several tables.

Triggers

As an aside, there is a feature in many versions of SQL called a **TRIGGER** which, like the referential actions, will execute a block of procedural code against the database when a table event occurs.

The procedural code is usually written in a proprietary language, but some products let you attach programs in standard procedural languages. A **TRIGGER** could be used to automatically handle discontinued merchandise, for example, by creating a credit slip in place of the original order item data.

The advantages of triggers over declarative referential integrity is that you can do everything that declarative referential integrity can and almost anything else, too. The disadvantages are that the optimizer can't get any data from the procedural code, the triggers take longer to execute, and they are not portable from product to product.

Our advice would be to avoid them when you can use declarative referential integrity instead. If you do use them, check the code very carefully and keep it simple so that you won't hurt performance.

> There is a proposal for standardizing TRIGGERs in the current ANSI/ISO SQL3, using a procedural language based on ADA. The proposal is fairly complicated and no product has implemented it completely. You should look at what your particular vendor has given you if you want to work with TRIGGERs.

The Example Database: Revisited

The next step in our database design is to decide which clauses should be moved into constraints and which referential actions we want to have in the schema. Let's do it one table at a time, starting with the **Salespersons** table:

```
CREATE TABLE Salespersons
 (empid INTEGER NOT NULL PRIMARY KEY,
  ename CHAR(15) NOT NULL,
  rank INTEGER NOT NULL DEFAULT 1 CHECK (rank IN (1,2,3)),
  salary DECIMAL(7,2) NOT NULL
     DEFAULT 1000.00 CHECK (salary >= 1000.00));
```

No, we don't need to change this table. But, we might want to make the check clauses into table check constraints. With the table check constraints it would look like this:

```
CREATE TABLE Salespersons
 (empid INTEGER NOT NULL PRIMARY KEY,
  ename CHAR(15) NOT NULL,
  rank INTEGER NOT NULL DEFAULT 1,
  salary DECIMAL(7,2) NOT NULL DEFAULT 1000.00,
  CHECK (salary >= 1000.00),
  CHECK (rank IN (1,2,3))
 );
```

Now let's look at the **Customers** table:

```
CREATE TABLE Customers
 (custid INTEGER NOT NULL PRIMARY KEY,
  cname CHAR(15) NOT NULL,
  credit CHAR(1) NOT NULL CHECK (credit IN ('A','B','C')));
```

No changes needed here. Let's go to the **Inventory** table:

```
CREATE TABLE Inventory
(partid INTEGER NOT NULL PRIMARY KEY,
 description CHAR(10) NOT NULL,
 stockqty INTEGER NOT NULL,
 reorderpnt INTEGER,
 price DECIMAL(7,2) NOT NULL);
```

Again, no changes needed here. Let's go to the **Orders** table:

```
CREATE TABLE Orders
(orderid INTEGER NOT NULL PRIMARY KEY,
 empid INTEGER NOT NULL REFERENCES Salespersons(empid),
 custid INTEGER NOT NULL REFERENCES Customers(custid),
 salesdate DATE NOT NULL DEFAULT CURRENT_DATE);
```

We need some changes here. Firstly, let's get the **REFERENCES** clauses into **FOREIGN KEY** constraints, like so:

```
CREATE TABLE Orders
(orderid INTEGER NOT NULL PRIMARY KEY,
 empid INTEGER NOT NULL,
 custid INTEGER NOT NULL,
 salesdate DATE NOT NULL DEFAULT CURRENT_DATE,
    FOREIGN KEY empid REFERENCES Salespersons(empid),
    FOREIGN KEY custid REFERENCES Customers(custid));
```

But now we can add referential actions to this table. What would we do if a salesperson's employee identification number is changed? Well, we would cascade the change, so that the right person gets their commissions!

What do we do if a salesperson is killed by a runaway beer truck? We don't want to throw away his orders, and we can't set the **empid** code to **NULL** unless we change the declaration on that column. Time for an executive decision; we could change the **empid** declaration to include a **DEFAULT** **empid** value! This dummy account would be used for computing commissions.

```
CREATE TABLE Orders
(orderid INTEGER NOT NULL PRIMARY KEY,
 empid INTEGER NOT NULL DEFAULT 0,
 custid INTEGER NOT NULL,
 salesdate DATE NOT NULL DEFAULT CURRENT_DATE,
```

```
    FOREIGN KEY empid REFERENCES Salespersons(empid)
    ON DELETE SET DEFAULT
    ON UPDATE CASCADE,
    FOREIGN KEY custid REFERENCES Customers(custid));
```

So far, so good. Again, if a customer changes his customer identification number, we would want to cascade the change so that the right person would get the goods that were ordered.

What if a customer is hit by that runaway beer truck? Then there is nobody to pay for that order! We'd better cancel it. That gives us the final table:

```
CREATE TABLE Orders
(orderid INTEGER NOT NULL PRIMARY KEY,
 empid INTEGER NOT NULL DEFAULT 0,
 custid INTEGER NOT NULL,
 salesdate DATE NOT NULL DEFAULT CURRENT_DATE,
    FOREIGN KEY empid REFERENCES Salespersons(empid)
    ON UPDATE CASCADE
    ON DELETE SET DEFAULT,
    FOREIGN KEY custid REFERENCES Customers(custid)
    ON UPDATE CASCADE
    ON DELETE CASCADE);
```

Finally, let's look at the **OrderItems** table. If an order is deleted, then the details that went with it should go also, so we will cascade a deletion. Likewise, if the order identification number changes, we want to keep the **OrderItems** in sync. That would give us this declaration:

```
CREATE TABLE OrderItems
(orderid INTEGER NOT NULL,
 detail INTEGER NOT NULL,
 partid INTEGER NOT NULL REFERENCES Inventory(partid),
 qty INTEGER NOT NULL,
 PRIMARY KEY (orderid, detail),
    FOREIGN KEY orderid REFERENCES Orders(orderid)
    ON UPDATE CASCADE
    ON DELETE CASCADE);
```

What about the parts that appear on the order form? Again, if the part number changes, we want to cascade the change so that the buyer gets the right merchandise. But what do we do if the item on the order is dropped from the **Inventory**? There is no single right answer, but here are some choices:

1 When an item is dropped from inventory, leave it on the order. An application program will decide how to handle things such as placing a back order, making a substitution using another table, or whatever. This approach would require an external program and probably add another table for the allowed substitutions. While that would be what you would do in a real sales support system, let's not do it in this example.

2 When an item is dropped from inventory, replace the ordered item with a default item that happens to have a price of $0.00, a shipping weight of 0 kilograms, and so on. The problem is that all the dropped items would be replaced by this single default part number. You wouldn't be able to tell a missing screwdriver from a missing submarine (not to mention a missing beer truck driver).

3 When an item is dropped from inventory, drop that line from the order. We don't sell what we don't have, as a matter of company policy. That is pretty easy, so let's go with that decision for the final version of the table definition:

```
CREATE TABLE OrderItems
(orderid INTEGER NOT NULL,
 detail INTEGER NOT NULL,
 partid INTEGER NOT NULL,
 qty INTEGER NOT NULL,
 PRIMARY KEY (orderid, detail),
    FOREIGN KEY orderid REFERENCES Orders(orderid)
    ON UPDATE CASCADE
    ON DELETE CASCADE,
    FOREIGN KEY partid REFERENCES Inventory(partid)
    ON UPDATE CASCADE
    ON DELETE CASCADE);
```

Summary

This chapter has only begun to deal with the complex concepts of data normalization. You could get a whole book on the subject, so we've had to condense the topic considerably.

We looked firstly at the definition of a key and all the different types of key.

Next, we looked at what normalization is and the reasons you need to have a normalized database. We looked at the first three normal forms, explaining how to get from one form to another and then relating the concepts to one specific example, which we started from scratch.

We introduced the concept of referential integrity and what conditions must be present in a database for it to have referential integrity. We then introduced the specific aspects of SQL that deal with referential integrity such as **UNIQUE** and **PRIMARY KEY** constraints, **FOREIGN** keys, drop behavior and referential actions. If you still are not sure about any of these terms, I suggest you go back and make sure you familiarize yourself with them, before you continue.

We finally linked all of these things into our example database and created the final set of definitions, five in total, which you'll need for the example database. Now we have an empty database structure, that has referential integrity and is ready to have data entered into it. This is what we'll look at in the next chapter.

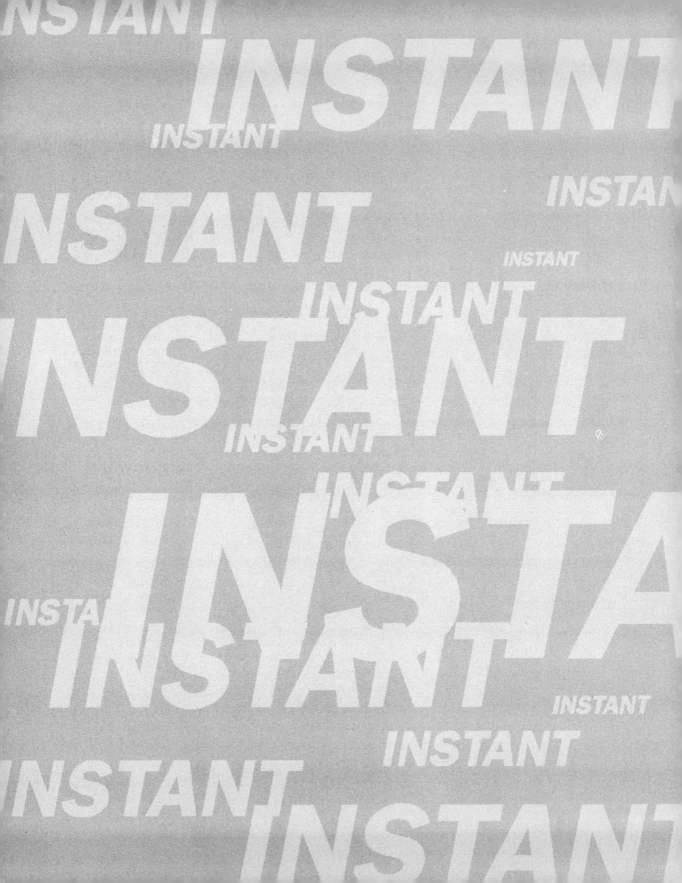

Chapter

5

Manipulating Database Information

Once an initial database table structure has been created, the next step is to physically insert the data into the tables. This may sound straightforward, but you will need to take care of the order in which you insert data into the example database, as one table might be dependent upon data from another. Therefore, we will look at the *structure* of the database before we actually **INSERT** the information into it. Once the information has been added, we will look at how you can delete obsolete records from the database, and finally we will discuss how you can alter it to change any out-of-date or erroneous information.

This chapter's tour takes in the following sights:

 The structure of the example database

 Inserting information into the example database

Deleting from the example database

Updating the example database

The Structure of the Example Database

So far, we've only talked about tables in terms of fields and records. It's important, however, to view the overall structure of the database and see how all the tables are interrelated. There are a total of five tables which have been created. It's a good idea to see how one table relates to another.

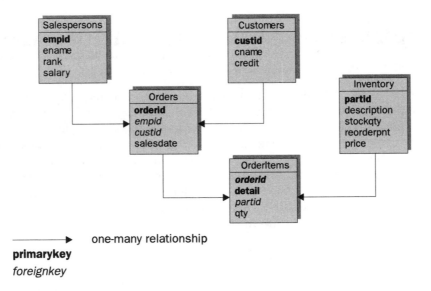

This diagram is purely an aid to helping you understand the structure of the database. There is no way to view the table structures that have been created, so it might be an idea to familiarize yourself with the database before you insert data into it.

There is one feature on the diagram that we haven't yet discussed: the concept of the **one to many** relationship. This is more database terminology, but it simply means that for every single entry in table X, there can be many corresponding entries in table Y. Looking at our example database, this means that one employee could be responsible for many orders.

However, each order can only have one employee dealing with it. The same goes for customers; there can be one customer who makes many orders, but each order can only have been made by one customer.

These relationships define the order in which tables can have data inserted. Some tables will require data from other tables. These dependencies were created in Chapter 4, when we included referential integrity in our database. When we specifically added foreign key constraints, it became impossible for us to put unrelated data into the database.

For example, the **Orders** table requires an employee identifier. Yet how could you insert data into the **Orders** table relating to the specific employee, if there was no data within the **Salespersons** table? It could well refer to an employee identifier that didn't exist. The SQL engine will therefore prevent you from doing this with an error message along the lines of 'no primary key value for the foreign key'. We will have to keep this in mind as we physically insert the data into the database.

Using the Interactive SQL Engine

This is where you can begin using the Watcom SQL engine which you will find on the disk provided at the back of the book. We're now moving on to the data manipulation language, which is available in its entirety on the disk. You'll find that all of the tables necessary for the example database have already been created, and also that the example database has already been partly populated. If you followed the instructions in Chapter 1 for connecting to the database, then you will be ready to start inserting the supplementary data. If not, you need to refresh yourself of the contents of Chapter 1 so that you know how to connect to the database.

The INSERT INTO Command

It's time to examine how we actually get data input into the example database. Standard SQL has one input statement, which itself has two forms. You can create and insert rows you define with a list of explicit values, or you can take the results of a query and insert that into the table. The syntax looks like this:

```
INSERT INTO <table name> [ (<insert column list>) ]
        <insert source>

<insert source> ::= VALUES (<value list>) | <query
expression>)
```

Value List Insertion

The simplest form of insertion uses a list of value expressions. If an insert column list is given, then SQL matches the columns in the value list to those in the table, by their positions. The first value in the value list is assigned to the first column named in the insert column list, the second is assigned to the second column and so on. Of course, the datatypes in the value list have to match the database datatypes. This means that you have to put quotes around character strings but not around numbers. The column names in the column insert list don't have to be in any particular order, but you can't repeat a column name. What about the columns in the table that were left out of the list? They get their default value or **NULL** assigned to them.

If no insert column list is given, then SQL will create a column list that has **ALL** the columns in the table, listed in the order they appear in the table. This means that the value list also has to have the number of columns as the target table.

Query Insertion

The query insertion executes the query and puts the result into the table. Again, the columns have to match up in position, number and datatype. All the rows from the query result are inserted into the target table at the same time. This is important as again this is the principle of sets! If just one row violates any constraint on the table, then the whole insertion fails.

Inserting Data into the Example Database

Let's put some data into a few of the tables, using the **INSERT INTO** statement. The first table we should consider populating is the **Salespersons** table which contains data about all of our sales employees. This isn't dependent on any other tables for its information.

The **INSERT INTO** statement needs to know which table to put the values into. Following the keyword **VALUES**, there should be a list of requisite values. It is also good practice to put the column names in after the table name, although this isn't strictly necessary. If you choose to ignore the column names, however, you could be creating more work for yourself at a later stage. Therefore, type in the following:

```
INSERT INTO Salespersons (empid,ename,rank,salary) VALUES (101, 'Andrew
Allen', 1, 1000);
```

Previously, in Chapter 4 we defined **empid** as a primary key, in the **CREATE TABLE** statement for the **Salespersons** table. If we now try to add another record with the same **empid**, it will be rejected by the database.

```
INSERT INTO Salespersons (empid,ename,rank,salary) VALUES (101, 'Larry
Larder', 1, 1000);
```

We can add records for which there is no **empid** with the same value, so another valid entry to this table would be the following:

```
INSERT INTO Salespersons (empid,ename,rank,salary) VALUES (110,'Larry
Larder',3,3500);
```

Similarly, if we try to add a record with too many or too few values specified for the **INSERT INTO**, this will also be rejected. For example, the statement:

```
INSERT INTO Salespersons (empid, ename, rank, salary)
VALUES (115, 'joe', 3)
```

and the statement:

```
INSERT INTO Salespersons (empid, ename, rank, salary)
VALUES(115, 'Joe', 3, 3500, 12)
```

will both fail.

Rather than get you to type in every entry into the database, once you have typed in this entry you will find that the rest of the data is already provided on the example disk, and is already present on the example database.

> If you are creating a database rather than using the one on the disk, then you should refer to Appendix B for the complete code.

The next table we would populate is the **Customers** table. All of the required customers data is stored in a straightforward list of **INSERT INTO** queries for the **Customers** table. This is also the case for the **Inventory** table data. We could actually have inserted the data into these three tables in any order, as none of them require information from another table.

However, when it's time to insert data into the **Orders** and **OrderItems** tables, we have to watch carefully the order of insertion. The **Orders** table needs to reference values from the **Salespersons** table and **Customers** table. Likewise, the **OrderItems** table references the **Orders** table and the **Inventory** table.

We could insert all the orders in their table first, then add all the items ordered. However, the correct way to do this is to first enter an order row and immediately follow it with the items:

```
INSERT INTO Orders (orderid,empid,custid,salesdate) VALUES (6099,101, 1,
'1995-12-15');
INSERT INTO OrderItems (orderid,detail,partid,qty) VALUES (6099,1,1002,3);
INSERT INTO OrderItems (orderid,detail,partid,qty) VALUES (6099,2,1003,3);
INSERT INTO OrderItems (orderid,detail,partid,qty) VALUES (6099,3,1004,3);
INSERT INTO OrderItems (orderid,detail,partid,qty) VALUES (6099,4,1009,3);
INSERT INTO OrderItems (orderid,detail,partid,qty) VALUES (6099,5,1010,1);
```

You will notice that all of the items are serially numbered within each order. This isn't obligatory, but the combination of **(orderid, detail)** has to be unique within the table. However, most front-end forms tools will use an auto increment function or the database itself may provide an auto-incrementing column. Both Sybase and SQL Server have an auto-incrementing keyword **IDENTITY** which can be used in the **CREATE TABLE** statement. Microsoft Access has a **COUNTER** datatype.

Selective INSERTing

You can probably guess that in many databases there is a lot of repetitive data that needs inserting, and rather than insert the data line by line, you can use a more powerful method. You can specify criteria for where data should be inserted, but we need to know how to **SELECT** data first. We will look at this in Chapter 6.

Import and Export of Bulk Data

The SQL standard doesn't have any construct for doing bulk data loads into tables, or for importing and exporting data from and to other file formats. Every vendor has a utility program or extension to his SQL for importing and exporting bulk data. The tools vary from product to product, and you will have to read your vendor manuals to find out the means by which they effect bulk data transfers.

Updating and Deleting Rows

SQL also lets you update and delete rows from a single table. However, remember that a change in one table can cascade via referential integrity constraints to other tables in the schema.

There are two ways to find the rows that you want to work with: by a logical search, or by a cursor. A cursor is a way of scanning a table to change or remove one row at a time. As they are dealt with by the host programming language and not by SQL, we won't deal with cursors in this book. SQL-89 and SQL-92 treat them in different ways which means that there are many different implementations available. We will therefore focus on the searched deletion and searched updates.

The DELETE FROM Statement

Firstly, let's look at how to get rid of unwanted data from your tables. The syntax for a searched deletion statement is as follows:

```
DELETE FROM <table name>
[WHERE <search condition>]
```

Notice that the **<table name>** can't have a correlation name according to the standard. However, this is a common extension to many vendor tools.

The subset of qualified rows defined by the search condition is removed from the table all at once. This is another example of the set orientation of SQL. The way that most SQL implementations do this is to make two passes through the table. The first pass marks all of the rows which tested **TRUE** for **WHERE** clause search condition; it skips those that tested **FALSE** or **UNKNOWN**. The second pass removes the marked rows. The important point is that while the rows are being marked, the entire table is still available for the **WHERE** clause to use in the search condition.

The **DELETE FROM** statement removes zero or more rows of one table. We'll deal with the rather odd concept of deleting zero rows in a moment. First we'll look at deleting a single row. Since we added Larry Larder's record, he has decided that this job is underpaid and he's moved on to better things. This query removes the one row that you have added. We specify his name, but if we searched by name we would also remove any other employees who coincidentally had the same name:

```
DELETE FROM Salespersons
WHERE empid=110;
```

A deletion that removes zero rows can seem a little strange, but remember that an empty set is still a subset. So a statement like this that removes anyone earning a salary of above $5000 is a valid query, even though there is no-one on our database who earns that much:

```
DELETE FROM Salespersons
WHERE salary>=5000;
```

Another important thing to remember is that the **WHERE** clause is optional. If there is no **WHERE** clause, then all rows in the table are deleted. A full set is a subset too.

At this point it seems wise to remind you to not forget the **WHERE** clause, unless you *do* want to delete the whole table. You would have to type all of the data in for that table, which is perhaps *not* what you want to do!

> The **<search condition>** can get quite complex, and it can include subqueries (which we look at in Chapter 9) which refer to other tables.

The UPDATE Statement

If you don't want to completely delete certain data, but just amend it slightly, then you can update specific fields or subsets of fields. The syntax for a searched update statement is as follows:

```
UPDATE <table name>
    SET <set clause list>
[WHERE <search condition>]
```

```
<set clause list> ::= <set clause> [{ , <set clause> }...]
<set clause> ::= <object column> = <update source>

<update source> ::= <value expression> | NULL | DEFAULT

<object column> ::= <column name>
```

The function of the **UPDATE** statement in SQL is to change the values in a block of one or more columns and zero or more rows of a table. The **UPDATE** clause simply gives the name of the table where the changes will be made. The **SET** clause is a list of columns and their changed values, and the **WHERE** clause tells the statement which rows to use.

The WHERE Clause

As we said earlier, the **WHERE** clause is optional. The subset of qualified rows defined by the search condition is changed all at once. If you look at the **Salespersons** table, (remember **SELECT * FROM SALESPERSONS;** will achieve this), then you will be able to see that all of the salaries of rank 2 employees are $2000. However, you are going to change this. We'll start with the record of Dale Dahlman who has had a raise after he convinced Wellesley Inc. that their life was incomplete without ten thingies. His new salary is now $2100. The update command specifies the actual table first, then you set the column value to 2100. However, you don't want every column being set to 2100, just Dale's, so you specify a restriction applying only to his record.

```
UPDATE Salespersons
SET salary = 2100
WHERE ename = 'Dale Dahlman';
```

There's nothing to stop you updating several columns at once, if you specify them within the restriction. If the top dogs of the company (those with rank 3), Faulkner Forest, Gloria Garcia, and Harvey Harrison had awarded themselves another raise from $2500 to $3000, this would need to be recorded. However, just to make it slightly more awkward, Kevin Kody already earns $3100, so his record won't need amending. The code that you would need is as follows:

```
UPDATE Salespersons
SET salary = 3000
WHERE rank = 3 AND NOT empid = 109;
```

The way that most SQL implementations do this is to make several passes through the table. The first pass finds all the rows which tested **TRUE** for the **WHERE** clause search condition; it skips those that tested **FALSE** or **UNKNOWN**. This pass makes a duplicate of each qualified row, which we will call the old and the new copy of the row.

The next several passes use the old copy and the **SET** clause statements to make changes in the new rows. The important point is that the entire original table is still available for the **WHERE** and **SET** clauses to use.

Finally, the new rows replace the old rows. If an error occurs during all of this, then the table is unchanged and the errors are reported.

This set orientation isn't like a traditional third generation programming language, so it might be hard to learn at first. This feature lets you write a statement which will swap the values in two columns, in this way:

```
UPDATE MyTable
SET a = b, b = a;
```

This works by making a copy of all the rows in a table called **NEW** and labelling the original columns table **OLD** in the first pass. There is no **WHERE** clause to test the columns against so all of the rows are copied across from the original table:

Pass One

```
OLD            NEW
a    b         a    b
======         ======
1    10        1    10
2    20        2    20
3    30        3    30
```

The second pass changes all of the values in the table **NEW**, column **a** to those of table **OLD**, column **b**. It will do this on a row by row basis, where the value for **a** is 1 in the first row of **NEW**, then it becomes the value for **b** in the first row of **OLD**:

Pass Two SET NEW a = OLD b

```
OLD            NEW
a    b         a    b
======         ======
1    10        10   10
2    20        20   20
3    30        30   30
```

The third pass changes all of the values in the table **NEW**, column **b** to those of table **OLD**, column **a**. Again, it will do this on a row by row basis, where the value for **b** is 10 in the first row of **NEW**, then it becomes the value for **a** in the first row of **OLD**:

Pass Three SET NEW b = OLD a

```
OLD            NEW
a    b         a    b
======         ======
1    10        10   1
2    20        20   2
3    30        30   3
```

The fourth pass just renames the table **NEW**, table **OLD** and the original table can be discarded:

Pass Four Replace OLD with NEW

```
OLD
a    b
======
10   1
20   2
30   3
```

This method of swapping of columns isn't the same as the following statements:

```
BEGIN
UPDATE MyTable
    SET a = b;
UPDATE MyTable
    SET b = a;
END;
```

In the first **UPDATE**, columns **a** and **b** will swap values in each row. In the second pair of **UPDATES**, column **a** will get all of the values of column **b** in each row, and then that same value will be written back into column **b**.

There are some limits as to what the value expression can be. The same column can not appear more than once in a **<set clause list>**, which makes sense given the parallel nature of the statement. Since both go into effect at the same time, you wouldn't know which **SET** clause to use.

However, the **<set clause list>** doesn't have to contain only simple values on the right of the assignments. You can also use arithmetic expressions to update the table. We will look at how to do this in Chapter 9.

If there is no **WHERE** clause, then all rows in the table are changed. The final state of the table can't violate any constraints on the table.

Summary

In this chapter, we took an overview of the all tables that we've created so far and the database structure as a whole. We looked at the process of inserting data into the database structure and why it's so important to make sure the tables are populated in a certain order. Once that order has been determined, the actual process of insertion becomes fairly simple. We also considered the methods by which specific records could be deleted from tables and how fields could be updated. We will return to all three methods of data manipulation in Chapter 9, when we consider how to use them in conjunction with **SELECT** queries. Next, we'll consider how you can extract the data you want from the database, now it's been stored correctly.

Exercises

1 Make up an order number, say 9999, and try to insert the items into the **OrderItems** table without first inserting a row in the Orders table. What happens?

2 Insert a row in the Orders table, using the following statement:

```
INSERT INTO Orders (orderid, custid) VALUES (9999, 10);
```

What happens?

(Hint: Remember that when the columns are not specified, the INSERT statement will try to use the DEFAULT values given in the table declaration.)

3 Black Cat Stores, customer number 33, has placed one order, with order number 6279. The items on it are:

```
detail qty partid description  price
====== === ===== =========== =======
1      1   1007  thingabob    12.50
2      1   1008  widget       25.00
3      1   1009  chachka      70.00
4      1   1010  thingie      80.00
5      1   1002  doohickey    25.00
6      1   1003  frammis       2.50
7      1   1006  gizmo        11.35
```

But as everyone knows, if you have a perfectly good 'thingie' then you don't need a 'thingabob'. Delete it from the order.

4 There has been a recall of gizmos! Yes, that unfortunate accident with all those dead fuzzy bunnies was a result of a defective gizmo. Delete all the orders.

5 Andrew Allen, employee number 101, was killed when he went to demonstrate a gizmo at the HappyLand Bunny Farm. We need to delete him from the database. Try to do that. What happens?

Querying the Database - the SELECT command

This chapter is one of a suite which looks at the crux of SQL, the **SELECT** command. The **SELECT** command is responsible for querying the database and returning the required information to the programmer. We shall start by looking at the composition of the **SELECT** command and how you would go about building up a query. From there we move on to the simple predicates and clauses that can be included within a **SELECT** query, the ones which can help with string matching and sorting. Finally, the chapter looks at how to sort your result table into order. Here is the outline of the what the chapter covers:

- **SELECT** command basics, including joins and projection
- The **WHERE** comparison
- Boolean search conditions
- The **BETWEEN**, **IN** and **LIKE** predicates
- Sorting, and the **ORDER BY** clause

SELECT Command Basics

The **SELECT** command is where you will do most of your SQL programming. This is "the big one" that queries the database. In a real sense, 80% to 90% of SQL is this one statement. Unfortunately for programmers new to SQL, this statement is highly detailed. We will break from our usual policy of giving you the whole syntax at once, and instead build the description of the **SELECT** statement one clause at a time.

In its simplest form, the **SELECT** command will simply return a whole table, or specific columns and/or specific rows. The syntax begins with a simple **SELECT** object **FROM** table. You specify what exactly it is that you want from a particular table and this information is returned to you. This is known as a **query**. Querying the database doesn't affect the structure of the database. Nor does it affect the ordering of the data; it simply presents it in a certain way to the user.

The **WHERE** clause acts as a filter. In the first chapter we said that for a query you would say "**SELECT** jobs paying over $5 an hour **FROM** the table of railway jobs." However, this isn't quite the whole truth. If you only wish to see certain data, then you can formulate a rule which only accepts the data you want to see. You then "stick" this rule on the end of the **SELECT** statement under the **WHERE** clause. Therefore, the new clause would read "**SELECT** jobs **FROM** table of railway jobs **WHERE** wage > $5."

Total Table

Job Type	Wage
Driver	$100 p/h
Guard	$10 p/h
Ticket Seller	$4 p/h
Trainspotter	$1 p/h

Result Table

Job Type	Wage
Driver	$100 p/h
Guard	$10 p/h

Another way of looking at this, is that you **SELECT** column/s **FROM** a table, and you use **WHERE** to specify row/s.

To build more complex queries, you just keep adding clauses. Imagine you want them in order with the highest wage at the top. In this case, you would add another clause at the bottom of the query, which would carry out the command **ORDER BY**. This command carries out a sort of the wage which can be specified in either ascending or descending order. The way it works is to simply take the job with the highest wage, display that row first, then look for the second highest job, display that, and so on.

Now imagine that you don't want information from only one table, you want it from several. The **SELECT** statement combines two relational operations, **join** and **projection**, in one statement. The following boxes and diagrams look at these operators in a little more detail. It will be worth your while getting familiar with them as they are pretty fundamental, and very useful.

> A join takes two tables and builds a new table from them by concatenating the rows from one table to the rows of the other.

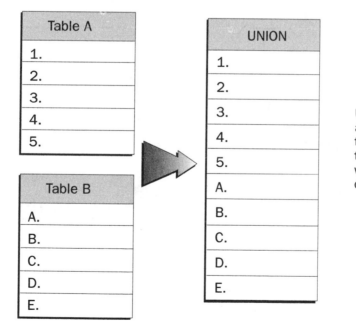

Union:
a set operator that combines two tables. Done with a UNION operator in SQL.

A projection removes unwanted columns from a table. It does this by generating an intermediate table, which the user never sees. This "invisible" table contains all of the columns listed in the query and removes those not mentioned (we will look at how SELECT * works in a moment). The final result table that the user gets to see after a projection then has any duplicate occurrences of rows removed.

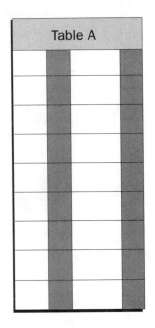

Table A

Projection:
a relational operator that removes columns from a table. Done with the SELECT clause of a SELECT statement.

The rules for using these operations are given as logical expressions. The expressions can be simple, or they can be very complex, but they can always be reduced to Boolean expressions with comparisons or function calls connected by **AND**, **OR** and **NOT**.

The real trick in SQL is learning to write a clear specification of what you want from the database in these logical expressions. The experienced programmer knows that analysts don't always give a clear specification from which to program. The burden on precision will inevitably be on the SQL programmer. We can handle it!

The Simple Single Table SELECT Statement

The simplest syntax of the **SELECT** statement is as follows:

```
SELECT [[ALL]|DISTINCT]{<columnorexpressionlist>|*}
FROM<table name>;
```

This statement is one whole command that will simply get all the rows in the single table, and display only those columns which are named in the **SELECT** clause expression or column list in the given order.

```
SELECT * FROM Salespersons;
```

Type this in and you will get a list of all the salespersons and all the corresponding information contained about them in the **Salespersons** table.

```
SELECT ename FROM Salespersons;
```

If you don't want all the information, (for example, you just want a list of the employee names), then you simply supply the column name, in this case **ename**.

```
SELECT ename, salary FROM Salespersons;
```

You can also select a list of specified column names, as long as you divide each name by a comma. The **SELECT *** option is the shorthand for a list of all the column names in the given table in the order in which they appear in the table declaration.

SELECT and ALTER TABLE

With some SQL products, problems can occur if you use **SELECT *** with **ALTER TABLE**. We'll start by looking at the working of the **SELECT *** option. The SQL-92 standard says that the **SELECT *** shorthand is expanded out as an actual list of columns. This means a statement such as **SELECT * FROM Salespersons** would be expanded out to:

	empid	ename	rank	salary
Row 1 Row 2				

For this table, the **SELECT *** statement is actually equivalent to the following code, and when you type **SELECT *** this is what is executed:

```
SELECT empid, ename, rank, salary FROM Salespersons;
```

This is where problems can occur. The **SELECT *** statement might display the column headings **empid**, **ename**, **rank** and **salary**. You then add the phone column into the table using the **ALTER TABLE** statement.

```
ALTER TABLE Salespersons ADD phone INTEGER NOT NULL;
```

	empid	ename	rank	salary	phone
Row 1 Row 2					

Because of the shorthand expansion rule, the addition of the new column is supposed to have no effect on any existing query expression. However, when you recompile query expressions, you will see the new column and it could change your results. Even though the same statement **SELECT *** effectively means the following, it might be that the Salespersons table now contains an extra column:

```
SELECT empid, ename, rank, salary FROM Salespersons;
```

This is the original table you created; the first version of the table, minus the new column you have since added. Or you might see the equivalent of this:

```
SELECT empid, ename, rank, salary, phone FROM Salespersons;
```

Check to see how your SQL product actually handles all this.

> This also affects the SQL-92 JOIN operators, which are discussed in Chapter 7.

In SQL-92, you could also use **TABLE <table name>** in place of **SELECT * FROM <table name>**, but not many products yet allow this shorthand.

Creating New Columns - the AS Operator

SQL allows you to put constants, expressions and function calls into the **SELECT** list (as well as column names). These constants, expressions and function calls will be evaluated for each row in the table. Such constructed columns can be given names in SQL-92 with the **<expression> AS <name>** operator.

```
SELECT ename || empid AS combine FROM Salespersons;
```

'||' is the concatenator we saw in Chapter 3. This statement takes **ename** and **empid** and adds them together as one string, which is displayed beneath the column heading **combine**. If both columns contained **INTEGER** or **DECIMAL** datatypes, then you could use arithmetical operators (+,-,*,/) instead of the concatenator.

How the SELECT Statement Works

It will help you to understand the working of the **SELECT** statement if you visualize what the statement is doing conceptually, rather than physically. The statement works by first building an empty result table using the names and expressions in the **SELECT** clause.

```
SELECT ename, salary FROM Salespersons;
```

The above code yields the following empty result table:

ename	salary

Empty Rows

We then go to the **FROM** clause and get the table listed there.

ename	salary
Andrew Allen	1000
Burbank Burkett	1000

Details from Salespersons

The **ALL** clause says that you keep duplicate rows, while the **DISTINCT** clause indicates that you remove redundant duplicates in the final results. The working table in the **FROM** clause is used to fill in the columns in the **SELECT** clause. In practice, the keyword **ALL** is never used, since it is the default of the clause.

Let's try a more complex one table query, using the following:

Foobar

a	b	c
1	23	10
1	23	10
2	17	11
3	32	12
4	41	NULL

You've already got all the necessary building blocks to create this table, so you can do it yourself. **SELECT * FROM Foobar** will enable you to check if you have created the table correctly.

> **The text which creates and fills this table can be found in the Appendix B.**

If you then type the following query:

```
┌─────────────────────────────────────────────────────────────────────┐
│ ─                       Watcom Interactive SQL              ▼ ▲       │
│ File  Edit  Command  Window  Help                                     │
├───────────────────────────────────────────────────────────────┬──────┤
│ ─                               Data                          ▼│▲     │
│ 'Blatz'                  a           b           fred                  │
│ Blatz                    1           23          230                  │
│ Blatz                    2           17          187                  │
│ Blatz                    3           32          384                  │
│ Blatz                    4           41          (NULL)               │
│                                                                       │
│                                                                       │
│                                                                       │
│                                                                       │
├───────────────────────────────────────────────────────────────┬──────┤
│ ─                            Statistics                       ▼│▲     │
│ Estimated 5 rows in query (I/O estimate 3)                            │
│ PLAN> TEMPORARY TABLE Foobar (seq)                                    │
├───────────────────────────────────────────────────────────────┬──────┤
│ ─                             Command                         ▼│▲     │
│  ┌──────────┐    SELECT DISTINCT 'Blatz', a, b, (b * c) AS fred    ↑  │
│  │ Execute  │        FROM Foobar;                                     │
│  └──────────┘                                                         │
│  ┌──────────┐                                                         │
│  │   Stop   │                                                         │
│  └──────────┘                                                      ↓  │
└─────────────────────────────────────────────────────────────────────┘
```

the first column is assigned a constant string value. Since we didn't use an **AS** clause to give it a name, it has none. However, for display purposes, most interactive query tools will use the same string as the column name.

The second and third columns keep their original names and their values.

The fourth column has a name because we gave it one with an **AS** clause. We also gave an expression for computing its values. The expression can involve operators, functions, and even subquery expressions, but let's keep it simple for now. Finally, when we have the whole answer table, the **DISTINCT** option removes one duplicate row from the results (expressly, the row 1, 23, 10).

This is how SQL is able to build its tables, one row at a time.

The WHERE Clause

We've now looked at **SELECT** in its simplest form. The next form of **SELECT** statement uses a new clause:

```
SELECT[[ALL]|DISTINCT]{<columnorexpressionlist>|*}
    FROM<tablename>
  WHERE<searchcondition>;
```

The **WHERE** clause is used to filter down the amount of information you get from a query. Without it, you'd just get every row in the file reeled off. In terms of relational database theory, the **WHERE** clause is called a **restriction**. It is another basic relational operation, like the two we met earlier.

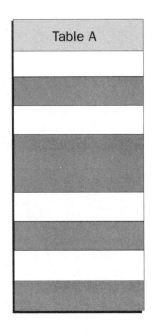

Restriction:
a relational operator that
removes rows from a table.
Done with the WHERE clause
of a SELECT statement.

A restriction serves the following purpose: if you only want certain information from a table, then you need to specify the information you want within the search condition. (A sample search condition might be **WHERE salary > 1000**, so that all values of salary below **1001** would evaluate to **FALSE**). A statement containing **WHERE** will get all the columns in the single table, and display only those rows which test **TRUE** when the search condition is applied to them. That also means that if the search condition is **FALSE** or **UNKNOWN**, that row will be removed from the results. Let's use this concept in conjunction with the **Foobar** table to ask the following:

```
┌─────────────────────────── Watcom Interactive SQL ──────────────────────▼─▲─┐
│ File  Edit  Command  Window  Help                                            │
│ ┌────────────────────────────── Data ───────────────────────────────────▼─▲┐│
│ │'Blatz'            a        b        fred                                   ││
│ │Blatz              2        17       187                                    ││
│ │                                                                            ││
│ │                                                                            ││
│ └────────────────────────────────────────────────────────────────────────┘│
│ ┌──────────────────────────── Statistics ────────────────────────────────▼─▲┐│
│ │Estimated 1 rows in query (I/O estimate 1)                                  ││
│ │PLAN> Foobar (seq)                                                          ││
│ └────────────────────────────────────────────────────────────────────────┘│
│ ┌───────────────────────────── Command ──────────────────────────────────▼─▲┐│
│ │ [Execute]  SELECT 'Blatz', a, b, (b * c) AS fred                           ││
│ │            FROM Foobar                                                     ││
│ │ [Stop]     WHERE (10 * a) >= b;                                            ││
│ └────────────────────────────────────────────────────────────────────────┘│
└──────────────────────────────────────────────────────────────────────────┘
```

The procedure is just as before, but the final step is to filter the working table in the **WHERE** clause. Imagine this as the working table (this is assuming the duplicate row has already been removed):

```
'Blatz'   a   b    fred
========================
'Blatz'   1   23   230
'Blatz'   2   17   187
'Blatz'   3   32   384
'Blatz'   4   41   NULL
```

The **WHERE** clause take the first row. It evaluates `(10*1)>=23`. The condition evaluates to **FALSE**. The row is removed. The second row `(10*2)>=17`. The condition evaluates to **TRUE**, so this row remains. The third row goes to `(10*3)>=32`, which is **FALSE** again and so that row is removed. The final row is also **FALSE**. Hence, there is only one row in the answer.

This query is both a restriction and a projection together in one SQL statement. The problem is that we are still working with only one table. You can't access the advantages of a relational database system until you can join more than one table to another.

Boolean Search Conditions

The search condition in the **WHERE** clause can use all of the comparison and Boolean operators we have discussed. Their use in SQL isn't much different from that within other programming languages, except when **NULL**s are involved. The precedence of the operators is to first do the comparisons, then the **AND**s and finally the **OR**s (warning to Pascal programmers: you are used to a different order of evaluation!).

If a column name appears in two tables, you have either to rename one of the columns with an **AS** clause, or fully qualify a column name. That is, you write it in the form `"<table>.<column>"` so that the SQL engine can tell them apart. If we use the last example, the `Foobar.a` would refer to the **a** column. This is known as a **qualified** column name.

> We will shortly discuss more complex predicates which involve subqueries, but they will all reduce to **AND, OR** and **NOT** combinations. You have to watch out for the **UNKNOWN** values due to **NULL**s in some of the columns.

NULLs in Comparisons

The problem with **NULL**s in comparisons and Boolean expressions is that the law of tricotomy doesn't apply.

> The law of tricotomy states for two numbers **x** and **y**, one and only one of the following is true: either $(x = y)$ or $(x < y)$ or $(x > y)$. e.g. as two is smaller than three, two can't be equal to or greater than three.

Therefore, you have to be careful. Consider the table **Foobar** and the query:

```
—                      Watcom Interactive SQL              ▼ ▲
 File  Edit  Command  Window  Help
—                            Data                          ▼ ▲
         a           b           c
         1          23          10
         1          23          10
         2          17          11
         3          32          12




—                          Statistics                      ▼ ▲
Estimated 3 rows in query (I/O estimate 1)
PLAN> Foobar (seq)
—                           Command                        ▼ ▲
  ┌─────────┐  SELECT *                                    ⬍
  │ Execute │    FROM Foobar
  └─────────┘   WHERE c > 10
  ┌─────────┐     OR c <= 10;
  │  Stop   │
  └─────────┘                                              ⬍
```

You would think that this query would return all the rows in **Foobar**. Intuitively you would deduct that each value of **c** must either be greater, smaller or equal to 10. However, you don't get the row **(4, 41, NULL)** because of the **NULL**. That **NULL** isn't equal, less than, or greater than, any value.

Predicates with the WHERE clause

Now we've considered how to use relational operators and boolean search conditions, within the **WHERE** clause, it's time to consider some other predicates that you can use in the same way. There are several predicates you can use to refine search conditions:

 The **LIKE** predicate. This is mainly of use when you only have a rough idea of what you want.

 The **IN** predicate specifies a list of objects in its search.

The **BETWEEN** predicate looks for everything that can be found within two specified objects or string patterns.

Let's have a look at these in more detail.

The LIKE Predicate

The **LIKE** operator is a string pattern matching predicate. The SQL-92 syntax is as follows:

```
<like predicate> ::=
    <match value> [NOT] LIKE <pattern>
        [ESCAPE <escape character>]

<match value> ::= <character value expression>
<pattern> ::= <character value expression>
<escape character> ::= <character value expression>
```

The expression "**M NOT LIKE P**" is equivalent to "**NOT (M LIKE P)**," which follows the usual syntax in SQL.

If you are an MS-DOS programmer, then you are used to the idea of wildcards for pattern matching. A **wildcard** is a special character that stands for some character or set of characters. The two wildcards in the **LIKE** predicate can only appear in the **<pattern>** string. They are the '**%**' and '**_**' characters. The '**_**' character represents a single arbitrary character and in this sense it is just like the '**?**' in an MS-DOS command file name. This translates to the following:

> 'Smith' LIKE 'S_ _ _ _' is **TRUE**
>
> 'Smith' LIKE 'S_ _ _' is **FALSE**-the pattern is too short
>
> 'Smith' LIKE 'S_ _ _ _ _' is **FALSE**-the pattern is too long

The underscore was a bad choice, but we are stuck with it. With today's clear, crisp laser printers, it is hard to count underscores by eye.

The '**%**' character represents an arbitrary substring pattern, possibly of length zero. Note that this isn't the same as the '*****' character in the MS-DOS command line! In MS-DOS, the asterisk expands to the full length of the file

name or file extension to which it is matched. In SQL, the percent sign, in
effect, generates trial strings of 0, 1, 2, .. (n) underscores and tries those
patterns against the **<match value>**. Thus:

```
'Bk' LIKE 'B%k' is TRUE
'Bok' LIKE 'B%k' is TRUE
'Book' LIKE 'B%k' is TRUE
'Block' LIKE 'B%k' is TRUE
'BBBBkkkk' LIKE 'B%k' is TRUE
'BkBkBk' LIKE 'B%k' is TRUE
'BkBkB' LIKE 'B%k' is FALSE
```

You can mix multiple underscores and percent signs together in a
<pattern>, but the matching takes more and more time. For example, if we
have a column called "**tenletters**," which is a string of ten characters,
then the following predicate

```
tenletters LIKE 'B%_K%'
```

is really the same as:

```
    (tenletters LIKE 'B_K_ _ _ _ _ _'
OR tenletters LIKE 'B_ _K_ _ _ _ _'
OR tenletters LIKE 'B_ _ _K_ _ _ _'
OR tenletters LIKE 'B_ _ _ _K_ _ _'
OR tenletters LIKE 'B_ _ _ _ _K_ _'
OR tenletters LIKE 'B_ _ _ _ _ _K_'
OR tenletters LIKE 'B_ _ _ _ _ _ _K_'
OR tenletters LIKE 'B_ _ _ _ _ _ _K')
```

The **<escape character>** syntax isn't yet widely implemented. The **<escape
character>** is used in the **<pattern>** to specify that the character which
follows it is to be interpreted as a literal character, rather than as a
wildcard. The escape character is always followed by another escape
character, an underscore, or a percent sign.

> **C programmers use a backslash for their escape character, so
> this is a good choice for SQL programmers too.**

LIKE Predicates and Queries

You can use the **LIKE** predicate within a query as follows. Your boss wants
to know the credit of the 'Black...' something stores, but she's forgotten
their precise name. This predicate, together with the wildcard, allows you to

match the bit your boss can remember to any entry in the **Customers** table that begins with the word "Black."

```
SELECT * FROM Customers WHERE cname LIKE 'Black%';
```

The only entry in the table commencing with Black is Black Cat Stores, so that must be the one.

NULLS and Empty Strings

As you would expect, a **NULL** in the predicate returns an **UNKNOWN** result. The **NULL** can be the **<match value>** or the **<pattern>**. I have no idea why you would set a **<pattern>** to **NULL**, but the **<match value>** is often a column from a table and it can be a **NULL**.

If the **<match value>** and the **<pattern>** are both character strings of length zero, then the result is **TRUE**. If only one of them is a zero character string, then you will get a **FALSE** result.

> **Things can be equal but not alike! A very important point that is often missed is that two strings can be equal but *not* alike in SQL. String equality in SQL first pads the shorter of the two strings with rightmost blanks, then matches the characters in each, one for one. Thus "Smith" and "Smith " (with three trailing blanks) are equal. However, the LIKE predicate does no padding in the <pattern>.**

The IN Predicate

The **IN** predicate asks if a value is in a set of other values e.g., Is the letter A in the set of vowels, or alternatively is the letter B in the set of vowels? You can use this as a criteria for selection, such as select all the products beginning with a vowel. The predicate would then have to check each letter in turn. The **IN** predicate has two forms, one with a list of values and one with a subquery. If you are a Pascal programmer, you already know the value list version of this predicate. The syntax for the expression list version is as follows:

```
<expression> [NOT] IN (<value1>, <value2>, ..., <valueN>)
```

This really is shorthand for the following:

```
(<expression> = <value1>
  OR <expression> = <value2>
    ....
  OR <expression> = <valueN>)
```

This predicate is handy in a **CHECK()** constraint to make sure that only the correct values get into the table. While not required by the standards, most implementations will scan the list for matches from left to right. Unfortunately, most people will order the list by sorting it numerically or alphabetically. If you put the mostly likely values in that order in the list, the query may run faster.

For example, did anyone order any of the items that we had on sale? Assuming that the items were as shown below, the query would be:

```
SELECT DISTINCT partid
  FROM OrderItems
 WHERE partid IN ('doodad', 'doohickey', 'frammis');
```

This will convert into the following:

```
SELECT DISTINCT partid
  FROM OrderItems
 WHERE (partid = 'doodad'
     OR partid = 'doohickey'
     OR partid = 'frammis');
```

If you wanted to know what else was sold, apart from these items, you could also use the **IN** predicate. The addition of the **NOT** operator to the statement is a method of searching for everything, excluding those pre-selected objects.

```
SELECT DISTINCT partid
  FROM OrderItems
 WHERE partid NOT IN ('doodad', 'doohickey', 'frammis');
```

It can subsequently be converted to the following:

```
SELECT DISTINCT partid
  FROM OrderItems
 WHERE (partid <> 'doodad'
     OR partid <> 'doohickey'
     OR partid <> 'frammis');
```

The BETWEEN Predicate

SQL has a shorthand which is a useful way of showing that one value lies within a range defined by two other values. This is the syntax:

```
<value expression> [NOT] BETWEEN <low value expr> AND <high
value expr>
```

This predicate is actually just a shorthand for the following expression:

```
((<low value expr> <= <value expression>)
        AND (<value expression> <= <high value expr>))
```

Beginners to SQL programming sometimes forget that this predicate works with any of the data types. It can even work for strings. This enables you to make alphabetical queries of a table. The query below would select all entries of the customer table which fell between A and C:

```
┌─────────────────────────────────────────────────────────────────┐
│ ─                      Watcom Interactive SQL              ▼  ▲   │
│  File   Edit   Command   Window   Help                           │
│ ┌───────────────────────────── Data ──────────────────────▼─ ▲─┐ │
│ │   custid  cname                      credit                  │ │
│ │      10  Acton Computers             A                       │ │
│ │      11  Agorist Distrib             B                       │ │
│ │      12  Alexandria Liqu             B                       │ │
│ │      15  Blumenfeld Educ             B                       │ │
│ │      16  Cardiff Industr             C                       │ │
│ │      33  Black Cat Store             C                       │ │
│ │      43  Berryville Supp             C                       │ │
│ │                                                             │ │
│ └─────────────────────────────────────────────────────────────┘ │
│ ┌──────────────────────────── Statistics ─────────────────▼─ ▲─┐ │
│ │ Estimated 1 rows in query (I/O estimate 1)                   │ │
│ │ PLAN> Customers (seq)                                        │ │
│ └─────────────────────────────────────────────────────────────┘ │
│ ┌──────────────────────────── Command ────────────────────▼─ ▲─┐ │
│ │ ┌─────────┐  SELECT *                                    ▲   │ │
│ │ │ Execute │  FROM Customers                                  │ │
│ │ ├─────────┤  WHERE cname BETWEEN 'aaa' and 'czz';            │ │
│ │ │  Stop   │                                                  │ │
│ │ └─────────┘                                              ▼   │ │
│ └─────────────────────────────────────────────────────────────┘ │
└─────────────────────────────────────────────────────────────────┘
```

New programmers also tend to forget that the range includes the end points, and that it has to be in the right order. Conversely, if you add a **NOT** operator you effectively reverse the meaning of the statement, so it looks for everything that doesn't fall between A and C, but for everything from D to Z, or that which begins with a numeric:

```
┌────────────────────────────────────────────────────────────────┐
│                      Watcom Interactive SQL                      │
│ File  Edit  Command  Window  Help                                │
│ ┌──────────────────────────── Data ─────────────────────────────┐│
│   custid  cname                    credit                         │
│       1   Stanwood Consul          A                              │
│       2   Vallecito Indus          B                              │
│       3   Wellesley Inc.           C                              │
│       4   White Court              A                              │
│      17   Del Toro Enterp          C                              │
│      18   DRT Marine Lab           A                              │
│      20   Fredericks and           A                              │
│      21   Kalakaua Corpor          A                              │
│      22   Ladera Enterpri          C                              │
│      25   Mission Hills I          B                              │
│      26   Monterey Univer          B                              │
│      27   Quinton College          B                              │
│      28   Rensselaer & Co          B                              │
│      29   Ridgewood-Berkm          B                              │
│ ┌──────────────────────────── Statistics ───────────────────────┐│
│ Estimated 19 rows in query (I/O estimate 1)                       │
│ PLAN> Customers (seq)                                             │
│ ┌──────────────────────────── Command ──────────────────────────┐│
│ [Execute]   SELECT *                                              │
│ [Stop]      FROM Customers                                        │
│             WHERE cname NOT BETWEEN 'aaa' and 'czz';              │
└────────────────────────────────────────────────────────────────┘
```

If any of the three value expressions is a **NULL**, then the answer follows directly from the definition.

- If both `<low value expr>` and `<high value expr>` are **NULL**, then the result is **UNKNOWN** for any value of `<value expression>`.

- If `<low value expr>` or `<high value expr>` is **NULL**, but not both of them, then the result is determined by the value of `<value expression>` and its comparison with the remaining non-**NULL** term.

> If `<value expression>` is **NULL**, then the results are **UNKNOWN** for any values of `<low value expr>` and `<high value expr>`.

While the **BETWEEN** is just a shorthand from a programmer's viewpoint, the SQL itself might not see it that way. Some products can do range searches in their indexes, so the **BETWEEN** is faster than its expansion. This is very product-dependent, but even if your SQL does the expansion, you have lost nothing and only gained a more readable query!

IS NULL, IS TRUE, IS FALSE and IS UNKNOWN

Finally, there are four other small predicates which are less commonly used, but might prove useful sometimes. The first is the **IS NULL** predicate which looks specifically for a **NULL** value. If you don't want **NULLs** in a specific column in your database, you could seek them out using this command. In the last chapter we inserted a **NULL** into the inventory table. We put it in the **reorderpnt** column, so now we can seek it straight out via this command:

```
SELECT description
FROM Inventory
WHERE reorderpnt IS NULL;
```

There should only be the one entry in the result table. Conversely, you can insert a **NOT** between the **IS** and **NULL** statement and look for all the entries in the **reorderpnt** that are not **NULL**.

The other three **IS** tests are all identical to each other in structure. The user provides a search condition and the result table is formed from all of the rows in the table that satisfy the **IS** condition. The following example looks for all the items in the inventory that cost more than $10:

```
                        Watcom Interactive SQL
 File  Edit  Command  Window  Help
                             Data
description
doohickey
gimmick
gizmo
thingabob
widget
chachka
thingie

                           Statistics
Estimated 2 rows in query (I/O estimate 1)
PLAN> Inventory (seq)

                           Command
 [ Execute ]    SELECT description
 [ Stop ]       FROM Inventory
                WHERE (price>10) IS TRUE;
```

The use of the other tests should be intuitive, you simply apply them in the same way. If you wish to reverse the test, you apply a **NOT** operator between the **IS** and second part.

The ORDER BY Clause

The **ORDER BY** clause isn't technically part of an SQL query, but rather belongs to the **CURSOR** statement. A cursor includes a **SELECT** statement and puts the results into a structure that can be accessed like a sequential file. However, since most of the tools that you use to access SQL will really have a cursor hidden in them, you will be using the **ORDER BY** clause.

This clause sorts the results into either ascending or descending order based on a list of column names. The syntax is as follows:

```
<order by clause> ::=
    ORDER BY <sort specification list>

<sort specification list> ::=
    <sort specification> [ { <comma> <sort specification>
}... ]

<sort key> ::= <column name> | <unsigned integer>

<ordering specification> ::= ASC | DESC
```

The **ORDER BY** clause goes at the end of the **SELECT** statement. The result table is sorted on the columns whose names are given in the **<sort specification list>**, ordering from left to right. The keywords **ASC** and **DESC** stand for ascending and descending order, respectively. The default is to assume ascending order on a column. Here's a quick query which simply flips the **Foobar** table you created earlier around the **a** column.

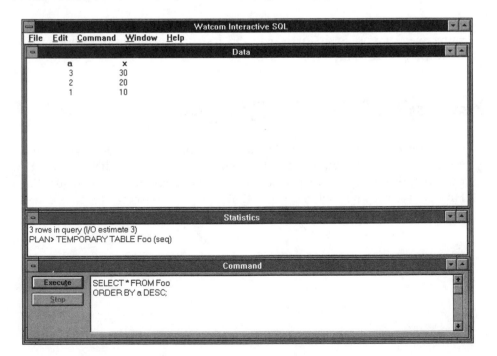

Notice that a column position number can be used in place of a column name. This is an old SQL-89 convention which is being phased out after SQL-92, so you shouldn't use it. The reason that it exists is that the SQL-89 standard did not have a way to name expressions in the **SELECT** clause list (the **<expression> AS <name>** syntax of SQL-92).

According to the standards, **NULL**s are grouped either before or after known values; the position is implementation defined. After the **NULL**s are in their position, the known values are sorted into ascending or descending order. However, you will find many implementations that treat **NULL**s as if they were values and will assign them a position in the collating sequence.

Summary

In this chapter you have introduced you to the **SELECT** statement. This statement queries the database, but doesn't alter the database in any way. That's the fundamental difference between a Data Manipulation Language and a Data Definition Language. The Data Definition Language gives you the building blocks to create your database-the Data Manipulation Language allows you to examine the structure and view it in different ways.

We have looked at the fundamentals of the **SELECT** command:

- We started with a basic introduction to the **SELECT** command.
- We looked at the logical operations projection, joining and restricting which go to make up a **SELECT** command.
- We have built up the different clauses of the **SELECT** command, **FROM** and **WHERE**, introducing the clauses individually.
- Within these clauses we have learned different predicates and methods for specifying search conditions **BETWEEN**, **LIKE**, **IN** and **ISNULL**. This gave us more power and flexibility when creating queries.
- Finally, we looked at the **ORDER BY** clause which is used for sorting the final result table.

In the next chapter we introduce the concept of joining two SQL tables together within a query.

Exercises

1 Select all of the details of our employees who are ranked over 1.

2 Select only the descriptions of the parts that cost more than $12.00.

3 Select all of the employees who earn between $1800 and $2500.

4 Select all our customers who begin with the letter 'D'.

5 Select all of the orders made before the 16th November 1995 and list them in order of date, with the most recent first.

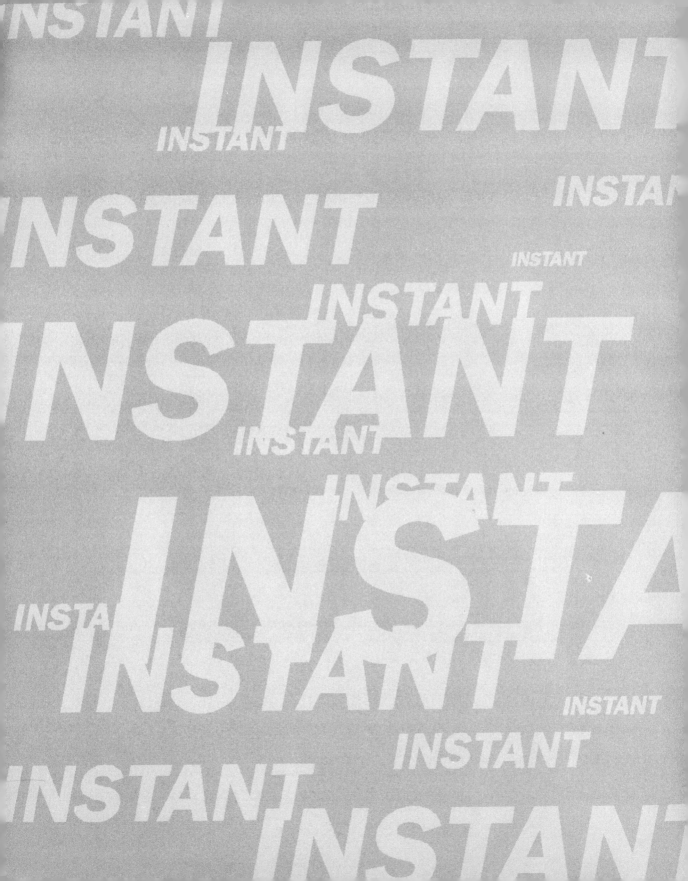

Chapter

Joining Tables

Up until this stage of the book, you have only been able to make rudimentary queries of one table. You'll soon find this too confining when you want to perform queries of any real complexity. If you want to compare data from two or more different tables, then you will have to start joining tables together. This is traditionally a difficult topic, so in this chapter the different types of join have been carefully separated to aid understanding. We'll also introduce the joins in order of complexity.

Here is what we will be covering:

- A quick reminder of Cartesian products
- The SQL equivalent of a Cartesian product, a cross join
- The equi join
- The theta join
- The self join
- The three table join
- The concept of inner and outer joins

Two or More Tables in a SELECT Statement

The most powerful use of a **SELECT** statement is the connecting or joining of two tables. Using joins, you can look down one column of a table and match it to the same row in another table. The purpose of doing this will become apparent later.

However, before we consider how to use joins in SQL, we need to recap on the theory of how to concatenate two tables and create a Cartesian product, as this is the method SQL uses to join tables.

> A quick reminder: the Cartesian product of two tables is all the possible combinations of the two tables in one.

Table 1

Column 1	Column 2
A	C
B	D

Table 2

Column 1	Column 2
1	3
2	4

Cartesian Product of Two Tables

Column 1	Column 2	Column 3	Column 4
A	C	1	3
B	D	1	3
A	C	2	4
B	D	2	4

Cross Joins

Cross joins are the basic level at which relationships between data tables are cemented. They are the fundamental background activity to all join processes. It is possible to determine a Cartesian product in SQL in one of two ways: with a comma or with the command **CROSS JOIN**. Here is the syntax:

```
SELECT { <column or expression list> | * }
    FROM <table1> { , | CROSS JOIN } <table2>;
```

As before, the statement goes to the **SELECT** clause to set up the columns for the final working table and then to the **FROM** clause to construct a working table. If your SQL product has SQL-92 features, then you can use either the keywords **CROSS JOIN**, or the comma. If your product uses SQL-89 syntax, it will only accept the comma. The **FROM** clause builds the Cartesian product of the two tables. This takes all the rows from one table and concatenates them to all the rows in a second table. The new rows in the resulting table have all the columns of both input tables, as well as all possible combinations of their concatenations. Let's use two small tables to illustrate this (if you're not using the Watcom run-time engine provided, then you can find code for the tables in Appendix B):

```
Foo             Bar
a    x          x    b
=======         ========
1    10         10   'A'
2    20         20   'B'
3    30         40   'C'
```

Now, we can execute the SQL-89 query:

```
SELECT * FROM Foo, Bar;
```

or the SQL-92 query shown in the command window, if it is available to you:

a	x	b	x
1	10	10	A
1	10	20	B
1	10	40	C
2	20	10	A
2	20	20	B
2	20	40	C
3	30	10	A
3	30	20	B
3	30	40	C

Estimated 9 rows in query (I/O estimate 2)
PLAN> Foo (seq), Bar (seq)

SELECT * FROM Foo CROSS JOIN Bar.

> Let's be honest - no SQL database product really does this
> step in the query, since it takes too long to execute, eats up
> storage space and gives you no real information. This is just
> a formal model.

If you wish to reference either of the two columns named 'x', then they
have to be qualified in a query by the names of their source tables. The
two columns named 'x' would have to be **Foo.x** and **Bar.x**, to distinguish
them.

Once this **CROSS JOIN** is built, it is the working table in the **FROM** clause
that the **WHERE** and **SELECT** clauses operate upon. The **WHERE** and **SELECT**
clauses have to be able to tell all the columns apart, so if the two tables
have columns with the same name, you have to use the fully qualified
<table>.<column> version of the column name. **Foo.x** distinguishes itself
from **Bar.x** by the addition of the table name.

If you have named an expression in the **SELECT** list with an **AS** subclause, then you can use that expression name in the **WHERE** clause since it was constructed in the **CROSS JOIN**.

> Always keep in mind that when two tables are joined, they are not physically connected. You are just viewing them as though they were. A join has no physical effect on the structure of your tables or database - it doesn't change them in any way.

Equi Joins

We have detailed some of the theory behind joins, but we need to expand on the simple **CROSS JOIN** and introduce the idea of matching information and records across tables.

Normalization tends to split data and create many small tables. Sometimes, normalization splits logically grouped information into two separate tables. Information, such as dates and details about orders, end up being separated from clients' names and addresses. This is because you would commonly get tables devoted to personal details, and tables specifically for orders. To be able to join the information and view the results in one table, there must be a common column, identical in both tables. You can join the tables by matching the record through this common column, where an entry in one table equals the entry in the same column of the other table. This is known as an **equi join**.

An Equi Join Example: at the Bank

Think about a bank database. One table might contain customer details, such as address and phone number, another table might contain monetary details. If the bank were to mail a client a credit statement, they would need both sets of details. An account number would be unique and would probably be used as a primary key, occurring in both tables. Knowing this, the bank could run an equi join using the account number. The customer record in one table would refer to the same customer's monetary details in the second table via the unique account number. When the account number in the first table is equal to the account number in the second table, you can equi join the tables accordingly:

BANK EXAMPLE

Personal Details Table

Account No.	Name	Address
12345678	John Doe	New York
12345679	Richard Roe	Virginia
12345680	Jane Doe	Washington

Equi join where
Personal Details Table
Account Number
=
Credit Details Table
Account Number

Account No.	Name	Address	Account No.	Credit	Credit Limit
12345678	John Doe	New York	12345678	$50	$500
12345679	Richard Roe	Virginia	12345679	$100	$1000
12345680	Jane Doe	Washington	12345680	$500	$1000

Credit Details Table

Account No.	Credit	Credit Limit
12345678	$50	$500
12345679	$100	$1000
12345680	$500	$1000

An Example from the Database

We'll now consider another simple example, this time utilizing the example database. Think about a situation where you need to know the date that a customer made a particular order. This sounds simple enough, but the information you need is contained in two separate tables. The customer name is in the **Customer** table and the sales date is found in the **Orders** table. You would need to use an equi join to match on the **Custid** column, as this is the common column and also a primary key.

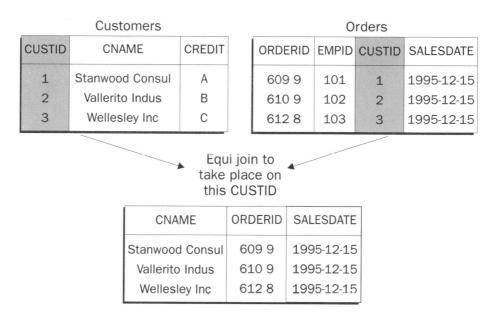

Customers

CUSTID	CNAME	CREDIT
1	Stanwood Consul	A
2	Vallerito Indus	B
3	Wellesley Inc	C

Orders

ORDERID	EMPID	CUSTID	SALESDATE
609 9	101	1	1995-12-15
610 9	102	2	1995-12-15
612 8	103	3	1995-12-15

Equi join to take place on this CUSTID

CNAME	ORDERID	SALESDATE
Stanwood Consul	609 9	1995-12-15
Vallerito Indus	610 9	1995-12-15
Wellesley Inc	612 8	1995-12-15

The necessary SQL for this join would be as found in the command window. The desired output is combined into one table. The first portion of the result table would look like this:

```
                            Watcom Interactive SQL
 File  Edit  Command  Window  Help
                                  Data
cname                    orderid    salesdate
Stanwood Consul              6099   1995-12-15
Vallecito Indus             6109   1995-12-15
Wellesley Inc.              6128   1995-12-15
Wellesley Inc.              6129   1995-12-15
Agorist Distrib             6148   1995-12-15
Alexandria Liqu             6155   1995-12-12
Alexandria Liqu             6157   1995 12 15
Blumenfeld Educ             6168   1995-12-15
Blumenfeld Educ             6170   1995-11-15
Cardiff Industr             6174   1995-12-12
Cardiff Industr             6175   1995-12-12
DRT Marine Lab              6196   1995-12-15
Kalakaua Corpor             6214   1995-12-12
Kalakaua Corpor             6215   1995-12-12
                                Statistics
Estimated 36 rows in query (I/O estimate 5)
PLAN> Orders (seq), Customers (Customers)
                                Command
 [Execute]    SELECT cname, orderid, salesdate
 [Stop]       FROM Customers, Orders
              WHERE Customers.custid=Orders.custid;
```

Now, let's look at an SQL-92 example of an equi join. If you were to join two tables on their **x** columns, you would get the following result:

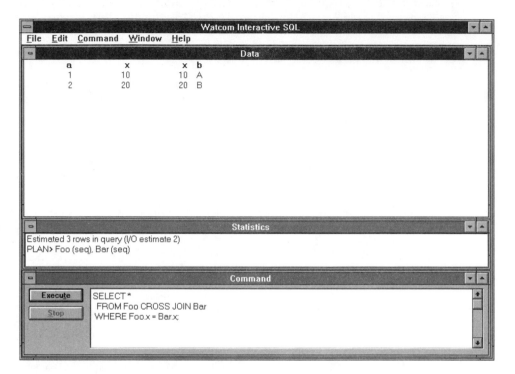

In this situation, the term equi join means that the search condition was based on equality. If the contents of one row 1 in table **Foo**, column **x**, match the contents of the equivalent row 1 in table **Bar**, column **x**, then that row is displayed in the result table of the equi join. Columns that are not equivalent are eliminated from the result table, and don't appear (although they are not eliminated from their actual tables). Compare this with the **CROSS JOIN**, where each row of **Foo** was matched to each row of **Bar**.

Non-equi Joins

Using equality in the **WHERE** clause is only one of many possible ways to join two tables together, but it happens so often that we give it the name equi join. There are other relational operators apart from equality that you can use. There is nothing wrong with writing a non-equi join in this way:

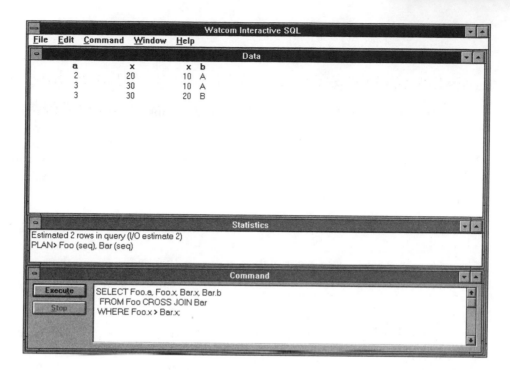

You can also introduce **NOT**, **AND** and **OR** operators with these joins to further restrict the query. We will look at using the Boolean operators in conjunction with joins later in this chapter.

Theta Joins

Both equi joins and non-equi joins, and indeed any type of join that uses a relational operator, are known collectively as **theta joins**. Theta joins compare the data of different tables or restrict the result table to a specific range of data. However, you should be careful when you construct theta join queries, since these queries can produce unexpected results and be accompanied by slow performance.

Self Joins and Aliases

The next type of join we will consider involves joining a table to itself. The purpose of this will become apparent in the next few examples, but to illustrate this rather cryptic idea, we need to refresh our memory as to how we rename columns.

Correlation Names

In the previous chapter, we mentioned the **AS** clause as a method of renaming columns. The **AS** clause can also apply to table names as well as column expressions, and it creates what is known as a **correlation name** for the life of the query. A correlation name can be thought of as an **alias** for a column or table name. In the following example, the correlation name or alias for **ename** is **employee**:

```
SELECT ename AS employee FROM Salespersons;
```

> If you give a table a correlation name in the **FROM** clause, then you must use it in the **WHERE** clause as part of the fully qualified column name.

Many people like to use correlation names as abbreviations or shortened names to save space when they type. A correlation name, however, is more than a simple alias when used with a table name. It makes a copy of the base table, which means that we can have multiple copies of the same data in a query under different names.

Joining a Table to a Copy of Itself

If we have multiple copies of the tables under different names, then we can join them together as if they were two separate tables.

Salespersons

EMPID	ENAME	RANK	SALARY
101	Andrew Allen	1	1000.00
102	Burbank Burkett	1	1000.00
103	Charles Cox	2	1000.00

EMPID	ENAME	RANK	SALARY
101	Andrew Allen	1	1000.00
102	Burbank Burkett	1	1000.00
103	Charles Cox	2	1000.00

Copy_of_Salespersons_Table

When we do a join on these copies, although we are effectively joining one copy of this table to another, we are actually joining a table to itself. This is called a **self join**. An example of why we might need to do a self join would be if we had to find all the matching pairs in one column. You would have to test each value in the column of one value to see if it was equal to the corresponding column of the table copy. If, for example, you wanted to investigate which pairs of employees were on the same rank, you would have to divide the table and join it as follows:

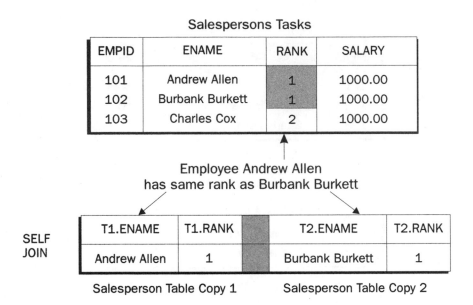

T1 and T2 are just aliases for the table **Salespersons**. Once you have created a copy of the table you wish to join, then you are ready to perform an equi join on it.

Pitfalls of Self Joins

Just like everything else in life, using self joins isn't as straightforward as you might imagine, so, in order to demonstrate some problems you might encounter, we'll make some deliberate mistakes on the way. Given an explanation of what a self join is, a fairly reasonable first attempt at the code might go like this:

```
SELECT T1.ename,T1.rank,T2.ename,T2.rank
FROM Salespersons AS t1, Salespersons AS t2
WHERE t1.rank = t2.rank;
```

If you try this, you'll find an immediate problem in the first record of the result table:

```
t1.ename    t1.rank     t2.ename    t2.rank
Andrew Allen    1       Andrew Allen    1
```

The result table has joined instances of each record to the identical record in the table copy. To eliminate this, you must stop the search from matching a record to itself, so you will have to introduce a new condition into the **WHERE** clause. The query must be able to identify that two records are identical, and the only way to do this is if the two records in question have the same primary or unique key. So the second condition must check if the primary or unique key from one table equals the equivalent primary or unique key from the table copy. In **Salespersons** the primary key is **empid**. So, when **empid** in **T1** doesn't equal **empid** in **T2**, you know that the records can't be identical:

```
SELECT T1.ename,T1.rank,T2.ename,T2.rank
FROM Salespersons AS t1, Salespersons AS t2
WHERE t1.rank = t2.rank
AND NOT t1.empid = t2.empid;
```

This still leaves a problem:

```
t1.ename    t1.rank      t2.ename    t2.rank
Andrew Allen     1      Burbank Burkett 1
Burbank Burkett     1      Andrew Allen     1
```

Each pair is matched twice. The query searches down table 1 and gets the first record, that of **Andrew Allen**. It searches down table 2 and finds that **Burbank Burkett** has the same rank. It's fine up to here. However, the query doesn't stop there. Once the record of **Andrew Allen** is finished with, the next record is that of **Burbank Burkett**. It compares the rank of **Burbank** with each record in table 2 and comes across the record of **Andrew Allen**, even though this pair has already been discovered. What can you do to prevent this?

The solution again involves the primary key **empid**. If we were to introduce the **empid** into the **SELECT** clause, then you might notice a way of selecting only one of the pairs:

```
SELECT T1.empid,T1.ename,T1.rank,T2.empid,T2.ename,T2.rank
FROM Salespersons AS t1, Salespersons AS t2
WHERE t1.rank = t2.rank
AND NOT t1.empid = t2.empid;
```

This gives the following result:

t1.empid	t1.ename	t1.rank	t2.empid	t2.ename	t2.rank
101	Andrew Allen	1	102	Burbank Burkett	1
102	Burbank Burkett	1	101	Andrew Allen	1

If the **empid** isn't identical in each record, then for one occurrence it must be smaller in one record than the other, and therefore larger for the other occurrence when the records are compared in reverse. So, if we use a non-equi join, where the records are only joined if **t1.empid** is smaller than **t2.empid**, then one of the two occurrences will be removed. The final result will look like this:

```
┌─────────────────────────── Watcom Interactive SQL ───────────────────────┐
│ File   Edit   Command   Window   Help                                      │
├───────────────────────────────── Data ────────────────────────────────────┤
│   rank     empid   ename              rank     empid   ename               │
│      1      101    Andrew Allen          1      102    Burbank Burkett      │
│      2      103    Charles Cox           2      104    Dale Dahlman         │
│      2      103    Charles Cox           2      105    Edward Everling      │
│      2      104    Dale Dahlman          2      105    Edward Everling      │
│      3      106    Faulkner Forest       3      107    Gloria Garcia        │
│      3      106    Faulkner Forest       3      108    Harvey Harrison      │
│      3      106    Faulkner Forest       3      109    Kevin Kody           │
│      3      107    Gloria Garcia         3      108    Harvey Harrison      │
│      3      107    Gloria Garcia         3      109    Kevin Kody           │
│      3      108    Harvey Harrison       3      109    Kevin Kody           │
├─────────────────────────────── Statistics ────────────────────────────────┤
│ Estimated 3 rows in query (I/O estimate 2)                                 │
│ PLAN> t1 (seq), t2 (seq)                                                   │
├──────────────────────────────── Command ──────────────────────────────────┤
│ ┌─────────┐  SELECT T1.rank, T1.empid,T1.ename,T2.rank,T2.empid,T2.ename   │
│ │ Execute │  FROM Salespersons AS t1, Salespersons AS t2                    │
│ └─────────┘  WHERE t1.rank = t2.rank                                        │
│ ┌─────────┐  AND t1.empid < t2.empid;                                       │
│ │  Stop   │                                                                 │
│ └─────────┘                                                                 │
└────────────────────────────────────────────────────────────────────────────┘
```

We will now move to a more complex example, where the join takes place on two columns. Imagine that you want to investigate purchasing patterns to discover if people buy doodads on the same day they buy chachkas. We would want to write a query to find pairs of orders from the same customer on the same day. We would use the two columns **orderid** and **salesdate** on which to perform the self join:

```
SELECT O1.custid, O1.orderid, O2.orderid
  FROM Orders AS O1, Orders AS O2
 WHERE O1.custid = O2.custid
   AND O1.salesdate = O2.salesdate
   AND O1.orderid < O2.orderid;
```

The **FROM** clause makes a copy of the **Orders** table and names it **O1**, then it makes a second copy and names it **O2**, and finally builds a working table with the **CROSS JOIN**. The first two predicates in the **WHERE** clause restrict the results to orders from the same customer on the same day. The last predicate is again to prevent pairs of the form (a, a), (a, b) and (b, a) from showing up in the results.

This is an example of where normalization can be a bit of a hindrance. We have a list of the **orderid**s, but not what the order was for. To find out what part was ordered we have to look in the **OrderItems** table. We can match the **orderid** to the **partid**, but even this doesn't tell us which part was ordered. For this, we have to trawl back to the **Inventory** to finally match **partid**s to descriptions.

Three Table Joins

In theory, there is no limit to the number of tables you can have in a query, but most products choke at 16 or more. As an example of a **three table join**, look at this query:

```
SELECT O1.empid, OI1.partid, (OI1.qty * I1.price) AS totalprice
  FROM Inventory AS I1, Orders AS O1, OrderItems AS OI1
 WHERE OI1.orderid = O1.orderid
   AND OI1.partid = I1.partid;
```

This example computes the total value of each item sold by each salesman. The three tables joined are the **Inventory**, **Orders** and **OrderItems** table. The **OrderItems orderid** is joined to the **orderid** in the **Orders** table. Imagine an intermediate table made from the **OrderItems** and **Orders** tables which contains a column for **partid**:

The **partid** in this intermediate table is then joined to the **partid** in the **Inventory** table. This creates a result table, which consists of three tables being joined:

Intermediate Table

empid	partid	qty
101	1002	3
101	1003	3
101	1004	3

Result Table

empid	partid	qty*price
101	1002	3 x 25.00
101	1003	3 x 2.50
101	1004	3 x 7.50

Inventory (I1)

partid	description	partid	qty	price
1002	doohickey	69	25	25.00
1003	2	23	30	2.50
1004	gadget	71	20	7.50

The query selects only what it needs to help create the final result table. The formal model of SQL says that the engine computes the **CROSS JOIN** on all the tables first, and then does the required restrictions. In the real world, this would simply take too long. What actually happens is that the SQL engine works with pairs of tables and tries to decide on the best sequence of steps, in order to reduce the execution time of the query, whilst still getting the right answer.

This means that the order of execution is out of your hands; the query optimizer does this. In this case, the optimizer could decide to assemble the join between **Inventory** and **OrderItems** first, then join that result to **Orders**, or it could join **Orders** and **OrderItems** first, then join that result to the **Inventory** table. How the optimizer decides how to do its job is an advanced topic, and we are not going to talk about it in this book. Basically, it looks at the available indexes and certain statistics to make its decision, but if you wish to know more, we suggest you check an advanced SQL title.

Joins in SQL-92 Syntax

What we have discussed so far are called **inner** joins. They are constructed in the **FROM** and **WHERE** clauses. SQL-92 allows us to write explicit join operations in the **FROM** clause of a **SELECT** statement, instead of having an equi join in the **WHERE** clause. The syntax for the **INNER JOIN** within the **FROM** clause is as follows:

```
FROM <table reference> INNER JOIN
    <table reference> [<join specification>]

<join specification> ::= <join condition>

<join condition> ::= ON <search condition>
```

This syntax isn't yet fully implemented in most SQL products, but you can expect to see more products using it in the future.

The **ON** clause specifies a chain of equality tests based on the common column names. In other words, we need to focus on how to use the **ON** clause in this statement. The **ON** clause is a flexible and general option, and it is being implemented in current releases of SQL products, such as Watcom SQL. Remember that once the result table has been constructed in the **FROM** clause, the **WHERE** clause will remove more rows.

The **INNER JOIN** statement is a more generalized version of what we have been doing in the **FROM** and **WHERE** clauses. Remember that an SQL-89 query can only accept the comma with which to join two tables. This SQL-89 query:

```
SELECT *
  FROM Foo, Bar
  WHERE Foo.x = Bar.x;
```

could be written in SQL-92 as:

```
SELECT *
   FROM Foo INNER JOIN Bar ON Foo.x = Bar.x;
```

This SQL-92 statement works by doing the same pruning of the **CROSS JOIN** as the **FROM** and **WHERE** clauses did in SQL-89. The differences are as follows:

1 You use parentheses to nest these statements inside each other and thus control the order of their execution. You can also use them with the other kinds of **JOIN**s which we will discuss later.

2 You can use an **AS** clause to give their results a name. You can also use an **AS** clause on each **<table reference>** to give them correlation names too.

Outer Join in SQL-92 Syntax

As we have just looked at an **INNER JOIN**, you have probably figured out that there is also an **OUTER JOIN**. Before you dive in, please note that not all SQLs support outer joins and those that do don't always support all the forms of outer join. They are, however, important to the discussion of joins, so we must consider them.

An outer join takes two tables and displays the records of one table where there is the matching record in the other table. The method by which an outer join is created depends on which table is referenced first within the query. A left outer join would display the records in the table referenced first (the 'left-hand' table), together with any matching entries from the table referenced second (the 'right-hand' table).

```
SELECT *
FROM Foo      <- 'left-hand' table
LEFT OUTER JOIN Bar ON Foo.x = Bar.x;
                  ^
                  | 'right-hand' table
```

The records in the left-hand table that don't match with any entries in the right-hand table are displayed. Records from the right-hand table that don't have a match on the left are not displayed. This, therefore, brings the need for a right outer join. This displays the records in the right-hand table, with or without a match in the left-hand table, and records that match in both tables.

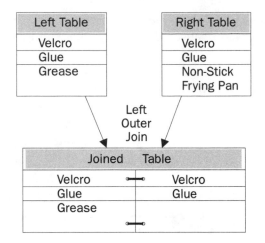

We will now illustrate the outer join with an example.

Imagine that we just added the Acme Company to our list of customers. Now we would like to do a join between the table of customers and the purchases they made to show us how much total business we did with each customer. One of the customers has just as many returns as purchases, so the total amount of business with them is zero dollars. However, compare this to the fact that we have not done any business with Acme - their total should be a **NULL**. Stop and think about this; there is a big difference between never having done business with Acme and the customer who cancels orders.

In an **OUTER JOIN**, one or both tables can be **preserved**. To understand the term 'preserved', we must first contrast this with what we already know about inner joins. An inner join looks down the column and matches each record according to the search criteria it has been given, such as each record with a salary value smaller than $1500. Everything that doesn't match this criteria is discarded. Preserving tables means that we will keep all the rows in the preserved table(s) when we do the join, and pad the unmatched columns in the working table with **NULL**s. Let's look at the syntax first:

```
<table reference> <outer join type> [OUTER] JOIN
    <table reference> [<join specification>]

<join specification> ::= <join condition>

<join condition> ::= ON <search condition>

<outer join type> ::= LEFT | RIGHT | FULL
```

Left Outer Join

Let's take a look at how the left outer join works first. Using the **Foo** and **Bar** tables we can write the query found in the command window:

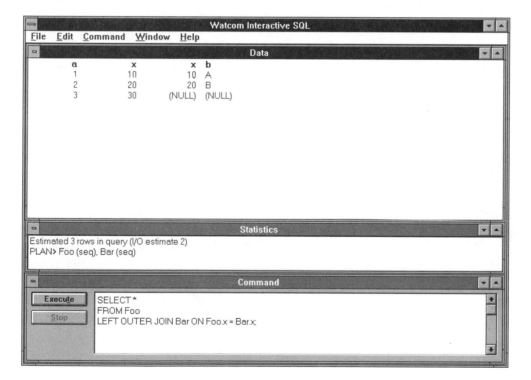

The table **Foo** was preserved. **Foo.x** matches **Bar.x** for the first two entries, as they both have the same values. When **Foo.x** had a value of **30**, that couldn't be matched to rows remaining in the **Bar.x** column. That row was padded out with **NULL**s.

Right Outer Join

We can do a right outer join in the reverse way. If you consider this query you can see that it will preserve table **Bar**. This time the table **Bar** is matched to **Foo** and as the value **40** can't be matched, the table **Foo** must be padded out with **NULL**s. This gives the following result:

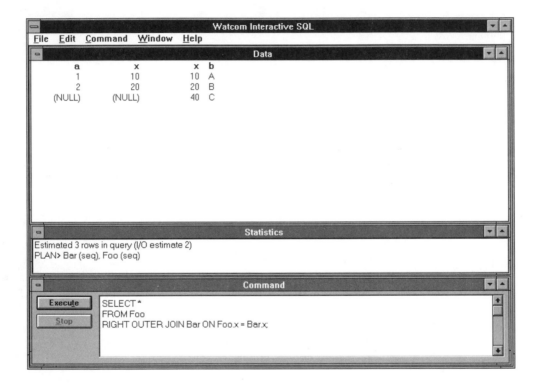

Full Outer Join

If we wanted to preserve both tables, then we would do a full outer join, which is a combination of a **LEFT OUTER JOIN** and a **RIGHT OUTER JOIN**. This isn't available on the Watcom product yet, but we'll run through it anyway:

```
SELECT *
FROM Foo
FULL OUTER JOIN Bar ON Foo.x = Bar.x;
```

We would get the following result:

```
Foo.a Foo.x Bar.x Bar.b
===== ===== ===== =====
    1    10    10     A
    2    20    20     B
    3    30  NULL  NULL
 NULL  NULL    40     C
```

Before the SQL-92 standard, many vendors implemented different syntax for outer joins, which involves using some sort of 'extended equality' comparison operator. However, they don't always work in some implementations and you should avoid them if you can. For example, this query:

```
SELECT *
  FROM Orders AS O1, OrderItems AS I1
 WHERE O1.orderid *= I1.orderid
   AND qty >= 2;
```

where "*=" means "preserve the left-hand table" can be equivalent to either this:

```
SELECT *
  FROM Orders AS O1 LEFT OUTER JOIN T OrderItems AS I1
       ON (O1.orderid = I1.orderid AND qty >= 2);
```

or this:

```
SELECT *
  FROM Orders AS O1 LEFT OUTER JOIN T OrderItems AS I1
       ON O1.orderid = I1.orderid
 WHERE qty >= 2;
```

The order of execution of the predicates matters! If we first remove all the **OrderItems** rows with a quantity not less than two, we will create rows that don't join to the **Orders** table. Consider this abbreviated version of the two tables:

```
Orders          OrderItems
    orderid         orderid qty
==========      ========== ===
       6099            6099   3
       6109            6109   1
       6128            6128   2
       6129
```

If we do the outer join first, we get:

```
orderid qty
===========
6099    3
6109    1
6128    2
6129    NULL
```

Then we apply the "qty >= 2" predicate to get the final answer:

```
orderid qty
===========
6099    3
6128    2
```

Now look what happens if we first apply the "qty >= 2" predicate, which affects only the **OrderItems** table, thus:

```
orderid qty
===========
6099    3
6128    2
```

Now perform the outer join with the **Orders** table:

```
orderid qty
===========
 6099    3
 6109 NULL
 6128    2
 6129 NULL
```

See the difference? Sybase and SQL Server do this one way, Oracle does it another and Gupta turned the method into a system parameter that could be set by the D.B.A. Queries with multiple outer joins, or queries where the same table appears both as preserved and unpreserved have serious problems with this notation.

Now you have an idea of the two major different types of joins - inner and outer joins. Every other type of join we have learned can occur within the context of an inner or an outer join. It is one of the most central concepts to the understanding of SQL and relational databases. Without a join, you can't have a relational database. Before we move on to the next chapter, which looks at the nesting of one **SELECT** statement within another, you must feel comfortable with the ideas discussed here, as they will continue to reoccur throughout the rest of the book.

Summary

Here is a list of the different types of join you can specify within a **SELECT** command and a quick summary of what they do:

- The cross join, which simply concatenates two tables and gives you an idea of how relationships between tables work at the most basic level.

- The equi join, which concatenates two tables according to a search condition specified by the user, such as **WHERE** column 1 = column 2.

- The non-equi join, which is identical to the equi join except that it uses the lesser than and greater than operators, rather than the equality operator.

- The self join, where you can specify a table by two different names and then join it to itself, using each name.

- The three table join, which is self-explanatory.

- Inner joins, which involve eliminating those rows which don't match.

- Outer joins, which preserve the rows that don't match and pad the remaining columns out with **NULL**s.

- Different types of outer join, which join the tables in different orders, such as a full outer join, a left outer join and a right outer join.

Now if you aren't worn out, you should have a go at the exercises over the page to see how much of this chapter has really sunk in!

Exercises

The boss just walked in and wants some queries to answer these questions:

1 Get me a list of the customers that we have done business with.

(Hint: the Salespersons table has Gloria's records, the Customer's table has the customers so where do you find the two together? Remember to remove duplicates!)

2 We have a formula for paying commissions to employees. We take the total number of the sales made by each employee and give them 1% times their rank. Print a report that will let me know what we owe Gloria Garcia.

3 Who ordered a 'doodad' and a 'doohickey' at the same time?

4 Who has ever ordered anything that begins with the letter 'g'?

5 Which items (not just their **partids**, but their whole descriptions) did we sell for Christmas 1995?

6 Which items (not just their **partids**, but their whole descriptions) did we sell on all the days, except Christmas 1995?

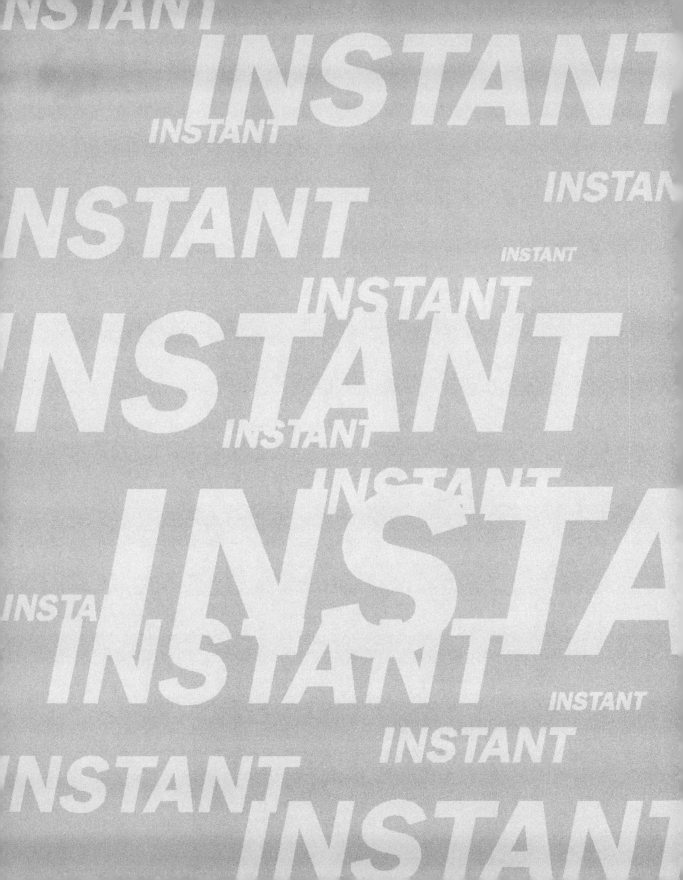

Chapter

8

Grouped Tables and Aggregate Functions

When tables are displayed, the result isn't organized in a logical way. The SQL engine will return results in no apparent order. If you wish to organize your results into categories, you must use another aspect of the Data Manipulation Language. This is known as a summary query, or the **GROUP BY** clause. To understand the **GROUP BY** clause fully, you must understand the concept of the working table, which is produced by SQL to help generate the final results. You can use aggregate functions in conjunction with the summary query. These allow you to perform some simple calculations on your tables, such as generating an average, total or a count of values in the table. You can also utilize simple maximum and minimum functions. Finally, we'll consider a restriction on the **GROUP BY** clause, the **HAVING** clause. The order of play for this chapter will be:

- The **GROUP BY** clause
- The working table
- The aggregate functions **COUNT**, **SUM** and **AVG**
- The extreme functions
- The **HAVING** restriction

The GROUP BY Clause

The **GROUP BY** clause is the only way SQL is able to summarize data. Its use is based on a method of simple partitions. Data from the table is divided up into different partitions, according to common characteristics. Let's use an abstract example: the organization of the NFL Imagine just one table of all the teams in the entire league. You can subdivide them into partitions such as the NFC and the AFC Within the NFC, there are separate groups of teams. You could further subdivide them into NFC East and NFC West, and so on. The **GROUP BY** clause allows you to subdivide tables in the same way, although you must specify the column which provides the categories for each group.

There are rules that govern how the partitions are divided. A partition of a set divides the set into subsets in the following ways:

1 The union of the subsets returns the original set.

2 The intersection of the subsets is empty.

Think of it as cutting up a pizza - each bit of pepperoni must belong to one and only one slice.

The Working Table

Another part of the working of the **GROUP BY** clause is that it builds a new table, held separately from the original. This is an important concept ! Let's work through a simple example in detail with our table of employees:

Salespersons Table

empid	ename	rank	salary
101	Andrew Allen	1	$1,000.00
102	Burbank Burkett	1	$1,000.00
103	Charles Cox	2	$2,000.00
104	Dale Dahlman	2	$2,100.00

Continued...

empid	ename	rank	salary
105	Edward Everling	2	$2,200.00
106	Faulkner Forest	3	$3,000.00
107	Gloria Garcia	3	$3,000.00
108	Harvey Harrison	3	$3,000.00
109	Kevin Kody	3	$3,100.00

As an example, we'll look at almost the most basic query you can make. It just groups the three different ranks in the table. You might think that we could achieve the same ends with the **SELECT DISTINCT** clause and you'd be right. However, it is imperative that you understand the concept of the working table, which is introduced next, via a very simple example. The most useful aspects of the **GROUP BY** clause are found when used in conjunction with other features, which will be introduced later. So we'll take this query first:

```
SELECT rank
  FROM Salespersons
 GROUP BY rank;
```

The query will go first to the **FROM** clause (and the **WHERE** clauses if there is one) to construct the working table specified therein. In this case, this is the full Salespersons table. It could be a very complex query, but the important point is that we get an unnamed working table first, then pass it along to the **GROUP BY** clause.

The **GROUP BY** clause will break the working table into groups which have identical values for the grouping columns. Since we are grouping by ranks, each group is a subset of rows which have the same rank.

There will now be a working table which is called a grouped table, and all operations are now defined on its groups rather than on the original rows. In effect, the original working table has disappeared. The order of the grouping columns in the **GROUP BY** clause doesn't matter, but since they have to appear in the **SELECT** list, you should probably use that same order to make it more readable. We'll get to that point in a little while. The grouped working table looks like this:

Working Table - GROUP BY

```
empid ename              rank  salary
===================================
  101   Andrew Allen        1  $1,000.00      Rank = 1
  102   Burbank Burkett     1  $1,000.00

  103   Charles Cox         2  $2,000.00      Rank = 2
  104   Dale Dahlman        2  $2,100.00
  105   Edward Everling     2  $2,200.00

  106   Faulkner Forest     3  $3,000.00      Rank = 3
  107   Gloria Garcia       3  $3,000.00
  108   Harvey Harrison     3  $3,000.00
  109   Kevin Kody          3  $3,100.00
```

The results give us three groups. As we only asked for the ranks to be grouped, the final result will be reduced to the single column that we asked for:

```
rank
====
  1
  2
  3
```

Let's consider a second example. This is what would happen were we to group on both rank and salary:

```
SELECT rank,salary
FROM Salespersons
GROUP BY rank,salary;
```

The subsets would be based on those two columns and we would get a separate group for Mr. Allen and Mr. Burkett, since they are both employees of **rank =1**, and **salary =$1,000**. However, each Mr Cox, Mr Dahlman and Mr Everling will get a separate group because, although they share a **rank =2**, they all earn different salaries. The table would look like this:

```
rank   salary
===============
  1    1000.00
  2    2000.00
  2    2100.00
  2    2200.00
  3    3000.00
  3    3100.00
```

> Never include a primary key in a GROUP BY clause. Since a key is always unique, you will always get one row per group.

Let's do another query and ask for the ranks which have people earning more than $2,000.00:

```
SELECT rank
  FROM Salespersons
 WHERE salary >= 2000.00
 GROUP BY rank;
```

As usual, the query will first go to the FROM clause, then to the WHERE clause and remove disallowed rows. At this point we have the following working table:

Working Table - WHERE

```
empid ename                rank  salary
=======================================
  104  Dale Dahlman          2  $2,100.00
  105  Edward Everling       2  $2,200.00
  106  Faulkner Forest       3  $3,000.00
  107  Gloria Garcia         3  $3,000.00
  108  Harvey Harrison       3  $3,000.00
  109  Kevin Kody            3  $3,100.00
```

Now we group the table by rank as before and we have only two groups:

Working Table - GROUP BY

```
empid ename                rank  salary
=======================================
  104  Dale Dahlman          2  $2,100.00   rank = 2
  105  Edward Everling       2  $2,200.00
  _____
  106  Faulkner Forest       3  $3,000.00   rank = 3
  107  Gloria Garcia         3  $3,000.00
  108  Harvey Harrison       3  $3,000.00
  109  Kevin Kody            3  $3,100.00
  _____
```

Now we can reduce the groupings to single rows:

```
rank
====
  2
  3
```

The important point to remember is that the original working table, with all the rows, has been replaced with a grouped table.

Common Problems with GROUP BY

There is a hidden catch to grouping records. To form the groups, the **GROUP BY** clause can only use column names from the working table. As the working table is formed from the **GROUP BY** clause, the column names must be specified within the **GROUP BY** clause if they are used to be within the **SELECT** list. Some versions of SQL will actively prevent you from doing, this while others such as Sybase won't, but the result that is generated will be meaningless. This is a little hard to understand at first, since a query like the following looks quite reasonable:

```
SELECT rank, ename
  FROM Salespersons
 GROUP BY rank;
```

Why do the grouping columns have to be in both the **SELECT** and **GROUP BY** clauses? The reason is that the **SELECT** list is now a description of the groups and can only contain group attributes. Group attributes are grouping columns and aggregate functions - we'll discuss this later in the chapter.

If you still can't grasp why this query is wrong, think about what value for the employee name column should be returned in each rank group. Should it be the longest name, the shortest name or a **NULL**? There are many employee names, yet only one rank in the result table. This query would probably be greeted with an error message. Therefore, the query makes no sense.

Let's take another example which also looks fairly reasonable.

```
SELECT rank, CAST ((salary/1000) AS INTEGER) AS thousands
  FROM Salespersons
 GROUP BY rank, thousands;
```

> Note that the ANSI/ISO standards allow truncation and rounding to be implementation-defined, so the answer could be truncated or rounded when the CAST()operator converts the expression to an INTEGER. You might want to look for a vendor-defined ROUND() or TRUNCATE() function instead.

The expression with the division is going to return the salary expressed in thousands of dollars. So why doesn't this work? The expression we named "thousands" is calculated in the SELECT clause. When we do the grouping, the SELECT clause has not yet been executed, so we can't see the calculation. You will probably be greeted with some form of error message, informing you that you need to have salary in the GROUP BY clause. Having said all of that, you will sometimes find SQL implementations which allow this as a vendor extension to the language. Avoid using this extension, as it destroys portability.

GROUP BY and NULLs

We have yet to consider how NULLs are treated in the GROUP BY clause. By convention, all the NULLs are put into a single group. This may well seem to fly in the face of the other rule that comparing NULL to NULL returns an UNKNOWN result that we considered in Chapter 3. It would seem to be more logical to put each NULL value into its own group - indeed, some of the first SQL implementations written before the ANSI/ISO standards did just that.

The practical problem that these early implementations found were that you quickly got too many groups and that the NULL was often used for a single class of missing values. For example, a hospital admission form would use a NULL in the diagnosis column to show that a diagnosis had not yet been made. While it's unlikely that each patient would have the same disease (and therefore be placed in the same group), it's reasonable to treat undiagnosed patients as a group. This is another area where SQL gives UNKNOWN the benefit of the doubt.

Right now, you may be thinking that a GROUP BY clause is a clumsy way of replacing a SELECT DISTINCT statement. Be patient - as mentioned earlier, the real use of the GROUP BY clause is with aggregate functions, which we'll discuss in the next section.

Aggregate Functions in Groups

Groups have other characteristics rather than just grouping columns. These group characteristics are called **descriptive statistics**, **aggregate functions** or **summary functions**. These functions are also called "set functions" in the SQL standard, but vendors, textbook writers and everyone else usually call them "aggregate functions", so we'll use that term.

> While statistics can get very complicated, SQL has only basic, well-understood functions - remember that SQL is a database language and not a computational language. You should also consult your particular product's manuals to find out the precision of the results for exact and approximate numeric data types.

The standard aggregate functions are the count (or tally), the average (or arithmetic mean), the sum (or total) and the extremes (minimum and maximum values in the set). The count and the extremes will work on any data type, but the average and the sum apply only to numeric values.

Obviously, we can count any distinct object. The extremes are based on the highest and lowest numeric value for numeric data types, the highest and lowest sorting order for character data types; and the earliest and latest chronological values for temporal data types. Average and sum would clearly make no sense for character and temporal data types.

NULLs in Aggregate Functions

The aggregate functions throw away **NULL**s before they do their calculations.

> It's a good idea for inexperienced programmers to get into the habit of explicitly saying "the average of the *known* weights", instead of simply "the average weight", to keep in mind that the **NULL**s have been dropped.

There are two options, **ALL** and **DISTINCT**, which are shown as keywords inside the parameter list. Putting keywords inside parameter lists is one of the strange things about the ISO/ANSI Standard SQL syntax, which makes SQL look different from other languages. You will see this in other places too.

If you don't specify a keyword, SQL automatically defaults to **ALL**. It means that you remove all the **NULLs** and keep the duplicate values when doing the calculations. The keyword **DISTINCT** tells the function to remove all the **NULLs** and all redundant duplicate values before doing the calculation.

The value expression used as a parameter in the function is usually a single column name, but it doesn't have to be. For example, you can write **SUM** (salary + commissions) to compute the sum of an employee's total pay.

Aggregate functions can't be nested inside each other; for example, **SUM (AVG (x))** is illegal. Nor can the value expression be any kind of subquery expression; for example, **AVG (SELECT column1 FROM SomeTable WHERE...)** is illegal. However, you must watch out for **NULL** values in the parameter if you use an expression, since the rules say that you do the work on the expression first. In this expression, a **NULL** commission for a non-sales employee will make the whole expression be **NULL** and the **SUM ()** function would remove it before doing the calculation.

For each of the functions we'll consider how they act with the **ALL** keyword, or default option. We'll then take a look at the **DISTINCT** keyword.

The COUNT Functions

COUNT (*) returns the number of rows in a table. It isn't like the other aggregate functions since it's the only one which uses an asterisk as a parameter. Unlike the other functions, **COUNT (*)** will also count **NULL** values, because this function deals with whole rows and not column values. **NULLs** are there, even if you don't know what they are. An empty table has a **COUNT (*)** of zero, which makes sense if you think about it.

COUNT ([ALL] <value expression>)

This returns the number of members in the **<value expression>** set. The **NULLs** have been thrown away before the counting took place, and an empty set returns zero. The best way to read this is as "Count the number of known (non-null) values in this expression," stressing the word *known*. For example, using the Salespersons table again, the following query:

```
SELECT COUNT (rank) FROM Salespersons;
```

or effectively the same query:

```
SELECT COUNT (ALL rank) FROM Salespersons;
```

would return a result of **9** because we have nine employees, all of whom have non-null values for rank.

The syntax for the **DISTINCT** sub clause is virtually identical to the previous syntax:

COUNT (DISTINCT <value expression>)

This returns the number of unique members in the **<value expression>** set. The **NULL**s have been thrown away before the counting took place and then all the redundant duplicates are removed. Again, an empty set returns a zero. However, the following:

```
SELECT COUNT (DISTINCT rank) FROM Salespersons;
```

would result a result of **3**, because there are three ranks (1, 2, 3) to which an employee can aspire.

The SUM Functions

SUM ([ALL] <value expression>)

This returns the numeric total of all known values. This function only works with numeric values, which again makes sense. An empty set returns a **NULL** result. This may seem a little strange to you if you are expecting to get a zero result, but if you give it further thought, there is a difference between an empty set and a set that sums to zero, such as (5, -5,-4, 4). An example query which would find the sum total of all of the salaries would be as follows:

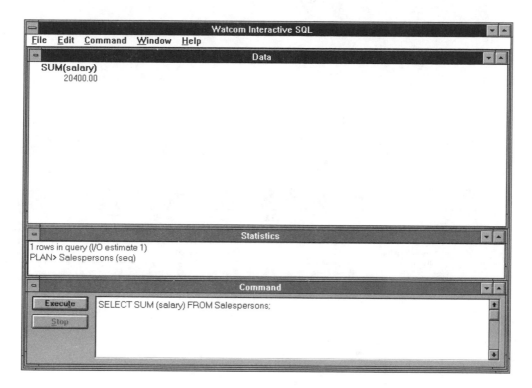

SUM (DISTINCT <value expression>)

This returns the numeric total of all known, unique values. The **NULL**s and all redundant duplicates are removed before the summation took place. As before, an empty set returns a **NULL**, not a zero. If you were to total only each distinct salary, then the query would run as follows:

```
┌─────────────────────── Watcom Interactive SQL ──────────────────── ▼ ▲ ┐
│  File  Edit  Command  Window  Help                                       │
│ ┌──────────────────────────── Data ─────────────────────────── ▼ ▲ ┐ │
│ │ SUM(distinct salary)                                                 │ │
│ │          13400.00                                                    │ │
│ │                                                                      │ │
│ │                                                                      │ │
│ │                                                                      │ │
│ │                                                                      │ │
│ │                                                                      │ │
│ │                                                                      │ │
│ └──────────────────────────────────────────────────────────────────┘ │
│ ┌────────────────────────── Statistics ───────────────────── ▼ ▲ ┐ │
│ │ 1 rows in query (I/O estimate 3)                                     │ │
│ │ PLAN> TEMPORARY TABLE Salespersons (seq)                             │ │
│ └──────────────────────────────────────────────────────────────────┘ │
│ ┌─────────────────────────── Command ──────────────────────── ▼ ▲ ┐ │
│ │ ┌─────────┐                                                          │ │
│ │ │ Execute │  SELECT SUM (DISTINCT salary) FROM Salespersons;         │ │
│ │ └─────────┘                                                          │ │
│ │ ┌─────────┐                                                          │ │
│ │ │  Stop   │                                                          │ │
│ │ └─────────┘                                                          │ │
│ └──────────────────────────────────────────────────────────────────┘ │
└───────────────────────────────────────────────────────────────────────┘
```

The AVG Functions

AVG ([ALL] <value expression>)

The above expression returns the average of the members in the value
expression set. An empty set returns a **NULL**. Remember that in general, **AVG
(x)** isn't the same as **(SUM (x) / COUNT (*))**, because while the **SUM (x)**
function has thrown away the **NULL**s in column x, the **COUNT (*)** has not.
SQL programmers who are new to the language often forget that **COUNT (*)**
counts the **NULL**s. This means that if you have **NULL**s in the value
expression, then **(SUM (mycolumn)/COUNT (*))** isn't the same as **(SUM
(mycolumn)/COUNT (mycolumn))** or **AVG (mycolumn).** If we wished to find
the average salary of the salespeople, we would use the following query:

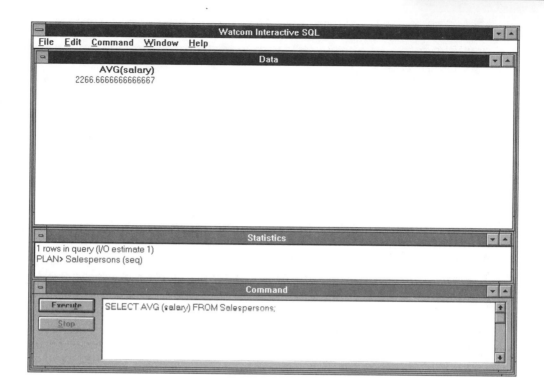

AVG (DISTINCT <value expression>)

As before, this returns the average of the distinct members in the **<value expression>** set. The SQL engine is probably using the same code for totaling in the **AVG ()** as it used in the **SUM ()** function. This leads to the same problems with rounding and truncation, so you should experiment with your particular product to find out what happens. This aspect of **AVG** is only of much use when used with the **GROUP BY** command. Here is a query which will find the average salary per rank:

```
┌─────────────────────────────────────────────────────────────────┐
│ ▬             Watcom Interactive SQL                    ▼ ▲        │
│ File  Edit  Command  Window  Help                                 │
│ ▬                        Data                           ▼ ▲        │
│     AVG(distinct salary)                                          │
│        1000.0000000000000                                         │
│        2100.0000000000000                                         │
│        3050.0000000000000                                         │
│                                                                   │
│                                                                   │
│ ▬                      Statistics                       ▼ ▲        │
│ Estimated 9 rows in query (I/O estimate 3)                        │
│ PLAN> TEMPORARY TABLE Salespersons (seq)                          │
│ ▬                       Command                         ▼ ▲        │
│  ┌─────────┐   SELECT AVG (DISTINCT salary)                       │
│  │ Execute │   FROM Salespersons                                  │
│  └─────────┘   GROUP BY rank;                                     │
│  ┌─────────┐                                                      │
│  │  Stop   │                                                      │
│  └─────────┘                                                      │
└─────────────────────────────────────────────────────────────────┘
```

In the `AVG (salary)` case, we are dividing by 9, since this is the number of rows involved. In the `AVG (DISTINCT salary)` case, we are dividing by 6, since that is the number of rows involved after we throw away duplicates.

The Extreme Functions

The "extreme functions" is simply a collective term for the `MAX` and `MIN` functions. These functions can be used on numeric, date and character data types. However, SQL has strange rules about comparing `VARCHAR` strings, which can cause problems. When two strings are compared for equality, the shortest one is right padded with blanks - they are then compared position for position. Thus, the strings 'John' and 'John<blank>' and 'John<blank><blank>' are equal. You will have to check your implementation of SQL to see which string is returned as the result of the `MAX()` and the `MIN()`, and if there is a pattern to it at all, or not.

The MAX Function

```
MAX ([ALL] <value expression>)
```

The above expression returns the greatest known value in the `<value expression>` set. Here is an example query which will find a maximum salary:

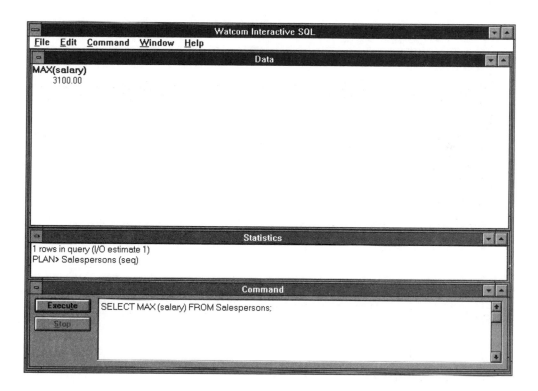

This function will also work on character data types to return the highest string in the collating sequence which will be the last one if you sorted the list. For temporal data types, it returns the one furthest in the future, *not* the most recent date, which would involve looking at the current date and time; this, then changes over time.

An empty set or all **NULL** sets returns a **NULL**. Technically, you can write **MAX (DISTINCT <value expression>)**, but this is the same as **MAX (<value expression>)**. This form is cited for completeness, but it's never used.

The MIN Function

```
MIN ([ALL] <value expression>)
```

The above expression returns the smallest known value in the **<value expression>** set. The **MIN** function has exactly the same format as the other functions:

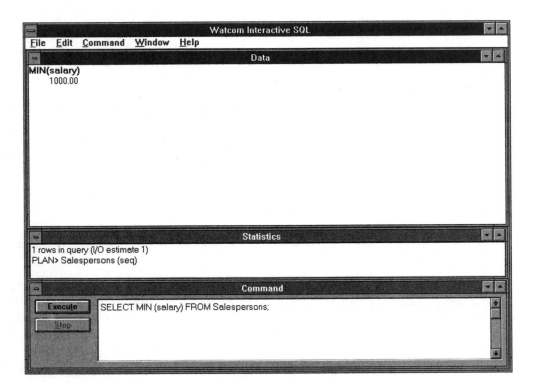

Because there is only one minimum value, this is all that is returned, even though there is more than one person earning that specific salary. Again, this function will also work on character data types to return the first string in the collating sequence, which will be the first one if you sorted the list. For temporal data types, it returns the earliest **DATETIME**. Just as before, **MIN(DISTINCT <value expression>)** exists, but it's cited only for completeness as it is hardly ever used.

GROUP BY and Aggregate Functions

The main reason for using a **GROUP BY** clause is to get aggregate functions for each of the groups. Since a descriptive statistic is a group property, it can go in the **SELECT** clause list of a grouped query. The results will be the grouping columns and the aggregate function results for each group. For example, using the Salespersons table again, we can ask the following, which will again first give us a grouped table:

```
SELECT rank, COUNT (*), SUM (salary), AVG (salary)
   FROM Salespersons
 GROUP BY rank;
```

Here is the grouped table from which the SQL engine will compute the aggregate functions within each group:

Working Table - GROUP BY

```
empid ename             rank  salary
======================================
 101   Andrew Allen       1   $1,000.00      Rank = 1
 102   Burbank Burkett    1   $1,000.00
 ___

 103   Charles Cox        2   $2,000.00      Rank = 2
 104   Dale Dahlman       2   $2,100.00
 105   Edward Everling    2   $2,200.00
 ___

 106   Faulkner Forest    3   $3,000.00      Rank = 3
 107   Gloria Garcia      3   $3,000.00
 108   Harvey Harrison    3   $3,000.00
 109   Kevin Kody         3   $3,100.00
 ___
```

The results would read:

```
rank COUNT (*) SUM (salary)  AVG (salary)
=========================================
  1      2      $2,000.00      $1,000.00
  2      3      $6,300.00      $2,100.00
  3      4     $12,100.00      $3,025.00
```

You can use any of the aggregate functions in expressions, but you should be careful. There is a big difference between **AVG (salary + commission)** and **AVG (salary) + AVG (commission)** when you have used **NULL**s for the commissions of employees who don't get commissions! Another problem is that although algebra might say that **SUM (salary/2)** is the same as **SUM (salary)/2**, your SQL compiler can get slightly different results, due to cumulative rounding errors.

Using our example, let's attempt a slightly more tricky query to discover whether or not we can find the total quantity of items that the customers have bought, and then compare them in descending order to find out who buys the most goods.

If it seems rather a large undertaking to perform all these actions at once, then we should break the task up into smaller steps and build the query up bit by bit. You need to decide what is required in the result table. You also need to total all of the items and group them by company name.

The initial problem is that the quantity of an item ordered and the customer details are in two different tables, with no common columns. That means they have to be joined via a common table. We only need the customer name and the sum of the quantities that they purchased. We then group these according to customer name. This provides a disorganized list, so we use the **ORDER BY** clause to sort the final result table. The complete query looks like this:

```
┌──────────────────────── Watcom Interactive SQL ─────────────────────▼▲─┐
│ File  Edit  Command  Window  Help                                      │
├──────────────────────────── Data ─────────────────────────────────▼▲──┤
│ SUM(qty)  cname                                                      ▲  │
│      78   Ladera Enterpri                                              │
│      65   DRT Marine Lab                                               │
│      47   Cardiff Industr                                             │
│      45   Kalakaua Corpor                                             │
│      43   Monterey Univer                                             │
│      38   Quinton College                                            │
│      37   Rensselaer & Co                                            │
│      36   Mission Hills I                                            │
│      35   Blumenfeld Educ                                            │
│      34   Wellesley Inc.                                              │
│      29   Berryville Supp                                            │
│      28   Mentone Enterpr                                            │
│      23   Alexandria Liqu                                            │
│      19   Ridgewood-Berkm                                           ▼  │
├──────────────────────────── Statistics ───────────────────────────▼▲──┤
│ Estimated 298 rows in query (I/O estimate 791)                         │
│ PLAN> TEMPORARY TABLE Orders (seq), Customers (Customers), OrderItems (orderid) │
├──────────────────────────── Command ──────────────────────────────▼▲──┤
│ ┌─────────┐  WHERE Customers.custid=Orders.custid                   ▲  │
│ │ Execute │  AND Orders.orderid=OrderItems.orderid                     │
│ └─────────┘  GROUP BY CNAME                                           │
│ ┌─────────┐  ORDER BY SUM(qty) desc;                                  │
│ │  Stop   │                                                        ▼  │
│ └─────────┘                                                            │
└────────────────────────────────────────────────────────────────────────┘
```

GROUP BY and HAVING

The **HAVING** clause is a restriction on groups, in much the same way that the **WHERE** clause is a restriction on rows. It's always performed after the **GROUP BY** clause, and **HAVING** is only used to restrict the final output (unlike the **WHERE** clause). It only has to use group characteristic columns because it's applied to the results of a **GROUP BY** statement. Let's write a query to find all the departments with more than three employees:

```
┌─────────────────────────────────────────────────────────────────┐
│ ─                 Watcom Interactive SQL                   ▼ ▲    │
│  File  Edit  Command  Window  Help                                │
│ ┌───────────────────────────────────────────────────────┬─────┐  │
│ │ ─                        Data                           ▼ ▲ │  │
│ │       rank                                                   │  │
│ │        3                                                     │  │
│ │                                                              │  │
│ │                                                              │  │
│ │                                                              │  │
│ │                                                              │  │
│ │                                                              │  │
│ │                                                              │  │
│ │                                                              │  │
│ ├───────────────────────────────────────────────────────┬─────┤  │
│ │ ─                     Statistics                        ▼ ▲ │  │
│ │ Estimated 9 rows in query (I/O estimate 3)                   │  │
│ │ PLAN> TEMPORARY TABLE Salespersons (seq)                     │  │
│ ├───────────────────────────────────────────────────────┬─────┤  │
│ │ ─                      Command                          ▼ ▲ │  │
│ │ ┌──────────┐  SELECT rank                              ▲    │  │
│ │ │ Execute  │   FROM Salespersons                       │    │  │
│ │ ├──────────┤   GROUP BY rank                                │  │
│ │ │  Stop    │  HAVING COUNT (*) > 3;                         │  │
│ │ └──────────┘                                          ▼    │  │
│ └───────────────────────────────────────────────────────┴─────┘  │
└─────────────────────────────────────────────────────────────────┘
```

The grouped working table for this query can compute a **COUNT (*)** for each group, and the **HAVING** clause checks that particular **COUNT (*)**, retaining only the groups which passed its tests.

> It's also worth noting that some older versions of SQL would require that the **SELECT** clause also has **COUNT (*)** in it. This is because they materialized the grouped table with all of the aggregate function expressions in the **SELECT** list first, and then passed that working table to the **HAVING** clause. This isn't standard SQL - check out your product to be sure.

Conceptually, the **SELECT** clause is always done last. The group characteristics can be thought of as existing in the grouped working table, waiting to be selected by the **SELECT** clause. You have probably figured out that using a **SELECT DISTINCT** with a **GROUP BY** is at best redundant; at worst, it will cause extra sorting and make your query take longer to run.

If there is no **GROUP BY** clause, then the **HAVING** clause will treat the entire table as a single group (according to the SQL-89 and SQL-92 standards). The easiest way to think of this is to imagine a nameless, mythical and invisible column which has only one value in it, and a mythical **GROUP BY** clause on it in your query. In practice, however, you will find that many older implementations of SQL require that the **HAVING** clause belongs to a **GROUP BY** clause.

While not required by the standard, most implementations will automatically sort the results of a grouped query. However, it's a good idea to sort the result with an **ORDER BY** clause, as implementations might change over time, or might not sort automatically. Internally, the groups were built by first sorting the table on the grouping columns, then aggregating them. The **NULL** group can sort either high or low, depending on the vendor.

It's also possible to give a name to an aggregate function result by using the SQL-92 `<aggregate function expression> AS <identifier>` in the **SELECT** list. This is handy for **VIEW**s and subqueries, which we'll consider in the next two chapters. However, you can't use that identifier in the **GROUP BY** or **HAVING** clauses since it doesn't exist until the **SELECT** clause is executed.

Summary

In this chapter we've considered how to tailor your output to a desired format. SQL doesn't provide good presentation facilities, and turning a query into a presentable report can require a little work. The **GROUP BY** clause, which we introduced first, is your main ally here. On its own, it provides little more use than a **SELECT DISTINCT** statement, but when combined with the aggregate functions **COUNT**, **SUM**, **AVG**, **MIN** and **MAX**, it provides a valuable way of organizing data for analysis. Finally, we introduced a new restriction, the **HAVING** clause, which can be used with the aggregate functions.

Exercises

1 What is the average salary for the Salespersons?

2 What is the average salary for the Salespersons by rank?

3 What is the value of each order?

(Hint: you need to mulitply the quantity ordered by the price of each item before you add them up).

4 What is the average value of each order?

5 How much money did we get from each customer? What was the average order for each customer?

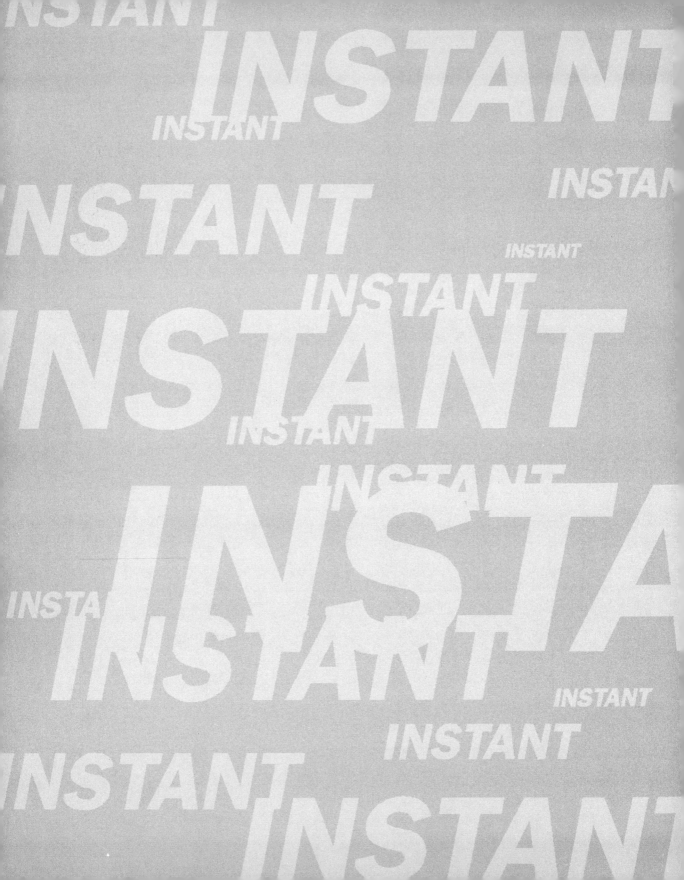

Using Subqueries

Once you are familiar with the **SELECT** command and its basic components, you can then move on to more complex queries. There's a special feature within SQL that lets you use the output from one query as part of another statement. This is known as a **subquery**. With subqueries, you can use the result of one query to answer the **WHERE** clause of another. They can be used to create very specific demands of the database. They are not confined to queries alone. You can also use subqueries with other features of the data manipulation language.

Here is what this chapter covers:

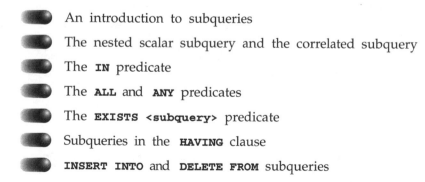

An introduction to subqueries

The nested scalar subquery and the correlated subquery

The **IN** predicate

The **ALL** and **ANY** predicates

The **EXISTS <subquery>** predicate

Subqueries in the **HAVING** clause

INSERT INTO and **DELETE FROM** subqueries

Subqueries

A subquery is a **SELECT** statement which is contained inside another statement. A subquery can be located in the following parts of the following statements:

- The **WHERE** or **HAVING** clause of a **SELECT** statement
- The **SELECT** clause of a **SELECT** statement
- The **WHERE** clause of an **INSERT INTO**, **DELETE FROM** or **UPDATE** statement
- The **SET** clause of an **UPDATE** statement

> **This nesting of queries within queries is where the original 'Structured [English] Query Language' got the word "structured" in its name.**

A subquery is always inside parentheses. In SQL-92, a subquery which returns a single value can be used as a scalar expression. If the subquery returns a single column, then it can be used as a list of constants. If the subquery returns a table result, then it can be used wherever a table is used in SQL-92.

Unfortunately, the rules for subqueries in SQL-89 were much more restrictive and elaborate than those for SQL-92. Also, they were not implemented uniformly in SQL products. Rather than discuss these old restrictions in painful detail, we have decided to ignore them as they won't matter for most products in a year or two.

The subqueries are used in special predicates which convert the results of the subquery into a chain of comparison predicates, connected by Boolean operators, at run time.

Queries with Subquery Predicates

The easiest way to introduce subqueries is within the **WHERE** clause of the **SELECT** statement. This is the most frequent use for subqueries, and once you understand how subqueries function here, you will understand how to use them in other statements. There are several different versions of these types of subqueries. We'll look at the most basic first.

The Nested Scalar Subquery

A scalar subquery is one which returns a single value. This can be used as an expression. You can use the result of the expression to return a **TRUE** or **FALSE** condition, when one variable is compared to a specific value. Those rows that return a **TRUE** condition are displayed in the final result table. For example, to find the customer who placed the highest order number issued on December 15th 1995, we could write the following query:

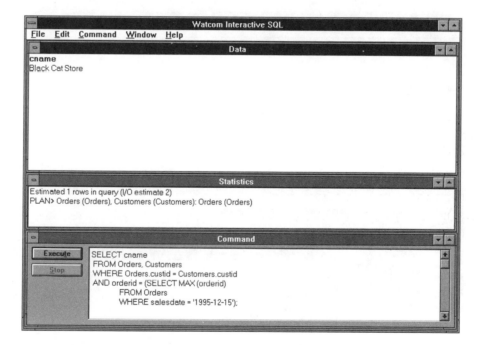

The nested query returns the highest order identification number in the **Orders** table. The second query then displays the customer name from the **Customers** table, which has to be linked with the **Orders** table first, which is in turn is linked with the highest order identification number calculated by the nested query.

Since the **MAX()** function will return only one value, the subquery can be used with a comparison operator. If you accidentally write a subquery which returns more than one value, you will get an error message, or else the system simply won't return an answer to you.

This shouldn't be confused with there being several values in the **Orders** table which match the one value returned by the nested query. In this case, all matches in this table are displayed, together with the corresponding values of **custid**. This scenario couldn't have happened for **orderid**, as **orderid** is a primary key within **Orders**. However, if you had been searching for the customers who had made an order with the employee with the highest **empid**, then your query would resemble the following:

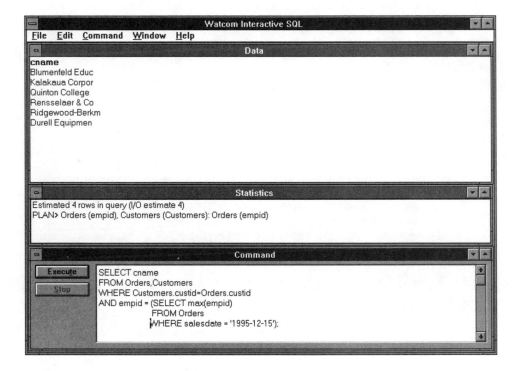

Predicates and Relational Operators

We've already met the **IN** predicate in Chapter 6. It can also be used in conjunction with subqueries. Remember that the **IN** predicate tests for set membership. In this example, the subquery tests for all customer identification numbers that made an order on December 12th, 1995.

```
SELECT cname
FROM Customers
WHERE custid  IN (SELECT custid
                    FROM Orders
                    WHERE salesdate='1995-12-12');
```

The **IN** predicate assumes the comparison operator is always an equality, and that the expanded Boolean operator is always **OR**. These next two predicates allow you to pick the comparison used, as well as how they are connected. They are called the quantified predicates, **ALL** and **ANY**.

The ANY Predicate

Let's start with the **ANY** predicate. It works along the lines of if there are **ANY** or **SOME** values which match a specified criteria; for example, are there **ANY** Salespersons on a salary < $1000 ? The syntax is as follows:

<expression> <comparison operator> [ANY | SOME] <subquery>

The **ANY** predicate can be used in conjunction with any of the relational operators used by SQL. The relational operator is used to compare the variable with every value in a specified column. Generally, there are four separate possible outcomes.

True Condition Returned

If any one of these values returns the condition **TRUE**, then so will the **ANY** predicate. If you think of an example where we might want to ascertain which customers made an order before November 15th, 1995, then you can use the **ANY** predicate to restrict the set. There are several **Customers** who made an order before this date, so the subquery would return their names:

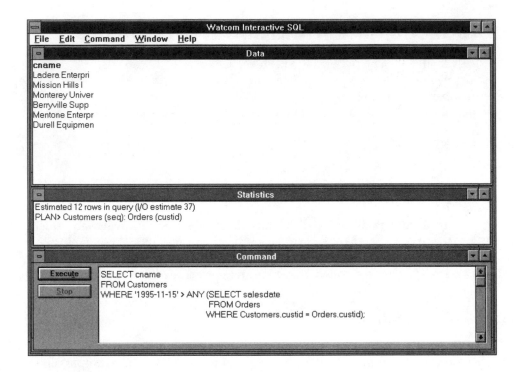

False Condition Returned

If the subquery is empty, then the **ANY** predicate returns **FALSE**. If we were to ask whether or not there were any orders before September 9th, then an empty result table would be returned, as there were no orders made before that date:

```
SELECT cname
FROM Customers
WHERE '1995-09-15' > ANY (SELECT salesdate
                          FROM Orders
                          WHERE Customers.custid = Orders.custid);
```

All NULL Values

If the subquery is all **NULL**s, then the **ANY** predicate returns **UNKNOWN**.

Some NULL Values and Some Non-NULL Values

If the subquery has non-NULL values, then the predicate becomes equivalent to the following:

```
((<expression> <comparison operator> <row1>)
 OR  (<expression> <comparison operator> <row2>)
  ...
 OR  (<expression> <comparison operator> <rowN>))
```

We'll now take two search conditions that look similar, but are *not* necessarily the same, and demonstrate how a subquery works without and with the ANY predicate. They will both return the same results unless there's a NULL value in the answer.

1 x >= (SELECT MAX(y) FROM SomeTable)

2 x >= ANY (SELECT y FROM SomeTable)

For this example let's assume that we are using a table which has three values in a column y, (1, 2, NULL). We'll call this table Sometable. Sometable will have both search conditions applied to it:

Sometable

y
1
2
NULL

Search condition number 1 is expanded into (x >= 2) because the MAX() function returns the largest **known** value from the column to the subquery, which is 2.

Search condition number 2 is expanded into ((x >= 1) OR (x >= 2) OR ((x >= NULL))). This is because it's selecting ANY value of y, not just one.

Let's assume that the value of **x** is zero, so that the **ANY** predicate expands into **((0 >= 1) OR (0 >= 2) OR ((0 >= NULL))**.This in turn becomes **(FALSE OR FALSE OR UNKNOWN)**. If you utilize the rules of **NULL**s and boolean operators which were discussed in Chapter 3, then you will discover that the result is expanded out into **UNKNOWN**, not **FALSE**! **(FALSE OR UNKNOWN** always goes to **FALSE)**

Tips

Note that you can also use the keyword **SOME** in place of **ANY**. This is a simple straight swap of keywords that doesn't change the results in any way. The main reason for using one keyword instead of the other is due mainly to personal preference.

Unlike other predicates, the quantified predicates don't have a **[NOT]** option. If you want to make a negative version, you simply change the comparison operator.

The ALL Predicate

The second quantified predicate is the **ALL** predicate. This, as you might imagine from the name, is the same as the **ANY** predicate except that all values in the subquery are tested for set membership. For example, which orders were there where **ALL** the quantities >1? The syntax for this is as follows:

```
<expression> <comparison operator> ALL <subquery>
```

Imagine that customers who order more than 30 items, in one order, gain special discounts. We'll use an example of the **ALL** predicate to discover which orders have been placed for more than 30 items. We break the query down into two stages. We need to know the total of items for each order. This we do in the subquery. To prevent the subquery from merely totaling the whole quantities ordered, we need to form a correlated subquery that relates it to the orders table, so that each order has a separate **SUM(QTY)** total. The second stage is to compare each of the totals generated to see if they are larger than 30. The resulting query would look and function like this:

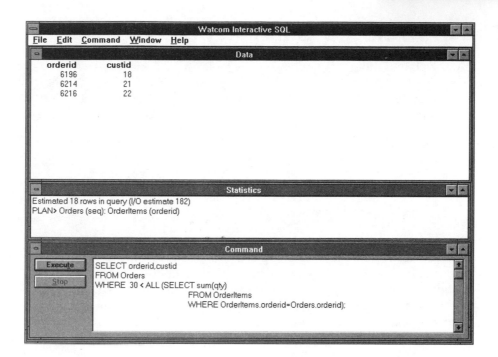

Special Cases

Like the **ANY** predicate, there are also four possible scenarios for the **ALL** predicate. We have just covered the first of them, where the predicate returns all the records matching the specified criteria. If the subquery is all **NULL**s, then the predicate returns **UNKNOWN**. If the subquery has non-**NULL** values, then the predicate becomes equivalent to the following:

```
(((<expression> <comparison operator> <row1>)
AND  (<expression> <comparison operator> <row2>)
  ...
AND  (<expression> <comparison operator> <rowN>))

<expression> <comparison operator> ALL <subquery>
```

If the subquery is empty, then the **ALL** predicate returns **TRUE**. This seems a little weird if you have not studied formal logic, where this rule is called 'existential import.' The idea is that if a set has no members, then anything you say about it is **TRUE** because you can't find a counter-example.

The Correlated Subquery

A correlated subquery references the table in the query in which it's contained. If the nesting is several levels deep, then it uses the nearest outer reference. This idea is easier to explain with an example. Let's find which customers ordered more than two thingabobs (**partid** number **1007**).

```
SELECT orderid, custid
  FROM Orders AS O1
 WHERE 2 < (SELECT qty
             FROM OrderItems AS I1
             WHERE O1.orderid = I1.orderid
             AND I1.partid = 1007);
```

The subquery will be executed once for each row in the **Orders** table. In the previous example of a subquery, the subquery was evaluated once and the results were made available to the outer query. With a correlated subquery, the outer query is processed and some information for each row is 'passed' to the correlated subquery. The important thing to notice here is that the **WHERE** clause of the subquery refers to **O1.orderid**. There is no **O1** table in the subquery's **FROM** clause. The value of **O1.orderid** comes from the current value in the **Orders** table.

If the subquery were to come back empty (nobody bought that many thingabobs!), then the subquery would become a **NULL**, and the **WHERE** clause result would be **UNKNOWN**.

Let's go one step further, and keep nesting. Did anyone order more than two units of the first item in alphabetical order of our catalog?

```
SELECT orderid, custid
  FROM Orders AS O1
 WHERE 2 < (SELECT qty
             FROM OrderItems AS I1
             WHERE O1.orderid = I1.orderid
             AND I1.partid = (SELECT partid
                               FROM Inventory AS V1
                               WHERE V1.partid = I1.partid
                               AND V1.description = (SELECT MIN(description)
                                                      FROM Inventory AS V2)));
```

This nesting is getting tricky. In the innermost subquery, we find the minimum description in the inventory table. This is a constant scalar value when we do the query 'chachka'. It might change over time, but right now it's a constant. This value is used by the next subquery as we move outward. Within this subquery, the **I1.partid** value is taken from the outer subquery for each row. From this point on, the unrolling of the nesting proceeds as before.

There's nothing to keep us from using an outer table again in a subquery. A good rule of thumb is to always give all tables in the **FROM** clauses of a nested subquery their own correlation names. This helps to reduce confusion. It's good to use the first letter of the table's name and a number to signal the nesting level of each appearance of the table.

EXISTS <subquery> Predicate

The **EXISTS** predicate is simple to understand. If the subquery has returned a result, then the predicate returns the value **TRUE**. If the subquery is empty and there's no match for the expression, then the value **FALSE** is returned. You must take note that **NULL**s count because they exist, even if you don't know what they are. Therefore, you can't get an **UNKNOWN** result. The **EXISTS** predicate can only use subqueries, as it has no equivalent relational operator. The syntax for this predicate is as follows:

```
[NOT] EXISTS <subquery>
```

Let's take a look at another example. If we wanted to ascertain which Salespersons made a sale on October 15th we would use the **EXISTS** clause in the following way:

```
┌─────────────────────────────────────────────────────────────────────┐
│ ▬                        Watcom Interactive SQL                  ▾ ▲ │
├─────────────────────────────────────────────────────────────────────┤
│  File   Edit  Command   Window   Help                                │
├─────────────────────────────────────────────────────────────────────┤
│ ▫                            Data                               ▾ ▲ │
├─────────────────────────────────────────────────────────────────────┤
│ ename                                                                 │
│ Charles Cox                                                           │
│ Dale Dahlman                                                          │
│ Edward Everling                                                       │
│                                                                       │
│                                                                       │
│                                                                       │
│                                                                       │
├─────────────────────────────────────────────────────────────────────┤
│ ▫                          Statistics                           ▾ ▲ │
├─────────────────────────────────────────────────────────────────────┤
│ Estimated 4 rows in query (I/O estimate 14)                          │
│ PLAN> Salespersons (seq): Orders (empid)                             │
│                                                                       │
├─────────────────────────────────────────────────────────────────────┤
│ ▫                           Command                             ▾ ▲ │
├─────────────────────────────────────────────────────────────────────┤
│ ┌─────────┐  SELECT ename                                          ▲ │
│ │ Execute │  FROM Salespersons                                       │
│ └─────────┘  WHERE EXISTS (SELECT *                                  │
│ ┌─────────┐          FROM Orders                                     │
│ │  Stop   │          WHERE Salespersons.empid=Orders.empid           │
│ └─────────┘          AND salesdate = '1995-10-15');                ▼ │
└─────────────────────────────────────────────────────────────────────┘
```

Since this predicate is based on rows, and not column values, you can use the **SELECT *** clause in the subquery. You must, however, note the extra line, which you might not intuitively add. The two tables have to be correlated by a join clause, so that **Salespersons.empid** from the outer query must equal **Order.empid**. The **empid** value is effectively passed as a parameter from the inner query to the outer query. Consider what might happen if you ignored this. The **SELECT** subquery would find the first occurrence of that particular salesdate and would return a **TRUE** to the **EXISTS** predicate. This would mean that every employee name would be selected from the table **Salespersons** as the two tables would be independent, and the two queries would *function* independently.

Conversely, you could simply reverse the query with the addition of **NOT** to find any Salespersons who didn't make a sale on October 15th. This, as you might expect, gives the list of all remaining salespeople not identified by the first query:

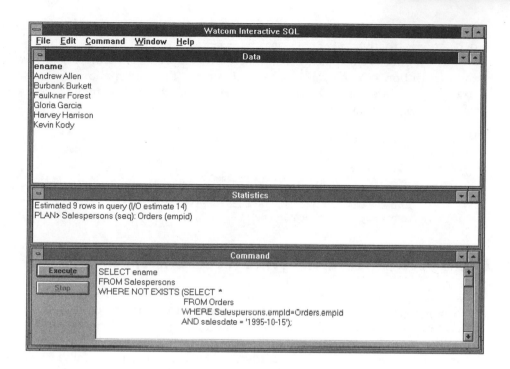

It's possible to make complex queries of the database using the **EXISTS** predicate. Imagine you were checking sales patterns, and you wanted to know on which dates orders were made for doodads. You would have to query three separate tables, so to make the query work you would need to create a join spanning two tables. This assumes that you did not know the **partid** for a doodad.

First, you must create the initial query, which will simply display the information you require. This is the sales date, and the **orderid** to make the output maybe a little more meaningful than simply a list of dates.

The subquery is a little more problematic. Consider that a doodad can only be located in the description column of the **Inventory**. However, there are no common columns between **Orders** table (which contains the sales date) and the **Inventory** table, but, the **OrderItems** table has fields common to both **Inventory** and **Orders**. If you created a join from the **Orders** table to

OrderItems table on the common **orderid** column, and created a join from **OrderItems** to the **Inventory** via the **partid** column, then the tables would be effectively linked. The rather unwieldy code is simply checking the description column for 'doodad'. It returns the information to the **EXISTS** predicate for each row of **Orders**, rather than just giving one answer from the subquery.

```
SELECT orderid,salesdate
FROM Orders
WHERE EXISTS (SELECT *
              FROM Inventory,OrderItems
              WHERE Orders.orderid=OrderItems.orderid
        AND OrderItems.partid=Inventory.partid
        AND description = 'doodad');
```

Subqueries in the HAVING Clause

It's also possible to use subqueries in the **HAVING** clause. The subquery works as part of the restriction carried out by the **HAVING** clause. Typically, they can be used in conjunction with the aggregate functions to restrict the final result. A typical use would be to calculate the average of a set of values, and then display the records that have a greater (or smaller) value than the average. If we wanted to examine the items that cost more than average in our stock, then a simple subquery to calculate the average price of the items in stock would achieve this:

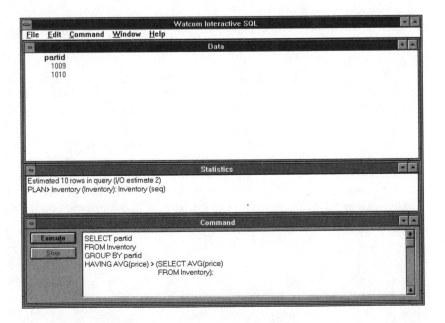

Note that the **GROUP BY partid** line won't be strictly necessary on all systems, as **partid** is already a primary key, and can only have one record per key entry. However, some systems require the **HAVING** clause to always be used with **GROUP BY**.

Using Subquery Predicates in Other Statements

These subquery predicates can also be used in expressions, **UPDATE**, **DELETE**, **FROM** and **INSERT INTO** statements. This is handy, but a little tricky.

Stand-alone Scalar Subqueries

A scalar subquery has to return a single value. If the subquery is empty, then it returns a **NULL**. Such subqueries can used anywhere that a scalar expression can be used in SQL-92.

One interesting use of this feature is in the **SELECT** clause of the containing query, which is helpful when writing tricky joins. For example, this is a query which would find the highest order number for each customer:

```
                       Watcom Interactive SQL
File   Edit   Command   Window   Help
─────────────────────────────── Data ───────────────────────────────
cname                          MAX(orderid)
Stanwood Consul                    6099
Vallecito Indus                    6109
Wellesley Inc.                     6129
White Court                       (NULL)
Acton Computers                   (NULL)
Agorist Distrib                    6148
Alexandria Liqu                    6157
Blumenfeld Educ                    6170
Cardiff Industr                    6175
Del Toro Enterp                   (NULL)
DRT Marine Lab                     6196
─────────────────────────────── Statistics ─────────────────────────
24 rows in query (I/O estimate 1)
PLAN> C1 (seq): TEMPORARY TABLE O1 (custid)
─────────────────────────────── Command ────────────────────────────
 [ Execute ]   SELECT cname, (SELECT MAX(orderid)
 [  Stop   ]          FROM Orders AS O1
                         WHERE O1.custid = C1.custid)
               FROM Customers AS C1;
```

If we look at the first eleven entries, we can see that **NULL** has been returned for the customers who haven't yet placed an order, as there can be no maximum order identification number.

Subqueries in DELETE FROM Statements

A subquery can let us use information from one table to delete rows in another. As a simple example, let's delete all the orders for items that begin with the letter 'd' by using the following:

```
DELETE FROM OrderItems
  WHERE partid IN (SELECT partid
                   FROM Inventory
                   WHERE description LIKE 'd%');
```

The subquery can also refer to the same table as the **DELETE** statement, so in such situations a correlation name becomes important. For example, to delete all the orders that total less than $500, you could write the following:

```
DELETE FROM OrderItems
  WHERE 500.00 > (SELECT SUM(qty * price)
                  FROM OrderItems AS O1, Inventory AS I1
                  WHERE O1.orderid = orderid
                    AND O1.partid = I1.partid);
```

Let's look at the subquery in detail. We are doing a self-join of the **OrderItems** table *to itself*. We give it the correlation name '**O1**' in the subquery, and join it to the **Inventory** table to get the price of each item. The total value of each order is the sum of the quantity multiplied by the price of each item.

The '**orderid**' in the first line of the **WHERE** clause refers to the outermost copy of the table in the **DELETE FROM** clause. This assures that the total we just computed is matched to the proper row which is being considered for deletion.

Subqueries in INSERT Statements

Scalar subqueries can be used as part of the **SELECT** statement that is providing values for an **INSERT** statement. This is a handy way to move values from one table to another. For example, let's assume that we have a table of contest winners which was built by a random drawing of order numbers. We are going to pay off the winners adding a $500 gift certificate to their orders (assume the $500 gift certificate is in the inventory as part number **9999**).

```
INSERT INTO OrderItems (orderid, detail, partid, qty)
  SELECT orderid,
         (SELECT MAX(detail) +1
            FROM OrderItems AS O1
           WHERE O1.orderid = P1.orderid)
         9999,
         1
   FROM Prizewinners AS P1
  WHERE orderid = P1.orderid;
```

This is another tricky statement. We go to the contest winner table and select the **orderid** that was used to identify this contestant. Next, we need to get a new detail number, so we use a scalar subquery that will put this row after the largest detail number in use for that order. The **partid** is a constant, as is the quantity.

Subqueries in UPDATE Statements

Subqueries can also be used to add information into tables using information gained from other tables. Take an example where the boss is in an exceptionally good mood on October 15th as it's his birthday. He decides that anyone who makes a sale on that day should get a $50 raise onto their salary. You can use a subquery with an **UPDATE** statement to achieve this. The two tables that you need to consider are the **Orders** table, which has the details of the dates on which sales were made, and the **Salespersons** table which contains the respective salaries of the salespersons. The subquery is used to locate all the orders made on October 15th, as well as to join the two tables. The main query updates each record respectively if a sale has been made by a salesperson on the 15th:

```
UPDATE Salespersons
SET salary = salary + 50
WHERE EXISTS (SELECT salesdate
        FROM orders
             WHERE Salespersons.empid=Orders.empid
             AND salesdate='1995-10-15');
```

> So that the information in the database corresponds to the output in the book, it's best to run this query again, substituting the plus sign for a minus sign, so that everyone is effectively restored their starting salaries!

Summary

There are several advantages of using subqueries, perhaps the key one being that they breakdown larger queries into logical steps. This means that you should be able to work out what each stage does separately, rather than having to write one large and incredibly complex query. They are intended to closely parallel the structure of the English language and there will be times when you have no choice but to use them.

We have dealt with several forms of subquery. The simple scalar subquery is the most common way of breaking down a query, and it returns a single value as a result. There are several predicates, **ALL**, **ANY** and **EXISTS**, which can all be used to tailor the results to your needs. The correlated subquery allows you to take short cuts with subqueries that would otherwise have to be repeated many times. Subqueries can also be used with the **INSERT INTO**, **UPDATE** and **DELETE FROM** statements which allows you to selectively alter the data contained within the database. The next thing we'll look at is how to selectively view only the parts of the database that you need to see.

Exercises

1 SQL doesn't have its own input and output, so you will probably use a front end tool that will paint an order form on a terminal screen. This form will take the fields on the screen, put the values into SQL statements, and execute those statements behind the scenes.

What single query would you need to get all the information in a typical order form on the screen?

(Hint: you need the customer data, the order data and the items in that order.)

2 Find all the orders which have both a 'doodad', and 'doohickey' on them. Don't look up their part numbers, and use the constants in the query.

3 Find all the orders which have both a 'doodad', and 'doohickey', and nothing else.

4 A more realistic example than deleting orders under $500 might be to delete rows from the **Orders** table when that particular order has no items in the **OrderItems** table. This could occur when the customer has called several times and canceled a line item each time, until he or she has nothing left.

(Hint: use an EXISTS predicate subquery.)

Chapter

Views

A view is a query which can be used in the same way as a table. However, a view doesn't actually exist in the database. It's used for security reasons, to prevent the user from seeing data for which he or she has no authorization. It can also be used to take data from many different tables and present it as one table, or to give the viewer his or her own personal look at the database. It does this by showing only specific records or fields that have been selected by the user. In this way it's the same as a **SELECT** query. Views differ from **SELECT** by the fact that they can also act like tables: parts can be updated and deleted. Unlike tables though, you can't see the whole of the information that is contained. The view is restricted by whatever conditions that are applied by the DBA.

This chapter covers the following subjects:

- An introduction to **VIEW**s
- Using **VIEW**s within the database structure
- Major functions of **VIEW**s
- Updating **VIEW**s: standards and vendor extensions
- The **WITH CHECK OPTION** clause
- Dropping **VIEW**s

Introducing VIEWs

When you use a **CREATE TABLE** statement, you *physically* create a structure within the database by which to see selected parts of the data. These structures are known as **base tables**. You can, however, use another method to look at the data contained within these tables. This method is known as **VIEW**, whereby you give yourself the ability to see different sections of different tables at the same time. A **VIEW** is sometimes called a **virtual table**, in order to distinguish it from a base table. A **VIEW** is a query which is given a name so that it can be used like a table. When the SQL engine sees the **VIEW** name, it goes to the description of the **VIEW**, executes the query, and returns with the result table. To draw an analogy between SQL and procedural languages, a **VIEW** is the closest thing that SQL has to an in-line macro, subroutine or procedure.

To give you a better idea of how a view operates within the database, we'll compare it to other database schema objects and their properties:

Schema Object	Physical Existence?	Accessed by User?
Table	yes	yes
View	no	yes
Index	yes	no

Those of you who are cynical might also add a line to this chart which defines a "back-up copy" as having neither existence nor accessibility.

Handling VIEWs

Upon finding a **VIEW** within an SQL statement, a database system can do one of two things:

 It can actually materialize a **VIEW** as a physical table in the database.

It can go to the system tables which hold the text of the **VIEW** definition and work them into the parsing of the query (like an in-line macro expansion in other programming languages).

However, the standard says that a **VIEW** always has to act as if it were materialized. By *materializing* we mean that the SQL query which creates the **VIEW** must be executed, and the results stored in a temporary table. When you create a **VIEW**, it's very like assigning a name to a particular **SELECT** query, in the way we assigned different names to tables we created in Chapter 2. Once the **VIEW** has been created, it can be treated in the same way as a table, in that you can make **SELECT** queries of it, you can **INSERT INTO** it, you can **UPDATE** it, and you can even perform joins upon it.

The CREATE VIEW Syntax

Let's look at how to go about creating a **VIEW**. The SQL syntax for a **VIEW** definition is as follows:

```
CREATE VIEW <table name> [(<view column list>)]
AS <query expression>
[WITH CHECK OPTION]
```

> The full SQL-92 syntax added an optional `<levels clause>` in the **WITH CHECK OPTION**, but it this isn't yet widely implemented.

The name of the **VIEW** must be unique within the database schema, like a table name. The **WHERE** clause in the `<query expression>` can't reference the **VIEW** itself, but otherwise isn't restricted by complexity. The view definition can't reference itself since it doesn't yet exist. The **VIEW** definition can reference other **VIEW**s, but these **VIEW**s must eventually reference underlying base tables. All of these restrictions make sense; if there were no permanent base tables involved, what would you actually be viewing?

Let's compare how the two different methods of **VIEW**s work, taking first an example of a materialized **VIEW** and then compare how an in-line **VIEW** expansion would deal with the same query.

Materialized VIEWs

Let's define a **VIEW** of the items costing over $10.00 in **Inventory**. We'll give it a meaningful name of **OverTen** so as not to confuse:

```
CREATE VIEW OverTen
AS SELECT *
    FROM Inventory
    WHERE price > 10;
```

This creates a **VIEW** which is simply all of the columns in the `Inventory` table and all of the records that have a price value greater than **10**. To find the expensive items whose quantity in stock is greater than **20**, we could write the query as follows:

```
                           Watcom Interactive SQL
File   Edit   Command   Window   Help
                              Data
  partid  description              stockqty
    1002  doohickey                      69
    1005  gimmick                        24
    1006  gizmo                          87
    1008  widget                         59
    1009  chachka                        95
    1010  thingie                       110
    1011  dibdob                         25




                            Statistics
Estimated 1 rows in query (I/O estimate 1)
PLAN> Inventory (seq)

                            Command
 Execute     SELECT partid, description, stockqty
  Stop          FROM OverTen
                WHERE stockqty > 20;
```

The materialization method would construct the **OverTen** table, then execute the query.

In-line VIEWs

Compare the in-line method which would, in effect, convert the query to the following:

```
SELECT partid, description, stockqty
FROM (SELECT *
      FROM Inventory
      WHERE price > 10) AS OverTen
WHERE stockqty > 20;
```

This is a legal expression in SQL-92, but isn't yet implemented in many products, including Watcom SQL. The optimizer could then rearrange the expansion to give the following equivalent statement:

```
SELECT OverTen.partid, OverTen.description, OverTen.stockqty
FROM Inventory AS OverTen
WHERE price > 10
AND stockqty > 20;
```

In this case, this expression would be able to use all the indexes and other features on the **Inventory** table and should give a fast answer. This makes in-line expansion look pretty good, but there are always trade-offs. Consider a **VIEW** which gives us the average quantity of each item ordered:

```
CREATE VIEW AvgQtyPerOrder (partid, avgqty)
AS SELECT partid, AVG(qty)
     FROM OrderItems
   GROUP BY partid;
```

We want to figure out who the above average customers for each product are. This monster query has to get data from three tables:

259

```
┌─────────────────────────────── Watcom Interactive SQL ──────────────────────┐
│ File  Edit  Command  Window  Help                                            │
├───────────────────────────────────── Data ──────────────────────────────────┤
│   partid  cname                     SUM(l1.qty)                               │
│    1001   Cardiff Industr                6                                    │
│    1001   Kalakaua Corpor               12                                    │
│    1001   Monterey Univer                5                                    │
│    1001   South Burlingam              10                                     │
│    1002   Blumenfeld Educ              13                                     │
│    1002   Cardiff Industr               7                                     │
│    1002   Durell Equipmen               3                                     │
│    1002   Kalakaua Corpor               3                                     │
│    1002   Ladera Enterpri               7                                     │
│    1002   Monterey Univer               5                                     │
│    1002   Rensselaer & Co              10                                     │
│    1002   Stanwood Consul               3                                     │
│    1003   Alexandria Liqu               3                                     │
│    1003   Berryville Supp               2                                     │
├───────────────────────────────── Statistics ────────────────────────────────┤
│ Estimated 280 rows in query (I/O estimate 179)                               │
│ PLAN> TEMPORARY TABLE O1 (seq), C1 (Customers), I1 (orderid): OrderItems (partid │
│ )                                                                            │
├────────────────────────────────── Command ──────────────────────────────────┤
│ ┌─────────┐  SELECT I1.partid, C1.cname, SUM(I1.qty)                         │
│ │ Execute │    FROM Customers AS C1, Orders AS O1, OrderItems AS I1          │
│ └─────────┘   WHERE C1.custid = O1.custid                                    │
│ ┌─────────┐     AND I1.orderid = O1.orderid                                  │
│ │  Stop   │   GROUP BY I1.partid, C1.cname                                   │
│ └─────────┘   HAVING SUM(I1.qty) > (SELECT avgqty                            │
│                       FROM AvgQtyPerOrder AS AQ1                             │
│                       WHERE AQ1.partid = I1.partid);                        │
└──────────────────────────────────────────────────────────────────────────────┘
```

If the final subquery expression is expanded into in-line code, the subquery
will be re-calculated for each row in the containing query, and it will run
like molasses in winter. If the **VIEW** is materialized, however, then the
HAVING clause becomes a simple correlated query on a small table that will
probably buffer into main storage. The materialized version should run
several hundred to several thousand times faster than the in-line expansion
in most current SQL implementations.

Updatable and Read-Only VIEWs

You can use **VIEW**s to **INSERT**, **UPDATE**, and **DELETE** into the base table from which it is built. This only applies under certain conditions in SQL, however.

> An updatable **VIEW** is one which can have each of its rows associated with exactly one row in a single, underlying base table.

This means that if you selected three columns X, Y and Z as a view of a table then there could only be three columns in the base table for that view to be updatable. Changes that are made within the view must be passed on to its underlying base table unambiguously. This is vital as when you are updating the view, you are effectively updating the table underneath it. If you change column X in a view then column X must correspond to a column in the base table. If there were four tables in the base table, how would the SQL engine know which column in the table should be updated? It's the same principle as in Chapter 5 where we simply inserted data into the database. We couldn't insert data for only four columns into a table with five columns, the **NOT NULL** constraints prevent us from doing this.

Let's look at an example of how we could pass the changes on from a view to the base table. If we wanted to add a new product to our view of **Inventory** items worth more than $10 which also had more than 20 items in stock, then we could write the following query:

```
INSERT INTO Overten (partid,description,stockqty,reorderpnt,price) VALUES
(1011, 'dibdob',25,10,24.00);
```

Although the values are inserted into the view, all of the values are passed onto the base table, **Inventory**. If you were now to query the **Inventory** table in this way:

```
─                          Watcom Interactive SQL                    ▼ ▲
File  Edit  Command  Window  Help
─                                   Data                             ▼ ▲
    partid  description       stockqty    reorderpnt      price
     1001   doodad               100          20          10.00
     1002   doohickey             69          25          25.00
     1003   frammis               23          30           2.50
     1004   gadget                71          20           7.50
     1005   gimmick               24          10          10.65
     1006   gizmo                 87          30          11.35
     1007   thingabob             10          30          12.50
     1008   widget                59          10          25.00
     1009   chachka               95          25          70.00
     1010   thingie              110          25          80.00
     1011   dibdob                25          10          24.00


─                                Statistics                          ▼ ▲
11 rows in query (I/O estimate 1)
PLAN> Inventory (seq)

─                                 Command                            ▼ ▲
   ┌─────────┐  SELECT * FROM Inventory;                             ▲
   │ Execute │
   └─────────┘
   ┌─────────┐
   │  Stop   │                                                       ▼
   └─────────┘
```

you would see that the entry for **dibdob** exists in the **Inventory** table, as well as the view **Overten**. However, as a result, updatable **VIEW**s are defined only for queries on one table, with no **GROUP BY** clause, no **HAVING** clause, no aggregate functions, no calculated columns, and no **SELECT DISTINCT** clause. Also, any columns excluded from the **VIEW** must be **NULL**able or have a **DEFAULT** in the underlying base table, so that a whole row can be constructed for insertion. By implication, the view must also contain a key of the table.

This is very restrictive and there are many other conditions under which a **VIEW** could be updatable. The SQL standard simply decided to play safe.

View Column List

The `<view column list>` is optional, and when it isn't given, the **VIEW** will inherit the column names from the query. In this example query had the `<view column list>` not been specified on the top line, the column list would have been assumed to be the same as that in the **SELECT** statement:

```
CREATE VIEW OverTwenty (partid,description,stockqty,reorderpnt,price)
AS SELECT partid,description,stockqty,reorderpnt,price
    FROM Inventory
   WHERE price > 20;
```

The number of column names in the `<view column list>` must be the same as the query expression. The same column name can't be specified more than once in the `<view column list>`. This is because there would be no way of differentiating between the two columns. This is the same as for the **CREATE TABLE** statement.

WITH CHECK OPTION Clause

If **WITH CHECK OPTION** is specified, then the viewed table has to be updatable. The **WITH CHECK OPTION** is part of the SQL-89 standard, which was extended in SQL-92. Have a look at a **VIEW** defined in the following way:

```
CREATE VIEW V1
AS SELECT *
   FROM Foo
   WHERE a = 1;
```

Now, **UPDATE** it with the following:

```
UPDATE V1
   SET a = 9;
```

The **UPDATE** will take place without any trouble, but the rows which were previously seen in the **VIEW** now disappear when we reuse **V1**:

```
SELECT * FROM V1;
```

They no longer meet the **WHERE** clause condition! Likewise, an **INSERT INTO** statement with **VALUES (a = 9)** would insert just fine, but its rows would never been seen when you reuse this **VIEW**.

VIEWs created this way will always have all the rows that meet the search condition, and that can be very handy. For example, you can set up a **VIEW** of records with a status code of "to be done," work on them, change a status code to "finished," and they will disappear from your view. The important point is that the **WHERE** clause condition was checked only at the time the **VIEW** was invoked.

The **WITH CHECK OPTION** makes the system check the **WHERE** clause condition upon each **INSERT** or **UPDATE**, verifying the **VIEW** over again. Thus, the previous **UPDATE** statement would get an error message, and you couldn't change certain columns in certain ways.

For example, consider a **VIEW** of salaries under $250, and another **VIEW** of employees getting between $100 and $250 per week:

```
CREATE VIEW Lowpay
AS SELECT *
    FROM Salespersons
  WHERE salary <= 250;

CREATE VIEW Mediumpay
AS SELECT *
    FROM Lowpay
  WHERE salary >= 100;
```

If neither **VIEW** has a **WITH CHECK OPTION**, then the effect of updating **Mediumpay** by increasing every salary by $1000 will be passed without any check to **Lowpay**. **Lowpay** will pass the changes to the underlying **Salespersons** table. The next time **Mediumpay** is used, **Lowpay** will be rebuilt in its own right and **Mediumpay** rebuilt from **Lowpay**.

However, if the **CREATE VIEW** statement for **Mediumpay** had a **WITH CHECK OPTION** on it, the **UPDATE** would fail. Medium pay has no problem with such a large salary, but it would cause a row in **Lowpay** to disappear, so **Mediumpay** will reject it.

Dropping Views

VIEWs, like tables, can be dropped from the schema. The SQL-92 syntax for the statement is as follows:

```
DROP VIEW <table name> <drop behavior>

<drop behavior> ::= [CASCADE | RESTRICT]
```

The **<drop behavior>** clause did not exist in SQL-89. (It doesn't exist in Watcom SQL either.) The usual way of storing VIEWs is in a schema level table is with the view name, the text of the view, and any other information that the SQL engine might need for reference purposes. When you dropped a VIEW, the engine usually removed the appropriate row from the schema tables. You found out about dependencies when you tried to use VIEWs built on VIEWs which no longer existed. Likewise, dropping a base table could cause the same problem when the VIEW is accessed.

The new SQL-92 **CASCADE** option will find all other VIEWs which use the dropped VIEW and also remove them. If **RESTRICT** is specified, then the VIEW can't be dropped if there's anything which is dependent upon it. It's a good idea to first use **RESTRICT** to see what is happening, then remove schema objects in an orderly way.

If we decided that we didn't really want the to use the view of **Inventory** to see products which cost more than $10, then we could use the following code to get rid of it in Watcom SQL. Like tables, however, this version of the statement must be used with caution as it affects any other related VIEWs. In this example, we know there are no other related VIEWs that we have created:

```
DROP VIEW Overten;
```

Hints on Using VIEWs

 Don't nest **VIEW**s too deeply; the overhead of building several levels eats up execution time, and the extra storage for materialized **VIEW**s can be expensive. Complex nestings are also hard to maintain.

 One way to figure out which **VIEW**s you should have is to inspect the existing queries and see whether or not certain subqueries or expressions are repeated. These are good candidates for **VIEW**s.

The best way to approach **VIEW**s is to think of how a user wants to see the database and then give them a set of **VIEW**s which make it look as if the database were designed for their applications alone.

The CREATE SCHEMA Statement

The SQL-92 standard, and most versions of SQL, also have a **CREATE SCHEMA** statement. This is needed to group objects for authorizations. You would put together a schema for one group of users and have in it only the table definitions that they were allowed to see.

While the SQL-92 standard has a **CREATE SCHEMA** statement, each vendor will have a little different version of it. The reason for this is that schema creation depends upon how the SQL engine uses physical storage. Some products have to allocate special storage space for the schema all at once, while others use the operating system and allocate storage as needed. Read your manual and look for a utility program specific to your database.

Summary

In this chapter, we have looked at how to create **VIEW**s via one of two methods, the first being with materialization, the second being the on-line method. We discussed what physical effect **VIEW**s had on the database. We also looked at how you can update **VIEW**s and physically update the base tables of the database at the same time. Then we worked on how you can drop **VIEW**s and noted the similarity with dropping tables. Finally, we looked at a few do's and don'ts with views, and how they are used to provide different users with different **VIEW**s of the database.

Exercises

1 In the chapter on subqueries, we talked about building a query which you would need to get all the information in a typical order form on the screen. Put that query into a **VIEW**, called **OrderForm**.

2 Use the **OrderForm** view to find all the orders which have both a **doodad**, and **doohickey** on them.

3 Use the **OrderForm** view to find all the orders which have both a **doodad**, and **doohickey** - and nothing else.

4 We need a view which will show the customer number, salesman's number, the order number and the total value of the order. Use the **OrderForm** view to make it.

5 Take the view you made in question 4 and use it to make a view with the customer name, salesman's name, the order number and the total value of that order.

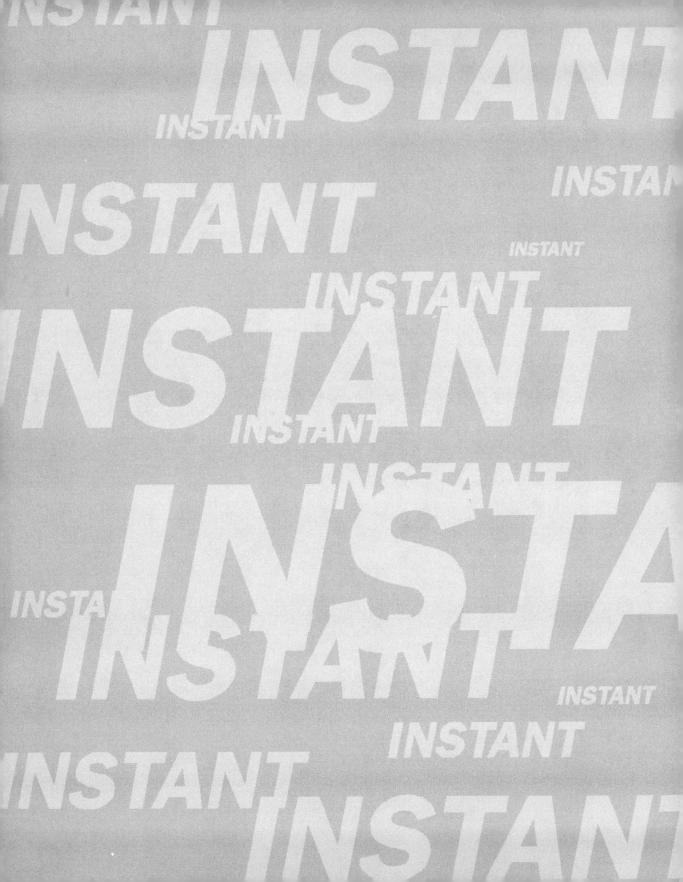

Chapter

Embedded SQL

We begin this chapter with a look back at all of the standard features of SQL that we've learned so far. However, one drawback should be apparent, and that is that SQL doesn't work by itself. You can't write stand-alone applications with pure SQL. What you must do instead is to embed SQL into a host language program and get it to pass data between the host language program and the database. You must send this mixed language program to a pre-compiler which looks at the program and can extract the SQL and convert it into the host language. The way the results of the SQL are passed back and forth is in structures known as **CURSOR**s which act like sequential files. You can use these structures to query and update the underlying base table.

This chapter delves into:

- An overview of the first 10 chapters
- Embedded SQL
- SQL Descriptor Area and SQL Communications Area
- **Cursor**s
- Update and Delete by positioned **CURSOR**s
- An example of a C-embedded SQL program

Where Are We Now?

Your head should really be hurting by now. We've looked at all the major features in the SQL Data Manipulation Language (DML) in a whirlwind tour. The first 10 chapters have given you an overview of the whole SQL language and all its different features:

 When you want to change a table, you have to do it with set oriented operations. The possible changes are insertions, deletions and updates. A join takes rows from two or more tables and concatenates them into a new row.

 A projection picks the columns that we want to look at.

 The **SELECT** statement builds joins and projections from logical expressions (predicates or search conditions). The predicates can refer to relationships between columns within the same table, or columns in different tables.

 By using subqueries (queries within a query), you can build more elaborate search conditions. The subquery is expanded at execution time, and transformed into a list or a single value that can be used in a Boolean expression.

 Subqueries can contain other subqueries and the nesting can be quite elaborate.

 You can make a query that you re-use quite a lot into a **VIEW** in order to make your programming easier.

So far, you've been relying on whatever interactive query tool was supplied by your DBMS vendor to issue your queries. However, if you don't want the user to type SQL in directly, you'll need to write some code in a high-level programming language.

Embedded SQL

SQL by itself is pretty useless, in fact the joke is that the initials stands for 'Scarcely Qualifies as a Language' because it doesn't work by itself. In fact, there's no way for SQL to input or output data to the operating system and the user. Instead, SQL sits quite happily between the database and a host language program passing data back and forth. The host program takes responsibility for communicating with the outside world.

The host language can be an ANSI or ISO procedural language like COBOL, FORTRAN, PL/1, Pascal, C, C++ and BASIC. In fact, the ANSI and ISO standards committees for these languages helped to define the actual interfaces for SQL.

Today, there are also front end tools on PCs which are designed to use SQL. Powerbuilder from Powersoft, SQL Windows from Gupta and Delphi from Borland International are fine examples. There are also 4GL products, such as Informix and Progress, which have switched from their original proprietary database languages to SQL.

Problems of Using SQL in a Procedural Host Language

There are two immediate problems in trying to use SQL in a procedural host language:

 The first problem is that SQL has a very rich collection of datatypes which might not match those available in the host language program. If the **NULL**, for example, doesn't exist in the host language, it's a real problem.

 The second problem is that SQL uses a set model of data and *not* a file model. This is referred to as 'impedance mismatch' in the literature. A file is read, updated, deleted from and inserted into one record at a time, while in contrast, the same operations in SQL are performed on a set and happen all at once.

How Embedded SQL Operates

These problems are solved with embedded SQL. The idea of embedded SQL is fairly simple: special SQL statements are inserted into the host program with the keywords **EXEC SQL** in front of them. A **pre-compiler** reads the mixed language program and converts all such SQL statements into appropriate host language procedure calls. This intermediate program is then ready to go to the host language compiler so that it can be compiled in the usual manner.

The host language database calls are low-level routines which operate directly on the SQL engine. These routines are part of what is called an API (Application Program Interface) library and are very specific to each SQL product and host language.

If the application programmer knew what the procedure calls were, he could write the program himself with these library routines. This isn't as easy as it sounds, however. The parameters are often complex and the results can be very hard to read. An embedded SQL program is much easier to read and thus to maintain. When a SQL product is upgraded, a program using the API may not be able to take advantage of changes without being re-written. If the vendor changes the pre-compiler, an embedded program may automatically get new features if it's recompiled.

Regardless of how it happens, you will finally have an executable host language program which can get data from an SQL database. The user has to connect the program to the database. Each product will have a different way of doing this, but they all involve identifying the database by name and the user by a password.

There will be a work area in the host program which passes data and messages between the host program and the SQL database. Some SQL statements, such as a **DELETE FROM**, will only send messages into the work area, whilst others will send data as well. The data which is sent back and forth is automatically converted into the appropriate host and SQL datatypes. In practice, there's really not that much data conversion done since the SQL implementation and the host language exist on the same platform, they very often use the same hardware features for numerics and character strings with few differences.

These work areas are the first thing we need to look at.

SQLDA

The **SQLDA** is another pre-defined structure called the 'SQL Descriptor Area', which holds parameters for the connection between the database and the host program. The SQL descriptor area is allocated and maintained by the system with the following statements:

```
<allocate descriptor statement>

<deallocate descriptor statement>
```

```
<set descriptor statement>

<get descriptor statement>
```

This isn't something that the programmer usually worries about, so we'll skip over it and tell you to read your manual.

SQLCA

The **SQLCA** is a pre-defined data structure called the 'SQL Communications Area', which passes messages from the database to the host. The most important parts of this structure for the programmer are the **SQLSTATE** and **SQLCODE**. The **SQLCODE** is an integer which returns a code for the results of the last action against the database. The **SQLSTATE** is new in SQL-92 and will replace the old **SQLCODE**.

SQLSTATE is a five character field which also returns a code for the results of the last action against the database. The first two characters are the general class of the message and the last three give the details. Vendors are allowed to add to the basic encoding scheme to provide even more details.

Declarations

The area where data passes one row at a time between the host and the SQL database is defined with a collection of host language variable declarations blocked off with the pre-compiler phases **EXEC SQL BEGIN DECLARE SECTION** and **EXEC SQL END DECLARE SECTION**.

If the SQL variable is **NULL**able, then it also needs an **INDICATOR** variable associated with it. An **INDICATOR** is an integer used as a flag to signal the host program when a **NULL** has been read. References to the host variables in the SQL statements always begin with a colon in front of their name.

There is also an **<embedded exception declaration>** statement which specifies the action to be taken when an exception is raised by by the last SQL statement executed. The syntax is:

```
WHENEVER <condition> <condition action>

<condition> ::= SQLERROR | NOT FOUND
```

```
<condition action> ::= CONTINUE | <go to>

<go to> ::= { GOTO | GO TO } <goto target>
```

SQLERROR is True whenever any error code is raised by the last SQL statement executed. The **NOT FOUND** condition is raised when no rows were returned by the last SQL statement executed.

The **<condition action>** clause instructs the program to either **CONTINUE** and proceed with the normal order of execution, or to jump to another part of the program where the **<goto target>** is a host language label.

If you need more control over the embedded SQL, then you can use the **SQLSTATE** just as you would any other host language variable and take any action you wish. If anything went wrong during the transfer, errors are reported back in a character field called the **SQLSTATE**. This will replace the older numeric field, **SQLCODE**, specified in the SQL-86 standard. Right now, you'll often see both of these in products so as to maintain compatibility with older programs.

SQLSTATE is a standardized set of warning and error messages in which the first two characters define the class and the last three characters define the subclass of the error. The author refers to this as the 'Dewey Decimal system of Data Disaster', but this is just a personal tick, not a technical term.

Vendors can add to the standard to provide messages that are particular to their product. The more important classes are the following:

Code	Description
00	Successful completion, which has only subclass 000
01	Warnings which aren't fatal to the operation
02	No data returned
08	Connection exception
0A	Feature unsupported
21	Cardinality violation
22	Data exception
2A	Syntax error
40	Transaction rollback

The old **SQLCODE** for successful completion was **0**, for a non-fatal warning it was **100**, and all errors were negative numbers defined by the vendors. This is why the **SQLSTATE** uses strings that can be easily converted into those numbers for success and warning codes. Beginners to SQL programming often try to get a **'00000'** **SQLSTATE** and they're happy. More experienced SQL programmers learn to use the information that comes back in the **'01xxx'** and **'22xxx'** **SQLSTATE** codes in their programs.

Using the principle of working in sets, SQL can return more than one **SQLSTATE** by putting them into a host language diagnostics area. For example, on a really bad day, a programmer might try to divide by zero in a table for which he doesn't have authorization, and then compound the error by making a syntax error during the process. How many messages this area can hold is up to the vendor (as is the point at which the engine stops looking for errors).

CURSORs

Structures, called **CURSORS**, will convert the result sets from SQL queries into records that can be passed one at a time through the work area. **CURSORS** behave much like simple sequential files in the host language. You open and close cursors like a file. You can read rows as you would records with the **FETCH** statement. And if it's an updatable cursor, you can write via the cursor to the underlying base table. SQL-92 also has provisions for navigating rows the way that you would with a random access file. They can act like pointers insofar as they're moved through a set of rows, where the program gets to access each row individually.

The DECLARE CURSOR Statement

The syntax for the **<declare cursor>** is rather complex and looks like this:

```
DECLARE <cursor name> [ INSENSITIVE ] [ SCROLL ]
CURSOR FOR <cursor specification>

<cursor specification> ::=
    <query expression> [ <order by clause> ]
        [ <updatability clause> ]
```

```
<updatability clause> ::=
    FOR { READ ONLY | UPDATE [ OF <column name list> ] }

<order by clause> ::=
    ORDER BY <sort specification list>

<sort specification list> ::=
    <sort specification> [ { <comma> <sort specification> }... ]

<sort specification> ::=
    <sort key> [ <collate clause > ] [ <ordering
specification> ]

<sort key> ::=
    <column name> | <unsigned integer>

<ordering specification> ::=
    ASC | DESC
```

This is the full SQL-92 specification which many vendors haven't yet implemented, although Microsoft SQL Server 6.0 is one major exception. The cursor works by executing the query inside it to get the rows of the result set. The **ORDER BY** clause will sort those rows on the given columns in ascending **(ASC)** or descending **(DESC)** order. If no **ORDER BY** clause is given, then you can't depend on any order in the result set.

If the query was on only one table and included a set of key columns for that table, then the cursor is assumed to have an implicit **FOR UPDATE** clause. These are the same rules SQL uses for updatable views. We will talk about special versions of the **UPDATE** and **DELETE** statements for updatable cursors a little later, but for now we'll just say that it means that you can use the cursor to update the underlying base table because every row in the cursor is associated with exactly one corresponding row in the underlying base table.

If the cursor isn't updatable, then there's an implicit **READ ONLY** clause on the cursor. When a cursor is **READ ONLY**, then you can also have **INSENSITIVE**, **SCROLL**, or **ORDER BY** clauses.

The **INSENSITIVE** option specifies that the cursor is either **READ ONLY** or that we're treating it that way. The operations of **UPDATE** and **DELETE** aren't allowed for **READ ONLY** cursors.

The **SCROLL** option allows the cursor to move from row to row under program control. Normally, a cursor can only be read one row at a time in a forward direction, like a deck of punch cards (lucky readers under the age of 40 who have never seen a deck of punch cards are asked to consult their computer history books).

The OPEN CURSOR Statement

The syntax of this is simply **OPEN <cursor name>** and we assume that the cursor is closed when we open it, otherwise we'll get an unwanted error message.

While we've been telling you that the cursor is like a file, this isn't strictly accurate as not all file systems behave in the same way.

Some SQL products materialize the results of the query when they execute the **DECLARE CURSOR** statement and some only materialize the results when they execute the first fetch statement - not when they open the cursor. This means that some errors can't be detected when the **OPEN** statement is executed.

When the cursor is opened, it's positioned before the first row of the result set. At this point, the cursor isn't positioned on a row, so you'll get an invalid cursor state message.

The FETCH Statement

Here is the syntax for the **FETCH** statement:

```
FETCH [ [ <fetch orientation> ] FROM ]
    <cursor name> INTO <fetch target list>

<fetch orientation> ::=  NEXT | PRIOR | FIRST | LAST
    | { ABSOLUTE | RELATIVE } <simple value specification>

<fetch target list> ::= <target specification>
    [ { <comma> <target specification>}... ]
```

If the **<fetch orientation>** is omitted, then **NEXT** is implicit; that means that you can read one row at a time in a forward direction, like a punch card reader. If the cursor was declared to be scrollable, then you can position the cursor on the **NEXT, PRIOR, FIRST** or **LAST** row. The **ABSOLUTE** option positions the cursor on a particular row, identified by its position number. The **RELATIVE** option lets you move forward or backward a number of positions from your current row. A positive integer means read forward, while a negative integer means read backwards.

It's possible for the **FETCH** statement with a **NEXT, ABSOLUTE** or **RELATIVE** option, to position the cursor after the last row of the result set. Likewise, a fetch with a **PRIOR, ABSOLUTE** or **RELATIVE** that jumps back before the first row will position the cursor before the first row. In both cases, the cursor isn't positioned on a row, so you'll get an invalid cursor state message.

Entry-level SQL-92 **<fetch statement>**s don't have **<fetch orientation>** options. Most products don't have this either although again Microsoft SQL Server 6.0 is an exception, but you can expect it to become much more popular in the near future.

The CLOSE CURSOR Statement

The **<close statement>** syntax is simply:

```
CLOSE <cursor name>
```

and this assumes that the cursor was in the open state when you closed it. This statement also destroys the **<cursor specification>**, so you can reuse the cursor name if you wish.

The Single Row SELECT Statement

The single row **SELECT** statement is a handy shorthand which will load one row into the host program without having the overhead of setting up a cursor, opening it and doing a **FETCH**. It has the following syntax:

```
SELECT [ <set quantifier> ] <select list>
INTO <select target list>
<table expression>

<select target list> ::=
<target specification> [ { <comma> <target specification> }... ]
```

If the cardinality of the query result set is greater than one, then you'll get a cardinality violation error. It's implementation dependent whether or not data values are assigned to the targets identified by the `<select target list>`.

If the query is empty, then no data values are assigned to any targets identified by the `<select target list>`, and a completion condition of no data is raised. Otherwise values in the row of the query are assigned to their corresponding targets.

Update and Delete by Position on Updatable Cursors

The following statements only work on updatable cursors. The restrictions are obvious - the cursor cannot be **READ ONLY**, or positioned either before the first row or after the last row.

The Positioned DELETE Statement

The positioned **DELETE** statement has the following syntax:

```
DELETE FROM <table name>
WHERE CURRENT OF <cursor name>
```

The row in the base table from which the current row of the cursor is derived is marked for deletion. If another operation also marks the same row for deletion, then you'll receive a warning that you have a possible cursor operation conflict. All rows that are marked for deletion are effectively deleted at the end of the statement and prior to any integrity constraint checking.

If the positioned **DELETE** statement deleted the last row of the cursor, then the position of the cursor is situated after the last row; otherwise, the position of the cursor is prior to the next row in the result set.

The Positioned UPDATE Statement

The positioned **UPDATE** statement will update a single row of a table. The syntax for this is as follows:

```
UPDATE <table name>
    SET <set clause list>
    WHERE CURRENT OF <cursor name>

<set clause list> ::=  <set clause>
    [ { <comma> <set clause> }... ]

<set clause> ::=  <object column>
    <equals operator> <update source>

<update source> ::= <value expression> | <NULL
    specification> | DEFAULT

<object column> ::= <column name>
```

The cursor remains positioned on its current row, even if an exception condition is raised during the derivation of any **<value expression>** associated with the object row. However, there are rules to keep you from using the cursor to subvert the integrity of the database.

If the cursor is an ordered cursor, then you're not allowed to directly or indirectly change the ordering columns. This means that you cannot update the columns in the **ORDER BY** clause.

The **<value expression>**s are effectively evaluated before updating the object row. If a **<value expression>** contains a reference to a column of the underlying table, then the reference is to the value of that column in the row before any value of the row is updated.

A **<value expression>** in a **SET** clause can't directly contain an aggregate function. The reasons for this restriction are a little hard to explain, but they have a great deal to do with possible self-referencing problems.

An Example of C-Embedded SQL

We've now considered how SQL can return error codes and how it can use **CURSORS** to handle the transfer of results sets, in a manner similar to the method that the host language would use sequential files. However, we haven't considered any examples of how SQL is called up within a host language program.

Rather than give a separate example after each part of the syntax, we've included them all in one C program. It doesn't matter if you don't understand C or if you don't understand the program given here, as it's not meant to be compiled. This is simply to demonstrate how SQL is called throughout an example program in a host langauge. Throughout the program we've highlighted the **EXEC SQL** calls in gray. These are the bits that the pre-compiler would need to translate into equivalent host language calls.

It's possible that you won't be able to run the following program since pre-compilers tend to deviate from the standard and offer distinctly alternative versions of the statements we've outlined. If you did wish to compile it you would need to run the pre-compiler on the program first. You would also need to gain a pre-compilation version of the program which would then be able to be compiled.

You'll find that the program is fully commented throughout:

```
/*
 * This is an incomplete example. Its sole purpose is to
 * show some uses of Embedded SQL in a C language program.
 * This program retrieves order info, and, optionally order
 * item info and displays it on the screen.
 *
 *
 */
#include <stdio.h>
#include <stdlib.h>
#include <string.h>

/* #include any header files specific to your product !%!% */

#define FAILURE 1
#define SUCCESS 0
```

```
/*     Function prototypes    */
long   getLong(char *prompt);
int    getStr(char *prompt, char *dest, int lim);
void   printError(void);

/* define the communication region */
EXEC SQL INCLUDE SQLCA;

int main()
{
    /* declare host variables referenced in Embedded SQL */
    EXEC SQL BEGIN DECLARE SECTION;

        long int wk_orderid;

        /* Order data */
        long   order_id;
        long   order_empl;
        long   order_cust;
        char   order_date[11];

        /* Misc descriptive data */
        char   cust_name[31];
        char   empl_name[16];
        char   part_desc[11];

        /* OrderItems data */
        long   item_orderid;
        long   item_detail;
        long   item_partid;
        long   item_qty;


    EXEC SQL END DECLARE SECTION;

    /* other variables used by program */
    int i;
    int ix;
    int result = 0;

    char action[2];
    char response;

    /* set error handler to bail out if we can't connect */
    EXEC SQL WHENEVER SQLERROR
        {
        printError();
        return FAILURE;
        };

    /*    Connect to the database */
    EXEC SQL CONNECT USER "dba" IDENTIFIED BY "sql";
```

```
    /* declare a cursor to search the order items */
    EXEC SQL DECLARE details_cursor CURSOR
        FOR SELECT orderid, detail, partid, qty
            FROM OrderItems
            WHERE orderid = :order_id
            ORDER BY detail
        FOR READ-ONLY;

    /*   Ask for an order number */
while ((wk_orderid = getLong("Order Number or <cr> to exit")) != -1L)
    {

    /*
    *  On SQL Error or Not Found, set error result
    *  and break out of loop
    */
    EXEC SQL WHENEVER SQLERROR
        {
        result = FAILURE;
        printError();
        break;
        };

    EXEC SQL WHENEVER NOTFOUND
        {
        printError();
        break;
        };

    EXEC SQL SELECT orderid, custid, empid, salesdate
            INTO :order_id, :order_cust, :order_empl,
                 :order_date
            FROM Orders
            WHERE orderid = :wk_orderid;

    EXEC SQL SELECT cname
            INTO :cust_name
            FROM Customers
            WHERE custid = :order_cust;

    EXEC SQL SELECT cname, ename
            INTO :cust_name, :empl_name
            FROM Customers, Salespersons
            WHERE custid = :order_cust
              AND empid = :order_empl;

    printf(
        "Order    Customer                    Sold by      Date\n");
    printf("%5ld %-30s %-15s %s\n",
        order_id, cust_name, empl_name, order_date);

    printf("\nDo you want to list Order Items? ");
```

```
        getStr("action [Yes, No, Quit]", action, 1);

        response = toupper(action[0]);
        while (response == 'Y')
            {

            EXEC SQL OPEN details_cursor;

            printf("Order Item  Part   Desc    Qty\n");
            /* set up to leave print loop when no more rows */
            EXEC SQL WHENEVER NOTFOUND
            {
             goto finish;
            };
            /*  prime the print loop */
            EXEC SQL FETCH details_cursor
                        INTO :item_orderid, :item_detail,
                             :item_partid, :item_qty;


            for (;;) /* Loop for ever; NOTFOUND terminates */
                {
                EXEC SQL SELECT description INTO :part_desc
                          FROM Inventory
                          WHERE partid = :item_partid;

                printf("%5ld %4ld %5ld %-10s %3ld\n",
                    item_orderid, item_detail, item_partid,
                    part_desc, item_qty);
                EXEC SQL FETCH details_cursor
                            INTO :item_orderid, :item_detail,
                                 :item_partid, :item_qty;

                }
finish:

            EXEC SQL CLOSE details_cursor;
            }

        if (response == 'Q')
            break;

    }


    EXEC SQL DISCONNECT;

    return SUCCESS;
}

/*
```

```
 *   getLong(char *prompt)
 *
 *      Prompts user to enter a string.
 *      Returns result of converting that input with atol().
 *      Returns -1L if no user input.
 */
long getLong(char *prompt)
{
    long r = -1L;
    char s[17];

    if (getStr(prompt, s, 16))
        r = atol(s);

    return r;
}


/*
 *   getStr(char *prompt, char *dest, int lim)
 *
 *      Prompts the user to enter a string.
 *      Copies up to <lim> characters into <dest>
 *      Returns number of characters input.
 */
int getStr(char *prompt, char *dest, int lim)
{
    static char workarea[512];
    int l = 0;

    if (*prompt)
        printf("Please enter %s: ", prompt);

    if (gets(workarea))
        {
        l = lim < strlen(workarea) ? lim : strlen(workarea);
        strncpy(dest, workarea, l);
        }

    dest[l] = '\0';

    return strlen(dest);
}

/*
 *   printError()
 *
 *      function to
 *      print a description of any SQL errors that bite us.
 */
void printError()
{
```

```
    static char buffer[200];

    /* here invoke product specific method of placing    !%!%
       error message in buffer */
    printf("SQL error -- %s\n", buffer)
       sqlerror_message( &sqlca, buffer, sizeof( buffer ) )
);
}
/*---< end >---*/
```

Summary

We've looked at the method SQL uses for passing data between the host language and the database. We looked briefly at the actual concept of embedded SQL, before moving on to how SQL uses the SQLCA structure to hold information about the completion status of embedded SQL statements. From the codes returned the user can deduce whether a statement was successful or not.

We also looked at **CURSORS** which are used to pass information back and forth between the database and the host language. We then looked at the different statements for controlling such **CURSORS**, including the **FETCH** statement which enables information to be passed, one row at a time. Finally we integrated all of the concepts into a C program with embedded SQL. Even if you aren't familiar with C, this should have given you an idea of how embedded SQL works in practise.

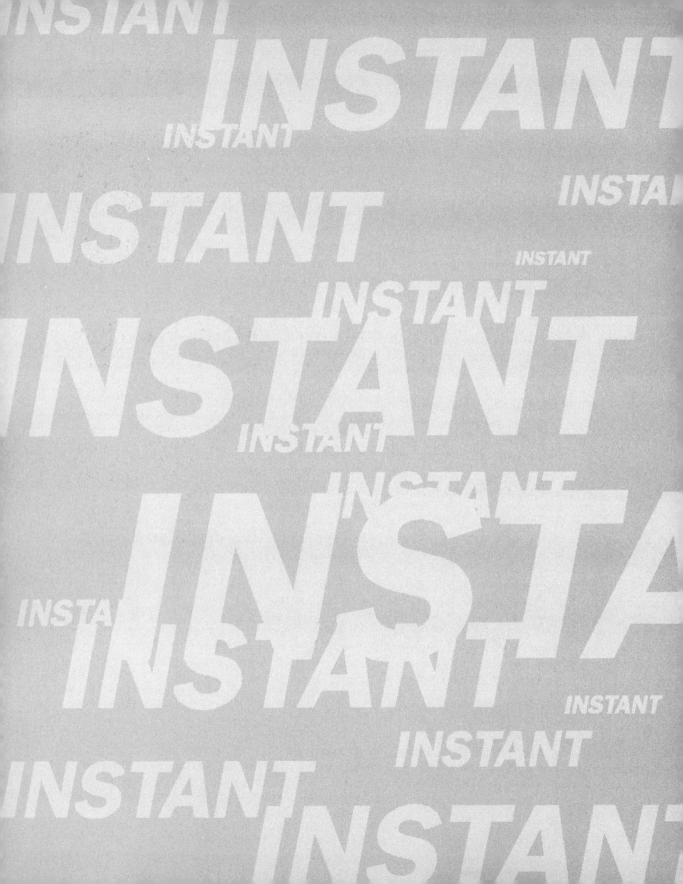

Optimization and Performance Tips

So far, we've only been concerned with the syntax of SQL and how to query the database via the Interactive SQL tool. Behind this tool, every time you query the database, the SQL database engine is put to work. We give you a very quick spin of the main features of the engine and how it works when given a query to carry out. We will then take a look at how the engine can use indexes to speed up access to the database. We consider two popular methods for doing this: the binary tree and hashing.

Finally, we focus on slightly different ways to enhance performance, mainly by improving the method by which you write SQL. We outline a method to create complex queries from simple English-like pseudo-code.

In this chapter we will be look at the following:

 The workings of the database engine

 Database access methods

Some hints on writing queries

The SQL Database Engine

A **database engine** is the actual program that acts on a database. There is no set way to write a SQL database engine. The standard only describes results which a conforming product must produce without covering the methods used to obtain them. However, in most products, there are some common high-level features and tools. Most SQL database engines include:

 Tools for manipulating the database schema

 Tools for compiling SQL statements

 Tools for developing efficient execution plans for the SQL code

Database Schemas

A set of table declarations (and other objects) make up a **database schema** (or just a **schema** for short). By analogy, this is a house without any furniture. A database is a schema with data in it; the house with furniture added.

A database engine can work with several different databases. The user has to connect the engine to the correct database before he or she can actually do anything. This usually involves a password or some other log-on procedure.

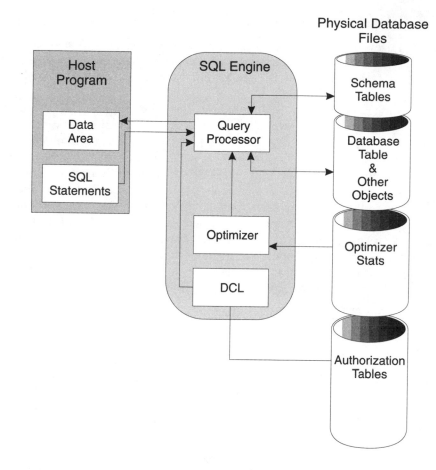

The engine is the traffic cop who will handle problems with multiple users trying to get to the same data at the same time. It checks and enforces privileges and rule violations, using the schema as its law book.

The Optimizer

The **optimizer** is the bit that figures out what sequence of **SELECT**s, **PROJECT**s, **JOIN**s and set operations will answer the request most efficiently. The actual techniques used by optimizers vary from DBMS to DBMS.

The optimizer includes an SQL compiler. Like the compilers you use for any procedural language, this compiler produces an executable program. But it differs in that parsing an SQL statement produces an **execution plan** instead of machine code. This execution plan is a description of how the query will be run against the database. The execution plan is built from the SQL statement using the optimizer which looks at table statistics, available indexes, and other things which may help it to find the best approach to the problem in hand. If indexes are added or dropped, if tables change size, or indeed, if any number of other things happen, then the same SQL statement can produce a completely different execution plan. This is a big difference from a procedural language which uses files. The procedural language program doesn't change upon being re-compiled just because its files have changed.

Queries

A request for data from a SQL database is usually called a **query** rather than a search. The reason why the word search is avoided is that it sounds too procedural, as though you were moving about in the woods looking for things. Querying is more appropriate as it sounds non-procedural: ask a question, and your loyal servant brings back the answer.

The SQL engine uses special tables which describe the schema in SQL. These tables are queried by the engine to check privileges, to get table and column names, to get information for the optimizer, the size of columns and any other required data. They're usually given distinctive names which begin with a prefix, such as '**sys-**' or '**SQL-**' and they're always kept away from users via the DCL (Data Control Language). You don't want anything but the SQL engine to change these tables!

The Information_schema Tables

The SQL-92 standard defines a version of these tables in some detail and refers to them as the **information_schema** tables. No vendor, though, has implemented it, nor are they very likely to do so. Each vendor will have different algorithms for doing things, which will require different data. You can usually find a description of the **information_schema** tables for your product in the database administrator documentation. On the bright side, you will probably also find a set of useful queries already written to extract helpful data from these tables.

Database Access Methods

You've probably realized by now that it's not really practical to implement SQL table operations by actually reading all the rows in all the tables involved, or constructing all the possible combinations of rows in the working tables of a query.

You want to work with the smallest number of rows required to answer a query, or to perform an insertion, update or deletion because physical access time is the slowest part of any computer system. The more work you can do in the central processor, the faster the system will run.

The two most common access methods used in SQL implementations are **indexing** and **hashing**. A SQL program never references an index or a hash table except to create or to drop it. The optimizer in the SQL engine decides how to use them and creates what is called an execution plan for the statement. Should an access structure be changed or dropped, then the execution plan has to be re-compiled, but the original statement doesn't.

When a row is inserted, deleted or updated, the SQL engine will also handle the changes in the data structures that hold these access methods. Older file systems didn't have this feature and the programmers had to write code to keep the indexes and their files synchronized.

Indexing a Table

Think of an old fashioned magnetic tape drive, moving a tape from reel to reel. This is an example of sequential file access; to get to a particular record in the file, the system has to physically read all of the records in front of it and check them until it finds the record that you requested.

When we finally got random access storage (that means disk drives), we could make a physical jump directly by moving a read-write head to the desired position and waiting for the disk to rotate underneath it. Similarly, the SQL engine can find the desired record without reading through all of the preceding records.

An **index** is a way to take search values and locate the records that go with those values. If you have an unabridged dictionary, then there is a good chance it has a thumb index cut into the sides of the pages. Rather than looking up a word by turning a page at a time, you can stick your thumb in a notch and flip to the start of the right section, bypassing all the unwanted sections.

Indexes are called 'primary' indexes if they are used to guarantee that a value is unique within a column as well as to speed up searching, and 'secondary' if they're only used to speed up searching on non-unique column values.

Keys and Indexes

There is a strong relationship between keys in SQL and indexes in SQL implementations, but they aren't the same. The SQL standard doesn't specify the use of indexes because the ANSI X3H2 Database Standards Committee felt that this was too vendor dependent and too physical to be part of a language standard. The standard uses keywords attached to the table declarations to specify keys and uniqueness, and lets the implementation decide how to handle physical access.

Index Defining

Defining indexes is usually a job reserved for the DBA. An index that benefits one job can hurt others, so the decision has to be made on a global level.

An Example of Indexing

How the indexes are built varies from one SQL implementation to another, but to give you an idea of how they work, let's assume that we're going to put an index on the `empid` column in the `Salespersons` table.

While vendors use different indexing methods, the X/Open consortium has specified syntax for **CREATE INDEX** and **DROP INDEX** statements, and their specification is currently the most common format in use. It looks roughly like this:

```
CREATE [UNIQUE] INDEX <index name>
    ON <table name> (<column name> { ASC | DESC }, ...);
```

and

```
DROP INDEX <index name>;
```

Almost every product has a **UNIQUE** option, since that's how SQL products were built before the standard insured primary keys. In SQL-92, a declaration of a primary key constraint on a table will often be implemented with an index which has a system generated name.

Another common extension is a sort order **(ASC, DESC)** option which will impose an ordering system on the index. This option lets the database engine know that when it uses the index, it will fetch rows in the specified order.

Clustered Indexes

Clustered indexes keep the table itself in sorted order. This is expensive to update and maintain, but knowing the ordering of the rows lets the database engine improve its strategy for planning sequential searches and joins.

Other Index Options

Other options in indexes might involve ignoring or not ignoring the case of letters, the physical storage method, the physical storage location, the indexing method and any number of other things. Some products have indexing structures which pre-define **JOIN**s between tables. This is the time to read your manual and perhaps take a vendor training course. These options can have *serious* effects on performance.

Binary Tree Indexing

Let's now do a greatly simplified example of an index using a binary tree approach. Each node in the tree has an **empid** value and a physical disk address of either another node or a record in a database. The SQL Engine will compare the target **empid** to the value in the first (or root) node. If the target value is less than the index records **empid**, then the SQL engine follows one pointer, otherwise it follows the other. It repeats this process until it either finds the desired record or finds that it doesn't exist in the table.

In a real index the system would probably use multi-way trees instead, but the principles still hold. The binary tree would look like this:

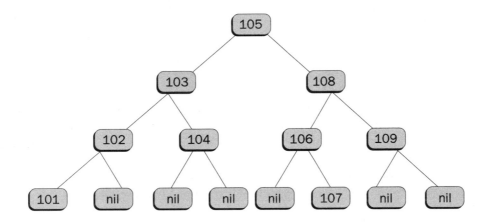

If we wanted to find the row for employee number 107, we would start at the top of the tree, then go to the right node, then the left node, and then finally to left again to arrive at a leaf node which would also have the physical address of the row **(107, 'Gloria Garcia', 3, $3,000.00)** in the **Salespersons** table.

If the SQL engine looks at all the possible paths, then the average number of nodes visited to find a particular record is 4.22 reads - remember that the SQL engine needs to read the table once after doing any index reads. If it were to read the rows one at a time from the **Salesperson**s table, it would take an average of 4.5 reads to find a single row.

If this were a real database indexing scheme, the tables would be much bigger and the savings in read time would be exaggerated, but the you can see the point, even in this toy example.

Indexing Techniques

What if we wanted to compute the total salary of all the employees? A sequential file read (or table scan to use SQL terminology) of all the rows will use a total of 9 reads. If we used the index to read all the rows, then it would take 38 reads - 29 in the index plus 9 reads in the **Salesperson**s table. One of the things the query optimizer needs to do is to decide when to use an index and when not to.

On the other hand, if the SQL engine wants to find the **MAX (empid)** or **MIN (empid)** functions, all the SQL engine has to do is look to the right or left side of the tree. Without the index, the SQL engine would have to read all 9 rows to be sure that the right value was found.

Indexes also give a boost to the **EXISTS** predicate. For example, if the SQL engine wants to find if a row with an **(empid > 105)** exists in the table, then all the SQL engine has to do is look to the right side of the tree, see a node with a value of 108, and never read the table at all. Without the index, the SQL engine would have to read rows in the table until it found one that met the criteria.

In the case of the **NOT EXISTS** predicate and no index, the engine would have to read all the rows to be sure. With an index, the tree is searched until it leads to a nil node (a node that has no branches) or a probe that goes outside the bounds of the tree.

> **NOT EXISTS** is a very expensive predicate, so it is best to try and avoid using it. The **EXISTS** predicate on the other hand is very fast and ideal for usage in a hashed index.

Hashing

Hashing takes the search value and passes it to a formula called the hashing function. The result of the hashing function is used as the subscript into a matrix of the physical locations of the rows.

Writing a good hashing function is a complicated mathematical task, but for our example let's just use a simple one - **Hash(empid) = empid MOD 3**. This would give us three 'buckets' - a term for the location of different search values with the same hash function result. Duplicate hash function results are called 'hash clash' and somehow have to be handled. One solution is to use a series of hashing functions until an unused location is found in the address matrix. Other methods use pointer chains or contiguous locations in the address matrix. Take the following:

```
Hash = 0     Hash = 1     Hash = 2
========     ========     ========
   102          103          101
   105          106          104
   108          109          107
```

To find the row with **(empid = 107)** apply the hashing function to the search value **(107 MOD 3 = 2)**, then read the corresponding bucket to locate the desired row. A sequential search of a bucket in this case would average 2.5 reads - remember you always have one read into the **Salesperson**s table.

This toy example is a little misleading in that you'll notice that hashing was faster on average than indexing and you might think that this is the general case. There are trade-offs however. Hashing is usually very fast for unique values, because you'll have a lot of very small buckets if you have a good hashing function. But if there are a lot of duplicate values, then the buckets can become very large, be slower to search than a sequential file and contain many unwanted rows. A clustered index would do a better job of finding all the duplicate values, since all the duplicates would be located together physically on the disk.

The hashing function will hardly ever use all the values in its address matrix, so you're trading increased storage for access speed. Furthermore, when rows are added or dropped from the table, the table should be re-hashed to minimize hash clashing. This takes more time than re-organizing an index.

The tips that we have offered so far are based generally on how you can improve the performance of the SQL engine, however another way to improve the time taken in queries is to improve the way that you actually write queries.

Hints on How to Write Queries

A lot of the trouble with a new programming language is not so much what you don't know as what you know that's not right. People tend to try to make the new programming language work like their old programming language. This isn't surprising since it also happens with natural languages too. When you first try to speak a foreign language, you use the new words, but with the word order and grammar of your first spoken language.

SQL has some general principles that will help you to write queries that will at least run, and as you get more experienced with the language, you can improve what you've done.

Let's use a moderately difficult problem and work it out in detail. The problem is basically to report the sum of the (n) largest orders placed by our customers.

Understanding the Question

This may sound absurdly simple, but failing to understand what is being asked for is the major source of problems. So let's start by explaining what the boss meant by 'the (n) largest orders' when he gave us that specification.

1 What if there are fewer than (n) orders - does he want the sum of the existing orders that we have? Probably, so let's make that a part of the problem specification.

2 When we're talking about the customers, do we mean the '(n) largest orders made by *each of* our customers *individually*' or do we mean the '(n) largest orders made by *all of* our customers *as a single group*' in this problem? Either way is quite reasonable, but let's assume that we mean each of our customers individually — one customer, one total.

3 However, if there were more than (n) orders, then one of our bosses said he wanted the sum the (n) largest amounts. That is, a customer who bought items for ($40, $40, $30, $20, $20, $10, $10, $10) would be reduced to the set of orders for ($40, $30, $20, $10) or a total of $100?

4 Another boss said that he wanted the sum the (n) largest orders. That means a customer who bought items for ($40, $30, $20, $20, $10, $10, $10) would be reduced to the set of orders for ($40, $40, $30, $20) or a total of $130?

5 Your solution is to keep both bosses happy by writing queries to do it both ways.

Once we've determined exactly what is wanted we can begin to write the query. However we won't start in SQL, we'll start with an English-like pseudo code, that hopefully is meaningful to you despite not being a legitimate programming language. We'll specify in very simple terms and expand each clause in turn:

```
SELECT <<data that the bosses want to know>>
FROM <<some tables>>
WHERE <<some conditions>>
GROUP BY <<some columns>>
HAVING <<some conditions>>;
```

Fill in the Select List First

This is usually pretty easy. We start with the customer identifier, **custid** and the total of the **top (n)** orders, which is all we want to know. In this case we know that the skeleton or pseudo code query will look like this:

```
SELECT custid, <<total of top (n) orders>> AS BigOnes
FROM <<some tables>>
WHERE <<some conditions>>
GROUP BY <<some columns>>
HAVING <<some conditions>>;
```

Imagine that it is the best of all possible worlds. Pretend that the SQL we're using has a library of functions, **f()**, which answer any of the tricky stuff we want to compute. The pseudo code query is just going to call those functions in the **SELECT** list with expressions of the form `<<function call>> AS <<name>>`. They're just a place holder for now. I can figure out that I have to do something with the customer, whom I identify by their **custid**, the price of the product and their quantity to compute the total of each order by customer.

```
SELECT custid, f(custid, orderid, price, qty) AS BigOnes
FROM <<some tables>>
WHERE <<some conditions>>
GROUP BY <<some columns>>
HAVING <<some conditions>>;
```

Put Table Names in the From Clause

Look at the schema and see which tables have the columns that you'll need to construct the **SELECT** clause list. You will probably get more tables than you need the first time. In this case, we can look at:

 Customers, for the customer id and name

 Inventory, for the prices

OrderItems, for the quantities

Orders, for the customer id

The only one we don't need in this problem is the **Employees** table, but in a larger database the number of tables excluded would typically be much higher than those included. The pseudo code query looks like this:

```
SELECT custid, f(custid, orderid, price, qty) AS
BigOnes
FROM Customers AS C0, Orders AS O0,
     OrderItems AS OI0, Inventory AS I0
WHERE <<some conditions>>
GROUP BY <<some columns>>
HAVING <<some conditions>>;
```

We could also put correlation names which end in zero on the tables at this point, more to save writing longer names than anything else. If some of the known result columns come from only one table, then attach the correlation names to those columns.

Joining Tables Together

Get the schema again and look at how the tables will have to be joined together. At this point, you can either do the joins in the **FROM** clause with the SQL-92 syntax or you can use the **WHERE** clause. Since the **WHERE** clause will work in both SQL-89 and SQL-92 products, lets use it.

The **OrderItems** table has the **qty** column and the Inventory table has the **price**. We know that **(qty * price)** is something that we have to calculate to get the totals we're after, so let's figure out how to join those two tables.

In the real world, most joins are usually an equi join performed on columns with a common name representing the same attribute. The common column here is **partid**. Put the join and formula in the pseudo code query like this:

```
SELECT custid,
       f(custid, orderid, (I0.price * OI0.qty)) AS BigOnes
FROM Customers AS C0, Orders AS O0,
     OrderItems AS OI0, Inventory AS I0
WHERE I0.partid = OI0.partid
AND/OR <<some conditions>>
GROUP BY <<some columns>>
HAVING <<some group conditions>>;
```

We need to gather these price extensions by order numbers so that we can get the totals. Using the same logic as before, we can see that the common column for a join is the **orderid**. Let's do that join as follows:

```
SELECT custid,
       f(custid, orderid, (I0.price * OI0.qty)) AS BigOnes
FROM Customers AS C0, Orders AS O0,
     OrderItems AS OI0, Inventory AS I0
WHERE I0.partid = OI0.partid
AND OI0.orderid = O0.orderid
AND/OR <<some conditions>>
GROUP BY <<some columns>>
HAVING <<some group conditions>>;
```

But look, we don't need the **Customers** table since we already have the **custid** in the **Orders** table; remove it and add correlation names to the columns we have thus far:

```
SELECT OO.custid,
       f(OO.custid, OO.orderid, (IO.price * OIO.qty)) AS
       BigOnes
FROM Orders AS OO, OrderItems AS OIO, Inventory AS IO
WHERE IO.partid = OIO.partid
AND OIO.orderid = OO.orderid
AND/OR <<some conditions>>
GROUP BY <<some columns>>
HAVING <<some group conditions>>;
```

Group the Table

Since we're asking for totals by customer, we know that somehow we have to come up with a **GROUP BY** clause based on customers and that we will have a **SUM()** function somewhere in the query. Add that to the pseudo code query:

```
SELECT OO.custid,
       f(OO.custid, OO.orderid, SUM(IO.price * OIO.qty)) AS
       BigOnes
FROM Orders AS OO, OrderItems AS OIO, Inventory AS IO
WHERE IO.partid = OIO.partid
AND OIO.orderid = OO.orderid
GROUP BY OO.custid
HAVING <<some group conditions>>;
```

The real question is do we also need to add **orderid** to the grouping columns. The answer is "No", but this isn't so obvious to a new SQL programmer. The orders are within the customers which is a hierarchy and the **GROUP BY** clause cannot deal with a hierarchy.

Design the Having Clause

Since we're looking for the top (n) orders for each customer, we have a vague feeling that the pseudo code query ought to have a **HAVING** clause with **MAX(<<something to do with totals>>)** or **COUNT(<<something to do with totals>>) <= (n)** in it. But now we're stuck. We know that somewhere we'll have to find a maximum of a sum and we know that we cannot nest aggregate functions in SQL.

Back Up and Decompose the Problem into Simpler Parts

Let's solve a simpler part of the problem and see if that helps. What if we could find the sum of **ordertotal** for each order:

```
SELECT OI0.orderid,
       SUM(I0.price * OI0.qty) AS ordertotal
  FROM OrderItems AS OI0, Inventory AS I0
 WHERE I0.partid = OI0.partid
 GROUP BY OI0.orderid;
```

We could put this in a **VIEW** and then use the **VIEW** in another query. That's often a handy trick, especially in situations where the same **VIEW** might be used by a lot of different queries. In fact, if you're using a SQL-89 implementation, you'll find that you almost have to use **VIEW**s for this sort of problem. However in SQL-92, we can treat this query as a subquery expression and use it directly.

Put the Simpler Parts Together

Let's go back to the original pseudo code query and plug in the subquery we've just developed. We need to tie in the customer data, so we can add the **Orders** table to get what we need:

```
SELECT O0.custid, O0.orderid,
       SUM(I0.price * OI0.qty) AS ordertotal
  FROM Orders AS O0, OrderItems AS OI0, Inventory AS I0
 WHERE I0.partid = OI0.partid
   AND OI0.orderid = O0.orderid
 GROUP BY O0.custid, O0.orderid;
```

The **GROUP BY** clause could be replaced with a scalar subquery expression that has an outside reference to the **orderid**, so the pseudo code query becomes:

```
SELECT O0.custid, O0.orderid,
       (SELECT SUM(I0.price * OI0.qty)
          FROM OrderItems AS OI0, Inventory AS I0
         WHERE I0.partid = OI0.partid
           AND OI0.orderid = O0.orderid) AS ordertotal
```

```
    FROM Orders AS OO, OrderItems AS OIO, Inventory AS IO
 WHERE IO.partid = OIO.partid
    AND OIO.orderid = OO.orderid;
```

But when we look at the **FROM** clause, we can see that we don't actually need the **OrderItems** or **Inventory** tables in it. And if we don't include the **OrderItems** or **Inventory** tables in the **FROM** clause, we cannot use them in the **WHERE** clause. The query now becomes:

```
SELECT OO.custid, OO.orderid,
       (SELECT SUM(IO.price * OIO.qty)
          FROM OrderItems AS OIO, Inventory AS IO
         WHERE IO.partid = OIO.partid
           AND OO.orderid = OIO.orderid) AS ordertotal
  FROM Orders AS OO;
```

Which query should we use? There are almost always several ways to write a query that will achieve the same results. The answer is that this depends on your SQL product. Some the queries won't work on some implementations. One version might perform well on one implementation and not so well on another.

We mention the scalar subquery as an option because it is new to SQL-92 (although some systems such as Sybase have already implemented this feature) and if the rules for computing that column were really tricky, then it could be a handy trick. But in this example we're doing simple extensions and totals, so let's assume that the **GROUP BY** version is the best choice.

But this query doesn't yet answer the original question about the top (n) orders per customer. We could stop here and then use a procedural program to sort and pull off the top (n) orders from each customer. But we don't want to do that - we're going to put the query into a **VIEW**, so that we can use it for other things too:

```
CREATE VIEW OrderSummary(custid, orderid, ordertotal)
AS
SELECT OO.custid, OO.orderid,
       SUM(IO.price * OIO.qty) AS ordertotal
  FROM Orders AS OO, OrderItems AS OIO, Inventory AS IO
 WHERE IO.partid = OIO.partid
   AND OIO.orderid = OO.orderid
 GROUP BY OO.custid, OO.orderid;
```

305

We also have another option - we could create a temporary table, (for those using the Watcom SQL engine provided, this temporary table has already been created):

```
CREATE GLOBAL TEMPORARY TABLE OrderSummary
(custid INTEGER NOT NULL,
 orderid INTEGER NOT NULL,
 ordertotal DECIMAL(12,2) NOT NULL,
 PRIMARY KEY (custid, orderid));

INSERT INTO OrderSummary
SELECT OO.custid, OO.orderid, SUM(IO.price * OIO.qty)
  FROM Orders AS OO, OrderItems AS OIO, Inventory AS IO
WHERE IO.partid = OIO.partid
   AND OIO.orderid = OO.orderid
GROUP BY OO.custid, OO.orderid;
```

The trade off for this is that the user will have to insert all the rows from the query into the temporary table himself. The engine will check its **PRIMARY KEY** constraint and any other constraint that might be added to the table. However, once the table is loaded, the SQL engine can use any indexes on that table for optimization.

Repeat the Process Iteratively and Recursively

Now that we have a **VIEW** with all the order summary information that we need, we can get on with the original problem of finding the top (n) orders for each customer.

Repeating our steps and pseudo code query, we can make an attempt at a query again. To find the total of all the orders for each customer, we could write the following query:

```
SELECT custid, SUM(ordertotal) AS total
  FROM OrderSummary
GROUP BY custid;
```

Maybe the answer is a modified version of this grouped query? What we need is a way to remove the lower priced orders from consideration before we do the summation. We could do that in a **WHERE** clause. Another hint is that when you have to extract a subset of a table, this usually implies a self-join. Now our pseudo code query looks like this:

```
SELECT custid, SUM(ordertotal) AS total
 FROM OrderSummary AS S0, OrderSummary AS S1
 WHERE <<f(S0, S1)>>
 GROUP BY custid;
```

Some of the characteristics of the top (n) items in a list without duplicates is that there are (n) of them. This implies that there is a highest value in the subset. We can build the subsets using **ordertotal** and one copy of the **OrderSummary** table to provide the highest element in each subset constructed from the other copy of the **OrderSummary** table. That's easier to see than to say:

```
SELECT S0.custid, SUM(S0.ordertotal) AS total
  FROM OrderSummary AS S0, OrderSummary AS S1
 WHERE S0.ordertotal >= S1.ordertotal
 GROUP BY S0.custid;
```

Since we're looking for subsets with (n) or fewer elements in them, this sounds like a job for a **HAVING** clause. To check this we need a test value for n, so we will use 3 from now on:

```
SELECT S0.custid, SUM(S0.ordertotal) AS total
  FROM OrderSummary AS S0, OrderSummary AS S1
 WHERE S0.ordertotal >= S1.ordertotal
 GROUP BY S0.custid
 HAVING COUNT(*) <= 3;
```

We still need to do one more step though:

Test and Repair Your Query

Let's keep (n = 3) and run it. Oops, there are problems here. When we get to customer #3, they only have two orders ($253.50 and $818.15), which totals to $1,071.65, but we're showing $1,889.80 as the answer. With a little math, we realize that we're getting (($818.15) + ($253.50 + $818.15)) which is the total of the running totals.

One way around this would be to get rid of the repeated values by making the **SUM()** into a **SUM(DISTINCT)** function, like this:

```
SELECT S0.custid, SUM(DISTINCT S0.ordertotal) AS total
  FROM OrderSummary AS S0, OrderSummary AS S1
WHERE S0.ordertotal >= S1.ordertotal
  AND S0.custid = S1.custid
GROUP BY S0.custid
HAVING COUNT(*) <= 3;
```

But this query will handle the case where a customer has separate orders
for identical amounts by reducing them to one purchase. That is probably
not what the boss wanted. How do we tell one order from another in the
database? By it's **orderid** of course! We're missing an important part of the
answer. In SQL-92, we could write

```
(S0.ordertotal, S0.orderid) >= (S1.ordertotal, S1.orderid) to
```

connect the total and id for an order together, but in SQL-89, we have to
break it apart:

```
SELECT S0.custid, SUM(S0.ordertotal) AS total
  FROM OrderSummary AS S0, OrderSummary AS S1
WHERE S0.ordertotal >= S1.ordertotal
  AND S0.orderid >= S1.orderid
  AND S0.custid = S1.custid
GROUP BY S0.custid, S1.orderid
HAVING COUNT(S0.orderid) <= 3;
```

Notice that we have to put the **S1.orderid** in the **GROUP BY** list to avoid
the repeated total problem.

Now we're getting a set of 1 to (n) rows which represent the largest single
order, the largest two orders, and so forth. But the code is getting to be a
bit of a mess. We can just put it in another **VIEW** which we can use for
other reports. This is also a chance to generalize the query by moving the
COUNT(S0.orderid) into the **SELECT** list, like thus:

```
CREATE VIEW TopN (custid, total, n)
  AS
  SELECT S0.custid, SUM(S0.ordertotal), COUNT(S0.orderid)
    FROM OrderSummary AS S0, OrderSummary AS S1
  WHERE S0.ordertotal >= S1.ordertotal
    AND S0.orderid >= S1.orderid
    AND S0.custid = S1.custid
GROUP BY S0.custid, S1.orderid;
```

Now the query can finally be written as:

```
SELECT custid, MAX(total)
  FROM TopN
 WHERE n <= 3
 GROUP BY custid;
```

Now if the boss wants to change (n) to another value, or just look at customers who placed exactly (n) orders or some other query based on running totals, we can appropriately change this little query.

Bag of Tricks

Obviously, this query was solved in a way that shows off as many SQL programming tricks as possible in one example. Let's make a list of those tricks and give a rule of thumb for each one:

1 Look for ways to join the tables that have the attributes you need for the query. Always consider more than one way and more than one table.

2 Don't use any more tables than you have to.

3 You can hide levels of aggregate functions in **VIEW**s.

4 Be careful with joins as they can be expensive. Make sure that the **WHERE** clause limits the selection sets as much as possible.

5 You can use temporary tables like **VIEW**s, but you are trading the time it takes to insert rows into them with extra storage space for indexing and constraints. The rule of thumb would be to do this when you need to create an index on columns that don't exist in the original tables (function calls and expressions), or you need to add constraints that don't exist in the original tables.

6 When you have to extract a subset of a table, you normally use a self-join. The self-join will use one copy of the table to pick a boundary value that partitions the other copy of the table into the desired subsets.

7 Test your query as you go along. Look for problems with empty tables, duplicate rows and NULLs.

8 You can build **VIEW**s with other **VIEW**s to hide complexity and to "fake" nesting aggregate functions. Try to write **VIEW**s which are understandable and useful in their own right so they can be reused in other queries.

Summary

We've looked at the different aspects of SQL that affect the performance and access times. The SQL engine takes a query and uses the optimizer to decide which set of SQL commands will answer the query most efficiently. It then produces an execution plan of how the query will run against the database. Next we considered two indexing methods which can be used by the optimizer to improve database access. Both binary trees and hashing are common methods used for storing data within many computer languages and we looked at how SQL implements these features. Finally we outlined a system for constructing complex queries from simple pseudo-code and we followed an example, building it up step-by-step.

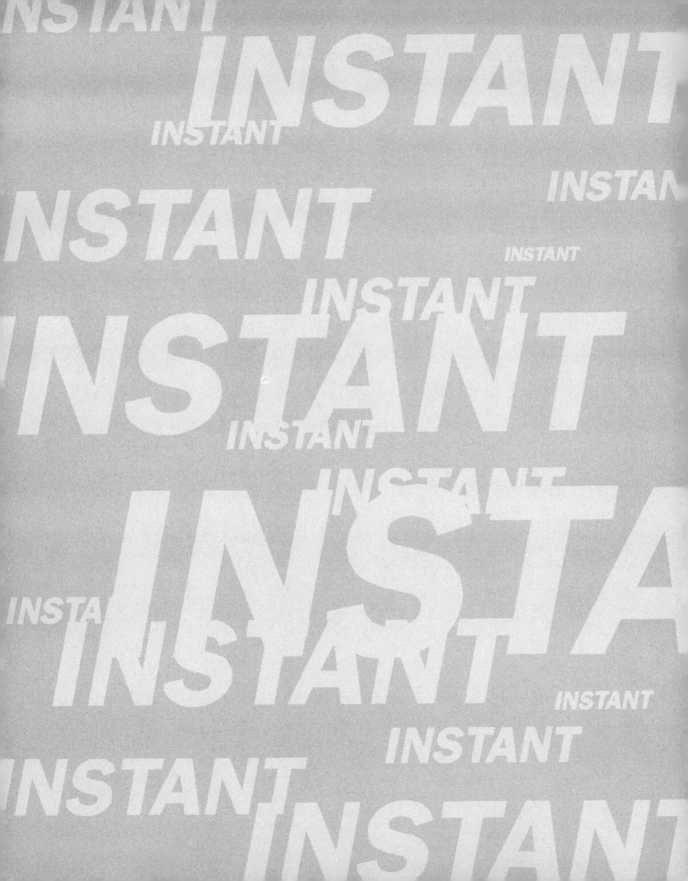

Where Do We Go From Here?

You may or may not have had opinions on or ideas about the SQL language before you read this book, but we're sure that you've found this tour an enlightening, informative and eye-opening experience. Not only have we tried to remove the excess stuffy baggage that traditionally drags programming material down, but we've also attempted to pack everything you need to know into a compact, cost-effective reference guide.

There's no doubt that SQL is the industry-standard database interrogation language, and there are several ways that you can progress from here. You can go deeper into the theory of database design, but this won't just mean planning what you're going to do beforehand. It will also involve you in an exploration of the methodologies essential to advanced database creation. Our title, Instant Database Design, due for publication in early 1996, will offer a radical new perspective on a traditionally hackneyed field, and it's an ideal companion-book should you take this route. However, if you wish to know more about SQL, Joe Celko writes regularly for a spread of specialist magazines and we've listed these in the front of this book - you'll find his columns stimulating reading. Finally, if you feel comfortable with the runtime version of Watcom SQL 4.0, then contact Watcom and buy yourself a copy of the registered edition of the language.

Now that you've had a taste of our refreshing style, would you like to know more about Wrox Press and our other publications? If you do, then why don't you ask for our latest catalog or check out our Web page. And remember, when you're down at your local bookstore, look out for our distinctive red binding - your guarantee of Wrox value.

Are you interested in writing or reviewing any of our future books? We warmly welcome any willing contributors that can help Wrox to publish *even* better books. If you're interested then contact us right away - see the details at the back of this book.

If you have any general comments about our books you can contact us via the reply card also at the back of this book, or get in touch with us by any of the following means:

Snail mail	Wrox Press Ltd, Unit 16, 20 James Road, Birmingham, B11 2BA, United Kingdom.
Electronic mail (e-mail)	feedback@wrox.com
World Wide Web	http://www.wrox.com
CompuServe	100063,2152
Telephone	(44121) 706 6826
Facsimile	(44121) 706 2967

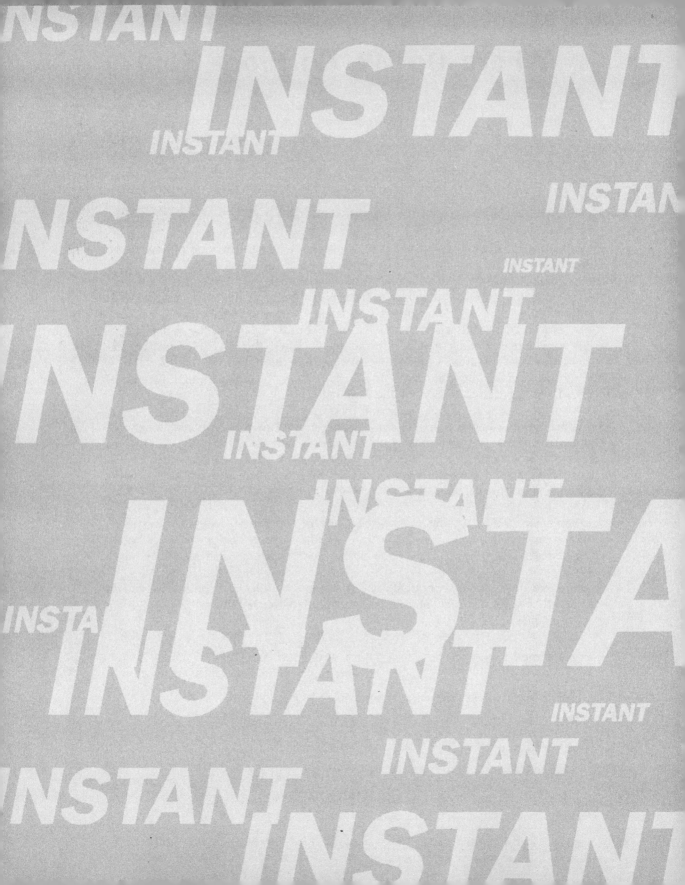

Conversion Notes for Different Vendor SQLs

In this appendix you'll only find the code describing the structure for the example database. The other examples should work just as you find them in the book, but if they don't, consult the implementation notes after the relevant code.

While there are often several declarations of a table in each chapter, each stage showing a progression, we'll only give you the final version of that table from that chapter. If the table has been defined in a previous chapter and there haven't been any amendments, then that table is also excluded from these notes.

Finally, the data for the example database isn't contained within this appendix - it can be found within Appendix B. This is because the one set of code can be run under all three vendor implementations, without any alterations.

Oracle

The code contained in the book is very similar to Oracle SQLPLUS, but there are a few differences to be chronicled.

Chapter 2 : Table Creation

The **Salespersons**, **Inventory**, **Customers** and **Orders** table definitions are as follows:

```
CREATE TABLE Salespersons
 (empid INTEGER NOT NULL PRIMARY KEY,
  ename CHAR(15) NOT NULL,
  rank INTEGER DEFAULT 1 NOT NULL
      CHECK (rank IN (1,2,3)),
  salary DECIMAL(7, 2)
      DEFAULT 1000.00 NOT NULL
       CHECK (salary >= 1000.00));

CREATE TABLE Inventory
  (partid INTEGER NOT NULL PRIMARY KEY,
  description CHAR(10) NOT NULL,
  stockqty INTEGER NOT NULL,
  reorderpnt INTEGER,
  price DECIMAL(5, 2) NOT NULL);

CREATE TABLE Customers
 (custid INTEGER NOT NULL PRIMARY KEY,
  cname CHAR(15) NOT NULL,
  credit CHAR(1) NOT NULL
    CHECK (credit IN ('A', 'B', 'C')));

CREATE TABLE Orders
 (orderid INTEGER NOT NULL PRIMARY KEY,
  empid INTEGER NOT NULL REFERENCES Salespersons(empid),
  custid INTEGER NOT NULL REFERENCES Customers(custid),
  salesdate DATE DEFAULT SYSDATE NOT NULL ,
  item1 INTEGER REFERENCES Inventory(partid),
  qty1 INTEGER,
  item2 INTEGER REFERENCES Inventory(partid),
  qty2 INTEGER,
  item3 INTEGER REFERENCES Inventory(partid),
  qty3 INTEGER,
  item4 INTEGER REFERENCES Inventory(partid),
  qty4 INTEGER,
  item5 INTEGER REFERENCES Inventory(partid),
  qty5 INTEGER);
```

Chapter 2 : General Implementation Notes

1 In Oracle the **DEFAULT** declaration must always appear before **NOT NULL**.

2 Instead of the **CURRENT DATE**, Oracle utilizes the data type **SYS DATE**.

3 Oracle requires that each clause is completed with a comma and each query or structure terminated with a semi-colon.

Chapter 3 : General Implementation Notes

1 In Oracle the **CONVERT()** function is equivalent to **CAST()**.

2 Oracle has no **COUNTER()** function.

3 In Oracle there are two variations on the **ROUND(x,p)** function, one as described in the text, and the other is used for dates taking the **ROUND(date,'format')** format.

4 **TRUNCATE** has a completely different function to the one outlined in Chapter 3. **TRUNCATE** removes all rows from a table. The equivalent function in Oracle is **TRUNC**, which like **ROUND** has two variations, one for numbers **TRUNC(x,p)** and one for dates **TRUNC(date,'format')**.

5 The **SUBSTRING** function is **SUBSTR(<string>,<start>,<count>)** in Oracle.

6 Instead of just having a single **TRIM** specification, Oracle has **LTRIM** and **RTRIM**.

7 The **INSTR** function in Oracle replaces the **POSITION** function.

8 Oracle has its own complete set of conversion functions for converting from one data type to another. A small selection are as follows :

> **TO_CHAR()** converts a number to act as a character
>
> **TO_DATE()** converts a number or character to act as a date
>
> **TO_NUMBER()** converts a character to act as a number

Chapter 4 : Code Details

Following the rules of normalization, the previous **Orders** table is split into two definitions; the **Orders** Table:

```
CREATE TABLE Orders
(orderid INTEGER NOT NULL PRIMARY KEY,
 empid INTEGER NOT NULL REFERENCES Salespersons(empid),
 custid INTEGER NOT NULL REFERENCES Customers(custid),
 salesdate DATE DEFAULT SYSDATE NOT NULL);
```

and the **OrderItems** table:

```
CREATE TABLE OrderItems
(orderid INTEGER NOT NULL REFERENCES Orders(orderid),
 detail INTEGER NOT NULL,
 partid INTEGER NOT NULL REFERENCES Inventory(partid),
 qty INTEGER NOT NULL,
 PRIMARY KEY (orderid, detail));
```

The redefinition of the **Salespersons** table including table constraints rather than column constraints is as follows:

```
CREATE TABLE Salespersons
(empid INTEGER NOT NULL PRIMARY KEY,
 ename CHAR(15) NOT NULL,
 rank INTEGER DEFAULT 1 NOT NULL ,
 salary DECIMAL(7,2) DEFAULT 1000.00 NOT NULL,
 CONSTRAINT pay_too_low CHECK (salary >= 1000.00),
 CONSTRAINT invalid_rank CHECK (rank IN (1,2,3)));
```

The redefinition of the **Orders** table, to preserve referential integrity is:

```
CREATE TABLE Orders
(orderid INTEGER NOT NULL PRIMARY KEY,
 empid INTEGER DEFAULT 0 NOT NULL,
 custid INTEGER NOT NULL,
 salesdate DATE DEFAULT SYSDATE NOT NULL,
 CONSTRAINT seller
   FOREIGN KEY (empid) REFERENCES Salespersons(empid),
 CONSTRAINT buyer
   FOREIGN KEY (custid) REFERENCES Customers(custid)
 ON DELETE CASCADE);
```

The redefinition of the **OrderItems** Table, also to preserve referential integrity would be:

```
CREATE TABLE OrderItems
(orderid INTEGER NOT NULL,
 detail INTEGER NOT NULL,
 partid INTEGER NOT NULL,
 qty INTEGER NOT NULL,
 PRIMARY KEY (orderid, detail),
```

```
CONSTRAINT right_order
  FOREIGN KEY (orderid) REFERENCES Orders(orderid)
ON DELETE CASCADE,
CONSTRAINT right_part
  FOREIGN KEY (partid) REFERENCES Inventory(partid)
ON DELETE CASCADE);
EXIT
```

Chapter 4 : General Implementation Notes

1 In Oracle the foreign key declaration must always be surrounded by these parentheses.

2 There are no declarative Oracle equivalents of the **ON DELETE SET DEFAULT** and **ON UPDATE CASCADE**. Database triggers can be used to implement these.

3 **CONSTRAINT**s must always be followed by a **CONSTRAINT** name.

Chapter 6 : General Implementation Notes

1 The keyword **AS** isn't required for aliases. You can write an equivalent query without the **AS** statement as follows:

```
SELECT DISTINCT 'Blatz',a,b,(b*c) fred
FROM Foobar;
```

Chapter 7 : General Implementation Notes

1 The **CROSS JOIN** clause isn't supported in Oracle.

2 The **INNER JOIN** clause isn't supported in Oracle.

3 The **LEFT OUTER JOIN**, **RIGHT OUTER JOIN** and **FULL OUTER JOIN** clauses aren't supported in Oracle, but this is a variant of the **LEFT** and **RIGHT OUTER JOIN**s that are supported by Oracle. The SQL necessary for a **LEFT OUTER JOIN** would be:

```
SELECT *
FROM Foo,Bar
WHERE Foo.x=Bar.x(+);
```

The SQL necessary for a **RIGHT OUTER JOIN** would be:

```
SELECT *
FROM Foo,Bar
WHERE Foo.x(+)=Bar.x;
```

4 The '***=**' notation isn't supported in Oracle.

Chapter 8 : General Implementation Notes

1 There isn't a **CAST** function in Oracle - the function **TO_NUMBER** can be used instead. The example query would read:

```
SELECT rank, TO_NUMBER(salary/1000) thousands
FROM Salespersons
GROUP BY rank,thousands;
```

Chapter 9 : General Implementation Notes

1 Oracle's default date format is **dd-MON-yy**. If you don't use this format then the **TO_CHAR** function would have to be used with the date format.

2 Subqueries aren't supported when the subquery is in the field selection list. So a query such as the following one wouldn't be supported:

```
SELECT cname,  (SELECT MAX(orderid)
                FROM Orders as O1
                WHERE O1.custid-C1.custid)
FROM Customers as C1;
```

This also affects the query:

```
INSERT INTO OrderItems (orderid, detail, partid, qty)
  SELECT orderid,
       (SELECT MAX(detail) +1
         FROM OrderItems AS O1
       WHERE O1.orderid = P1.orderid)
       9999,
       1
   FROM Prizewinners AS P1
  WHERE orderid = P1.orderid;
```

This would have to be performed by defining a view for the subquery and joining it with the prizewinner's table.

Chapter 10 : General Implementation Notes

1 Subqueries aren't supported in the **FROM** clause under Oracle.

Sybase

Sybase is very similar to Microsoft SQL Server. These are the notes and code you should use if you wish to use the examples on the Microsoft SQL Server.

Initialization

Before you can enter any **CREATE TABLE** statements in Sybase, you have to create the database and make that database *current* (with the **USE** statement). This rather unpleasant looking piece of code will do the necessary groundwork for you:

```
/* device creation and database creation for Install SQL
   Wrox Press
   requires a privilege to run
   assumes only sa will use the database

*/
use master
go

if not exists (select * from sysdevices
          where name = 'data_device_2')
     begin
          disk init
              name = 'data_device_2',
                physname = 'c:\sql10\data\data2.dat',
                vdevno=4,
                size=5120
     end
go

if not exists(select * from sysdevices
          where name = 'log_device_2')
     begin
          disk init
              name = 'log_device_2',
                physname = 'c:\sql10\data\log2.dat',
                vdevno=5,
                size=1280
```

```
        end
go


if exists (select * from sysdatabases
        where name = 'telesales')
    begin
            drop database telesales
    end
go

print 'creating database telesales'
go

create database telesales on data_device_2=10
        log on log_device_2=2
go
sp_dboption telesales, trunc, true
go
sp_dboption telesales, "select", true
go
use telesales
go
checkpoint
go
use master
go
use master
go
dump tran telesales with no_log
quit
go
```

Chapter 2 : Code Details

The **Salespersons** table definition is as follows:

```
CREATE TABLE Salespersons
(empid INTEGER NOT NULL PRIMARY KEY,
ename CHAR(15) NOT NULL,
rank INTEGER DEFAULT 1 NOT NULL
    CHECK (rank in (1, 2, 3)),
salary DECIMAL(7, 2) DEFAULT 1000.00 NOT NULL
    CHECK (salary >= 1000.00)
)
go
```

The **Customers** table definition would be:

```
CREATE TABLE Customers
(custid INTEGER NOT NULL PRIMARY KEY,
 cname CHAR(15) NOT NULL,
 credit CHAR(1) NOT NULL CHECK (credit in ('A', 'B', 'C')))
go
```

The **Inventory** table definition would become:

```
CREATE TABLE Inventory
(partid INTEGER NOT NULL PRIMARY KEY,
 description CHAR(10) NOT NULL,
 stockqty INTEGER NOT NULL,
 reorderpnt INTEGER NULL,
 price DECIMAL(5, 2) NOT NULL)
go
```

And the **Orders** table definition:

```
CREATE TABLE Orders
(orderid INTEGER NOT NULL PRIMARY KEY,
 empid INTEGER NOT NULL REFERENCES Salespersons(empid),
 custid INTEGER NOT NULL REFERENCES Customers(custid),
 salesdate DATETIME DEFAULT getdate() NOT NULL ,
 item1 INTEGER NULL REFERENCES Inventory(partid),
 qty1 INTEGER NULL,
 item2 INTEGER NULL REFERENCES Inventory(partid),
 qty2 INTEGER NULL,
 item3 INTEGER NULL REFERENCES Inventory(partid),
 qty3 INTEGER NULL,
 item4 INTEGER NULL REFERENCES Inventory(partid),
 qty4 INTEGER NULL,
 item5 INTEGER NULL REFERENCES Inventory(partid),
 qty5 INTEGER NULL)
go
```

Chapter 2 : General Implementation Notes

1 The major difference between other SQLs and Sybase is that Sybase doesn't by default use the semi-colon. Special effort is required to make it accept it, and then it will only accept it in its command-line **isql** (interactive sql) product.

2 SQL Server requires that the **DEFAULT** clause precede the **NULL/NOT NULL** specification.

3 SQL Server has **Money** and **SmallMoney** datatypes that would normally be used for the salary column. In this example use **SmallMoney** (max of 214,xxx.xx). **CHECK, DEFAULT, PRIMARY KEY** and **DECIMAL** aren't available in Microsoft SQL Server V4.2 and below or in Sybase SQL Server V4.9.x and below.

4 In Sybase, the **Order** definition will fail if the **Inventory** table hasn't already been created.

5 Since Sybase doesn't have a **DATE** datatype, it has a combined **Datetime** datatype. **getdate()** is the Sybase function that returns the system date.

6 If nullity is omitted in Sybase, **NOT NULL** is assumed (a grievous deviation from the standard), so you must state **NULL** if you want to permit null values.

7 In Sybase, there's no distinction between **NUMERIC** and **DECIMAL** data types.

8 Sybase doesn't provide **DATE** or **TIME** datatypes, just **Datetime**. Its **timestamp** datatype has nothing to do with real-world time - it's an update counter used to manage optimistic concurrency control.

9 Sybase allows a built-in function as well as a literal (**getdate()** for instance). This is probably because the only system value it provides is **USER**!

10 Sybase doesn't support **DROP <column>**.

11 Sybase uses a **REPLACE DEFAULT** phrase instead of **SET DEFAULT**.

Chapter 3 : General Implementation Notes

1 In Sybase, the **CAST** function isn't available, so use **CONVERT** instead.

2 **x MOD y** should be **x%y** in Sybase

3 In Sybase the **COUNTER()** function is accomplished by declaring a column to have the identity attribute. There is a global variable, **@@identity**, which contains the last value assigned.

4 Sybase permits both double and single quotes to delimit strings. In Transact-SQL, there would be no difference between '**INTEGER**' and "**INTEGER**"; both are character string constants.

5 Sybase syntax for **SUBSTRING** is **SUBSTRING(<string>, <start>, <length>)**.

6 Instead of just having a single **TRIM** specification Sybase features **LTRIM** and **RTRIM**.

7 A Sybase timestamp isn't temporal but isn't necessarily a sequential number either.

8 Sybase has functions that return parts of the date (the day or month for instance) , together with the names of those parts (Monday or January for example).

9 In Sybase, there's no **COALESCE()** - the equivalent function is **ISNULL()**.

Chapter 4 : Code Details

Following the rules of normalization, the previous **Orders** table is split into two definitions; the **Orders** table:

```
CREATE TABLE Orders
 (orderid INTEGER NOT NULL PRIMARY KEY,
  empid INTEGER NOT NULL REFERENCES Salespersons(empid),
  custid INTEGER NOT NULL REFERENCES Customers(custid),
  salesdate DATETIME DEFAULT getdate() NOT NULL )
go
```

and the **OrderItems** table:

```
CREATE TABLE OrderItems
 (orderid INTEGER NOT NULL REFERENCES Orders(orderid),
  detail INTEGER NOT NULL,
  partid INTEGER NOT NULL REFERENCES Inventory(partid),
  qty INTEGER NOT NULL,
  PRIMARY KEY (orderid, detail))
go
```

The redefintion of the **Salespersons** table with table constraints rather than column constraints is:

```
CREATE TABLE Salespersons
(empid INTEGER NOT NULL PRIMARY KEY,
ename CHAR(15) NOT NULL,
rank INTEGER DEFAULT 1 NOT NULL,
salary DECIMAL(7, 2) DEFAULT 1000.00 NOT NULL,
    CONSTRAINT pay_too_low CHECK (salary >= 1000.00),
    CONSTRAINT invalid_rank CHECK (rank in (1, 2, 3))
)
go
```

The redefinition of the **Orders** table, to preserve referential integrity is:

```
CREATE TABLE Orders
(orderid INTEGER NOT NULL PRIMARY KEY,
 empid INTEGER NOT NULL,
 custid INTEGER NOT NULL,
 salesdate DATETIME DEFAULT getdate() NOT NULL,
 CONSTRAINT seller
     FOREIGN KEY (empid) REFERENCES Salespersons(empid),
 CONSTRAINT buyer
     FOREIGN KEY (custid) REFERENCES Customers(custid))
go
```

The redefinition of the **OrderItems** Table, to preserve referential integrity is as follows:

```
CREATE TABLE OrderItems
(orderid INTEGER NOT NULL,
 detail INTEGER NOT NULL,
 partid INTEGER NOT NULL,
 qty INTEGER NOT NULL,
 PRIMARY KEY (orderid, detail),
 CONSTRAINT right_order
     FOREIGN KEY (orderid) REFERENCES Orders(orderid),
 CONSTRAINT part_ok
     FOREIGN KEY (partid) REFERENCES Inventory(partid)
)
go
```

Chapter 4 : General Implementation Notes

1 Sybase would also allow you to have a named constraint at the column level:

```
.
.
rank INTEGER DEFAULT 1 NOT NULL
    CONSTRAINT invalid_rank CHECK (rank in (1, 2, 3)),
.
.
```

2 Sybase requires the foreign key columns to be enclosed in parentheses.

3 Sybase only supports the **RESTRICT** rule for referential integrity. It doesn't permit the specification of **ON UPDATE/DELETE RESTRICT** in the **CREATE TABLE** statement. The desired operations would need to be handled in a trigger. (See **Order Items** table).

4 Sybase requires a constraint name when you use the word **CONSTRAINT**.

Chapter 5 : General Implementation Notes

1 In Exercise 5, since the referential constraints only support **restrict**, the delete will fail. In the example, the default **empid** will be used.

Chapter 6 : General Implementation Notes

1 If **SELECT *** is used in a view, trigger or stored procedure, the column list won't change until the object is deleted and recompiled.

2 Unlike the result given in this book, for this example query:

```
SELECT DISTINCT 'Blatz', a, b, (b * c) AS fred
    FROM Foobar;
```

The Sybase result won't label the constant:

```
        a     b     fred
-----  ----  ----   ----
Blatz  4     41     NULL
Blatz  1     23     230
Blatz  2     17     187
Blatz  3     32     384
```

3 Sybase does string concatenation with the + sign (overloading the arithmetic operator).

4 In Sybase, you can enclose the % or _ character in square brackets in order to treated it as the literal character. The escape clause is also supported in the most recent version.

Chapter 7 : General Implementation Notes

1 Sybase doesn't support the **CROSS JOIN** clause or any of the other SQL-92 syntax mentioned within the chapter.

Chapter 9 : General Implementation Notes

1 Sybase doesn't require the keyword **AS** for aliases. The code can be rewritten without it in the following format:

```
SELECT orderid, custid
   FROM Orders  O1
  WHERE 2 < (SELECT qty
               FROM OrderItems  I1
              WHERE O1.orderid = I1.orderid
                AND I1.partid = 1007)
```

2 The following query in Sybase will give a different set of results to the ones shown in the book:

```
SELECT cname, (SELECT MAX(orderid)
                 FROM Orders AS O1
                WHERE O1.custid = C1.custid)
FROM Customers AS C1;
```

Sybase doesn't include the ones with **NULL** in its result set.

3 The following code works in Sybase to the point where we get a constraint violation because there's no part **9999** in **Inventory** :

```
INSERT INTO OrderItems (orderid, detail, partid, qty)
  SELECT orderid,
       (SELECT MAX(detail) + 1
          FROM OrderItems  O1
         WHERE O1.orderid = P1.orderid),
       9999,
       1
   FROM Prizewinners P1
```

Chapter 10 : General Implementation Notes

1 Sybase has a richer set of updatable views. For example, you can update any of the tables in a join, as long as you do it one table at a time.

2 Sybase doesn't support the `<drop behavior>` clause.

Chapter 12 : General Implementation Notes

1 Sybase automatically builds this index (in fact, the key constraint syntax includes all the physical index characteristics). An attempt to build another index will fail if both are declared as clustered. It will succeed if one is clustered and the other isn't, creating potential havoc in update performance!

Sybase deletes triggers for `Orders` and `Inventory` to enforce **DELETE CASCADE**:

```
create trigger Inventory_d_tr
  on Inventory for delete as
begin
  /* Save for audit fields
  */
  declare @TS datetime, @UI smallint
  select @TS = getdate()
  select @UI = suser_id()

  /* DELETE of Inventory ROW
  ** CASCADES to OrderItems(partid)
  */
  delete OrderItems
  from OrderItems, deleted
  where OrderItems.partid = deleted.partid

end
go
create trigger Orders_d_tr
  on Orders for delete as
begin
  /* Save for audit fields
  */
  declare @TS datetime, @UI smallint
  select @TS = getdate()
  select @UI = suser_id()

  /* DELETE of Orders ROW
  ** CASCADES to OrderItems(orderid)
  */
  delete OrderItems
```

```
   from OrderItems, deleted
   where OrderItems.orderid = deleted.orderid

end
go
```

Access

Before the advent of Access 2.0 there was no way to create and/or modify table definitions. With Access 2.0 Microsoft has given us two methods of creating and modifying tables; one method is the Data Access Object (DAO) whilst the other is Data Definition Language (DDL). It's important to note that the Access DDL isn't fully developed and you'll need to go elsewhere within Access to complete the job.

DDL queries can be created in one of two ways, using the SQL view of the QBE window or by defining and executing a QueryDef. Access SQL supports four basic DDL statements:

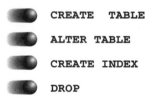

CREATE TABLE

ALTER TABLE

CREATE INDEX

DROP

and the **CONSTRAINT** clause for just the creation of indexes. Access SQL doesn't support the **NOT NULL** or **CHECK** contstraints, but may at a later date.

Before you can enter any **CREATE TABLE** statements in Access, you have to make the database available to you. The following code snippet will get you started:

```
Dim MyDatabase As Database
Dim ConnectString As String

ConnectString = "ODBC;UID=Fred;PWD=RHS;"

Set MyDatabase = DBEngine.Workspaces(0).Databases(0)
```

The following Access-SQL statements can be executed using Access Basic via DAO (Data Access Objects) or interactively using the Access QBE in SQL mode and typing SQL statements in the QBE then executing them as queries.

Chapter 2 : Code Details

The **Salespersons** table definition is as follows:

```
CREATE TABLE Salespersons
(empid INTEGER CONSTRAINT PrimaryKey PRIMARY KEY,
ename TEXT (15),
rank INTEGER,
salary CURRENCY);
```

The **Customers** table definition is:

```
CREATE TABLE Customers
(custid INTEGER CONSTRAINT PrimaryKey PRIMARY KEY,
cname TEXT (15),
credit TEXT (1));
```

The **Inventory** Table definition is:

```
CREATE TABLE Inventory
(partid INTEGER CONSTRAINT PrimaryKey PRIMARY KEY,
description TEXT (10),
stockqty INTEGER,
reorderpnt INTEGER,
price CURRENCY);
```

The **Orders** Table definition is:

```
CREATE TABLE Orders
(orderid INTEGER,
empid INTEGER CONSTRAINT tblSalespersonsFK REFERENCES Salespersons,
custid INTEGER CONSTRAINT tblCustomersFK REFERENCES Customers,
salesdate DATETIME,
partid INTEGER CONSTRAINT REFERENCES Inventory,
qty1 INTEGER,
CONSTRAINT PrimaryKey PRIMARY KEY (orderid, empid, custid);
```

Chapter 2 : General Implementation Notes

1 As you can see there are major differences between Access SQL and other SQLs. Access SQL has a limited support of the DDL requiring the use of other Access features to complete the creation of tables.

2 Access SQL doesn't support the **NOT NULL** or **CHECK** constraints.

Chapter 3 : General Implementation Notes

1 In Access SQL, the functions **CAST** or **CONVERT** aren't supported. However, Access Basic has a number of functions for converting to different data types.

2 Access allows both double and single quotes to delimit strings.

3 Access uses two functions to change the case of a string. **LCASE$** shifts all letters to lower-case and **UCASE$** turns all letters into upper-case letters.

4 For string manipulation Access uses several functions: **INSTR$**, **LEFT$**, **RIGHT$** and **MID$**.

5 The SQL function **SUBSTRING** isn't supported in Access.

6 Access uses **LTRIM** to remove leading blanks, **RTRIM** to remove trailing blanks and **TRIM** to remove both leading and trailing blanks.

7 **LEN** is used in Access to determine the length of a string. **INSTR** is used to return the position of a string within a string.

8 SQL functions **REVERSE** and **FLIP** aren't supported in Access.

9 Access doesn't support the **NULLIF** or **COALESCE** function of SQL-92. You can simulate the **NULLIF** function using the **ISNULL** and **IIF** functions in Access.

Chapter 4 : Code Details

Creating the **Orders** table is as follows:

```
CREATE TABLE Orders
(orderid INTEGER,
empid INTEGER CONSTRAINT tblSalespersonsFK REFERENCES Salespersons,
custid INTEGER CONSTRAINT tblCustomersFK REFERENCES Customers,
salesdate DATE,
CONSTRAINT PrimaryKey PRIMARY KEY (orderid));
```

Creating the `OrderItems` table is as follows:

```
CREATE TABLE OrderItems
(orderid INTEGER CONSTRAINT tblOrdersFK REFERENCES Orders,
detail INTEGER,
partid INTEGER CONSTRAINT tblInventoryFK REFERENCES Inventory,
qty INTEGER,
CONSTRAINT PrimaryKey PRIMARY KEY (orderid, detail));
```

Chapter 4 : General Implementation Notes

Access SQL doesn't support referential actions like **UPDATE**, **DELETE** or **CASCADE**. However by using features in Access Basic and the Relations Window, you can implement referential integrity by setting cascading update and delete options.

The **CONSTRAINT** clause in Access SQL doesn't support a way to create non-unique indexes within **CREATE TABLE** or **ALTER TABLE** statements. However, you can use the **CREATE INDEX** statement to create unique indexes.

Chapter 6 : General Implementation Notes

1 Since Access doesn't support **NOT NULL**, in Access-SQL the **ALTER TABLE** statement will look like this:

```
ALTER TABLE Salespersons ADD phone INTEGER;
```

2 Access-SQL doesn't support the "||" concatenator, to combine fields together using the "&" as follows:

```
SELECT ename & empid as combine FROM Salespersons;
```

or "+" as follows:

```
SELECT ename + empid as combine FROM Salespersons;
```

Even though you can use the "+" operator to concatenate two character strings, you should use the "&" operator for concatenation to eliminate ambiguity and provide self-documenting code.

3 Access-SQL doesn't support the SQL wildcard characters "_" or "%". Access does support "*" and "?" as wildcard characters.

4 Since Access-SQL doesn't support "%" as a wildcard character, the **SELECT** statement using the **LIKE** predicate should be written as:

```
SELECT * FROM Customers WHERE cname LIKE "Black*";
```

5 Access-SQL doesn't support the **IS TRUE** or **IS FALSE** predicates.

Chapter 7 : General Implementation Notes

1 Access supports both inner and outer joins. By default Access joins tables using an inner join. In addition Access supports both a left and right outer join.

2 Access-SQL doesn't support the **CROSS JOIN** syntax. However, the example can be written in Access-SQL using an **INNER JOIN** and the **ON** clause.

```
SELECT *
FROM Foo INNER JOIN Bar ON Foo.x = Bar.x;
```

3 Equi-joins can be simulated in Access-SQL by using an **INNER JOIN** with a **WHERE** clause. In most all cases it's the preferred case that you use the **INNER JOIN** with an **ON** clause instead of a **WHERE** clause:

```
SELECT *
FROM Foo INNER JOIN Bar
WHERE Foo.x = Bar.x;
```

4 Access-SQL will support a self-join, but it isn't a recommended procedure and should be used sparingly:

```
SELECT orders.custid, orders.orderid, orders_1.orderid
FROM Orders AS Orders, Orders AS Orders_1
WHERE orders.custid = orders_1.custid
AND Orders.salesdate = Orders_1.salesdate
AND Orders.orderid < Orders_1.orderid;
```

5 Access-SQL supports a slightly modified **OUTER JOIN** - the word **OUTER** isn't used when defining an **OUTER JOIN**. Access-SQL doesn't support a **FULL OUTER JOIN**. An example of a **LEFT OUTER JOIN** in Access-SQL would be:

```
SELECT *
FROM Foo
LEFT JOIN Bar On Foo.x = Bar.x;
```

An example of a **RIGHT OUTER JOIN** in Access-SQL would be:

```
SELECT *
From Foo
RIGHT JOIN Bar ON Foo.x = Bar.x;
```

6 Access-SQL doesn't support the "***=**" for creating an outer join.

Chapter 8 : General Implementation Notes

1 When implementing the **GROUP BY** clause in Access-SQL you have to perform some type of aggregating function on each field in the **SELECT** statement.

2 Access-SQL doesn't support the **CAST** function. The example **SELECT** statement can be written in Access-SQL as shown in the following statement:

```
SELECT rank, INT(salary/1000) as thousands
FROM Salespersons
GROUP BY rank, INT(salary/1000);
```

3 Access-SQL doesn't support the **DISTINCT** aggregrate function references. However Access-SQL is less restrictive than ANSI SQL in that Access allows for grouping on expressions and ANSI SQL doesn't.

Chapter 9 : General Implementation Notes

1 Access-SQL won't support queries containing an aggregate function such as **MAX()** in the **JOIN** statement. To create the example of a scalar subquery in Access-SQL without using an aggregate function within the **JOIN** statement, the code is as follows:

```
SELECT DISTINCTROW Orders.orderid, Orders.custid, Max(OrderItems.orderid)
AS MaxOforderid, OrderItems.salesdate
FROM Orders INNER JOIN OrderItems ON Orders.orderid = OrderItems.orderid
GROUP BY Orders.orderid, Orders.custid, OrderItems.salesdate
HAVING ((OrderItems.salesdate=#12/15/95#));
```

In this case the subquery would actually be the `OrderItems.salesdate`.

2 Access-SQL assumes the **ALL** predicate if you don't use the **DISTINCT**, **DISTINCTROW**, or **TOP** predicates when defining a **SELECT** statement.

Chapter 10 : General Implementation Notes

CREATE VIEW, **DROP VIEW**, and **CREATE SCHEMA** aren't supported in Access-SQL. You can use **SELECT** queries in place of **CREATE VIEW** for creating views of data for display, or if you want to create temporary tables to act as **VIEWS** then use a **SELECT** query with an **INTO** clause. An Access-SQL simulation of a **VIEW** may be created in two ways; for display only:

```
SELECT *
FROM Inventory
WHERE price > 10.00;
```

or if you want to create a temporary table that can be used in other queries:

```
SELECT  * INTO overten
FROM Inventory
WHERE price > 10.00;

SELECT partid, description, stockqty
FROM overten
WHERE price > $10.00
AND stockqty > 20;
```

This creates a temporary table called **AvgQtyPerOrder** to simulate a **VIEW**:

```
SELECT partid, AVG(qty) as avgqty INTO AvgQtyPerOrder
FROM OrderItems
GROUP BY partid;
```

By using the temporary table as a **VIEW** we can use it in another query to further refine the information needed:

```
SELECT I1.partid, C1.cname, SUM(I1.qty)
FROM Customers as C1, Orders as O1, OrderItems as I1
WHERE C1.custid = O1.orderid
AND I1.orderid = O1.orderid
GROUP BY I1.partid, C1.cname
HAVING SUM(I1.qty) > (SELECT avgqty
FROM AvgQtyPerORder as AQ1
WHERE FROM AQ1.partid = O1.partid);
```

Chapter 11 : General Implementation Notes

1 Access doesn't support the **GRANT** and **REVOKE** commands. To simulate these commands you would need to write code in Access Basic.

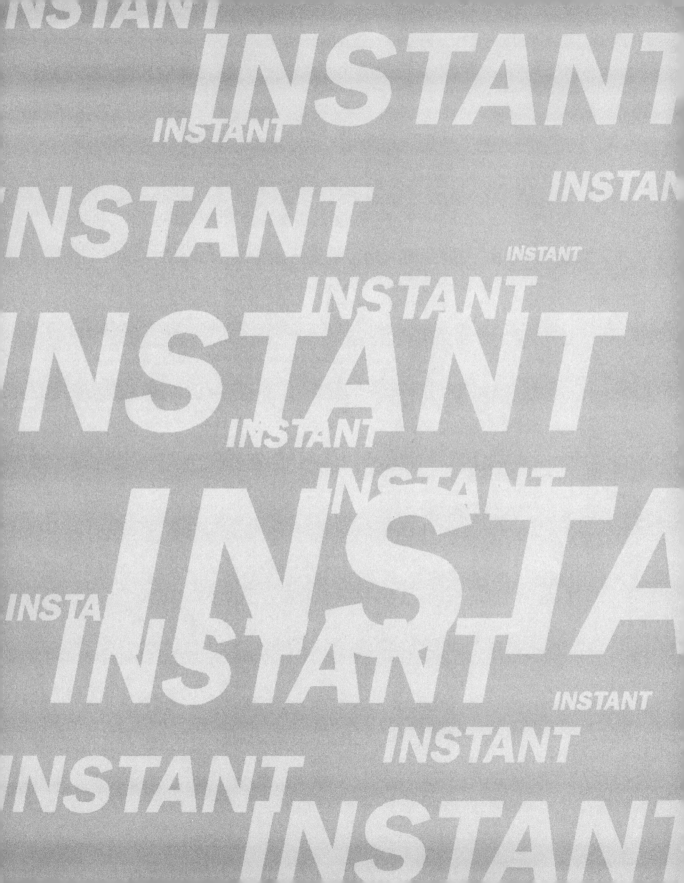

Appendix

Example Databases

How to Create the Example Database

The source code for the example database used in this book is available on the enclosed disk inside the back cover. You don't need it to run the exercises, but we will list it here to give you a rough idea of what size a small office database would be and also what it would look like. We have already discussed how to create the five tables so here is all the data for these tables.

> Note that the code represented here should work on most SQL implementations without any problems.

Inserting the Data

To insert the data into the tables you require the following code:

```
INSERT INTO Salespersons (empid, ename, rank, salary)
    VALUES (101, 'Andrew Allen', 1, 1000);
INSERT INTO Salespersons (empid, ename, rank, salary)
    VALUES (102, 'Burbank Burkett', 1, 1000);
INSERT INTO Salespersons (empid, ename, rank, salary)
    VALUES (103, 'Charles Cox', 2, 2000);
INSERT INTO Salespersons (empid, ename, rank, salary)
    VALUES (104, 'Dale Dahlman', 2, 2000);
INSERT INTO Salespersons (empid, ename, rank, salary)
    VALUES (105, 'Edward Everling', 2, 2200);
INSERT INTO Salespersons (empid, ename, rank, salary)
    VALUES (106, 'Faulkner Forest', 3, 2500);
INSERT INTO Salespersons (empid, ename, rank, salary)
    VALUES (107, 'Gloria Garcia', 3, 2500);
INSERT INTO Salespersons (empid, ename, rank, salary)
    VALUES (108, 'Harvey Harrison', 3, 3000);
INSERT INTO Salespersons (empid, ename, rank, salary)
    VALUES (109, 'Kevin Kody', 3, 3100);
```

```
INSERT INTO Customers (custid, cname, credit)
    VALUES (01, 'Stanwood Consulting', 'A');
INSERT INTO Customers (custid, cname, credit)
    VALUES (02, 'Vallecito Industries', 'B');
INSERT INTO Customers (custid, cname, credit)
    VALUES (03, 'Wellesley Inc.', 'C');
INSERT INTO Customers (custid, cname, credit)
    VALUES (04, 'White Court', 'A');
INSERT INTO Customers (custid, cname, credit)
    VALUES (10, 'Acton Computers', 'A');
INSERT INTO Customers (custid, cname, credit)
    VALUES (11, 'Agorist Distributors', 'B');
INSERT INTO Customers (custid, cname, credit)
    VALUES (12, 'Alexandria Liquor Co.', 'B');
INSERT INTO Customers (custid, cname, credit)
    VALUES (15, 'Blumenfeld Educational Corp.', 'B');
INSERT INTO Customers (custid, cname, credit)
    VALUES (16, 'Cardiff Industries', 'C');
INSERT INTO Customers (custid, cname, credit)
    VALUES (17, 'Del Toro Enterprises', 'C');
INSERT INTO Customers (custid, cname, credit)
    VALUES (18, 'DRT Marine Lab', 'A');
INSERT INTO Customers (custid, cname, credit)
    VALUES (20, 'Fredericks and Assoc.', 'A');
INSERT INTO Customers (custid, cname, credit)
    VALUES (21, 'Kalakaua Corporation', 'A');
INSERT INTO Customers (custid, cname, credit)
    VALUES (22, 'Ladera Enterprises', 'C');
```

```
INSERT INTO Customers (custid, cname, credit)
    VALUES (25, 'Mission Hills Inc.', 'B');
INSERT INTO Customers (custid, cname, credit)
    VALUES (26, 'Monterey University', 'B');
INSERT INTO Customers (custid, cname, credit)
    VALUES (27, 'Quinton College', 'B');
INSERT INTO Customers (custid, cname, credit)
    VALUES (28, 'Rensselaer & Co.', 'B');
INSERT INTO Customers (custid, cname, credit)
    VALUES (29, 'Ridgewood-Berkman Co.', 'B');
INSERT INTO Customers (custid, cname, credit)
    VALUES (30, 'South Burlingame Co.', 'A');
INSERT INTO Customers (custid, cname, credit)
    VALUES (33, 'Black Cat Stores', 'C');
INSERT INTO Customers (custid, cname, credit)
    VALUES (43, 'Berryville Supplies', 'C');
INSERT INTO Customers (custid, cname, credit)
    VALUES (53, 'Mentone Enterprises', 'C');
INSERT INTO Customers (custid, cname, credit)
    VALUES (79, 'Durell Equipment', 'A');
```

```
INSERT INTO Inventory (partid, description, stockqty, reorderpnt, price)
    VALUES (1001, 'doodad', 100, 20, 10.00);
INSERT INTO Inventory (partid, description, stockqty, reorderpnt, price)
    VALUES (1002, 'doohickey', 69, 25, 25.00);
INSERT INTO Inventory (partid, description, stockqty, reorderpnt, price)
    VALUES (1003, 'frammis', 23, 30, 2.50);
INSERT INTO Inventory (partid, description, stockqty, reorderpnt, price)
    VALUES (1004, 'gadget', 71, 20, 7.50);
INSERT INTO Inventory (partid, description, stockqty, reorderpnt, price)
    VALUES (1005, 'gimmick', 24, 10, 10.65);
INSERT INTO Inventory (partid, description, stockqty, reorderpnt, price)
    VALUES (1006, 'gizmo', 87, 30, 11.35);
INSERT INTO Inventory (partid, description, stockqty, reorderpnt, price)
    VALUES (1007, 'thingabob', 10, 30, 12.50);
INSERT INTO Inventory (partid, description, stockqty, reorderpnt, price)
    VALUES (1008, 'widget', 59, 10, 25.00);
INSERT INTO Inventory (partid, description, stockqty, reorderpnt, price)
    VALUES (1009, 'chachka', 95, 25, 70.00);
INSERT INTO Inventory (partid, description, stockqty, reorderpnt, price)
    VALUES (1010, 'thingie', 110, 25, 80.00);
```

The **Orders** table needs to use values from the **Salespersons** table and the **Customers** table. Likewise, the **OrderItems** table references the **Orders** and the **Inventory** tables. The order for insertion into both tables is as follows:

```
INSERT INTO Orders (orderid, empid, custid, salesdate)
    VALUES (6099, 101, 1, '1995-12-15');
INSERT INTO OrderItems (orderid, detail, partid, qty)
    VALUES (6099, 1, 1002, 3);
```

```
INSERT INTO OrderItems (orderid, detail, partid, qty)
    VALUES (6099, 2, 1003, 3);
INSERT INTO OrderItems (orderid, detail, partid, qty)
    VALUES (6099, 3, 1004, 3);
INSERT INTO OrderItems (orderid, detail, partid, qty)
    VALUES (6099, 4, 1009, 3);
INSERT INTO OrderItems (orderid, detail, partid, qty)
    VALUES (6099, 5, 1010, 1);


INSERT INTO Orders (orderid, empid, custid, salesdate)
    VALUES (6109, 102, 2, '1995-12-15');
INSERT INTO OrderItems (orderid, detail, partid, qty)
    VALUES (6109, 1, 1001, 1);
INSERT INTO OrderItems (orderid, detail, partid, qty)
    VALUES (6109, 2, 1007, 1);
INSERT INTO OrderItems (orderid, detail, partid, qty)
    VALUES (6109, 3, 1009, 1);
INSERT INTO OrderItems (orderid, detail, partid, qty)
    VALUES (6109, 4, 1010, 1);


INSERT INTO Orders (orderid, empid, custid, salesdate)
    VALUES (6128, 103, 3, '1995-12-15');
INSERT INTO OrderItems (orderid, detail, partid, qty)
    VALUES (6128, 1, 1004, 2);
INSERT INTO OrderItems (orderid, detail, partid, qty)
    VALUES (6128, 2, 1006, 10);
INSERT INTO OrderItems (orderid, detail, partid, qty)
    VALUES (6128, 3, 1007, 10);


INSERT INTO Orders (orderid, empid, custid, salesdate)
    VALUES (6129, 104, 3, '1995-12-15');
INSERT INTO OrderItems (orderid, detail, partid, qty)
    VALUES (6129, 1, 1004, 1);
INSERT INTO OrderItems (orderid, detail, partid, qty)
    VALUES (6129, 2, 1005, 1);
INSERT INTO OrderItems (orderid, detail, partid, qty)
    VALUES (6129, 3, 1010, 10);


INSERT INTO Orders (orderid, empid, custid, salesdate)
    VALUES (6148, 105, 11, '1995-12-15');
INSERT INTO OrderItems (orderid, detail, partid, qty)
    VALUES (6148, 1, 1004, 1);
INSERT INTO OrderItems (orderid, detail, partid, qty)
    VALUES (6148, 2, 1005, 10);
INSERT INTO OrderItems (orderid, detail, partid, qty)
    VALUES (6148, 3, 1006, 1);
INSERT INTO OrderItems (orderid, detail, partid, qty)
    VALUES (6148, 4, 1008, 1);
INSERT INTO OrderItems (orderid, detail, partid, qty)
    VALUES (6148, 5, 1009, 1);
```

```
INSERT INTO OrderItems (orderid, detail, partid, qty)
    VALUES (6148, 6, 1010, 2);
INSERT INTO OrderItems (orderid, detail, partid, qty)
    VALUES (6148, 7, 1001, 2);
```

```
INSERT INTO Orders (orderid, empid, custid, salesdate)
    VALUES (6155, 103, 12, '1995-12-12');
INSERT INTO OrderItems (orderid, detail, partid, qty)
    VALUES (6155, 1, 1005, 3);
INSERT INTO OrderItems (orderid, detail, partid, qty)
    VALUES (6155, 2, 1009, 3);
INSERT INTO OrderItems (orderid, detail, partid, qty)
    VALUES (6155, 3, 1010, 2);
INSERT INTO OrderItems (orderid, detail, partid, qty)
    VALUES (6155, 4, 1003, 3);
INSERT INTO OrderItems (orderid, detail, partid, qty)
    VALUES (6155, 5, 1004, 3);
```

```
INSERT INTO Orders (orderid, empid, custid, salesdate)
    VALUES (6157, 105, 12, '1995-12-15');
INSERT INTO OrderItems (orderid, detail, partid, qty)
    VALUES (6157, 1, 1008, 3);
INSERT INTO OrderItems (orderid, detail, partid, qty)
    VALUES (6157, 2, 1009, 2);
INSERT INTO OrderItems (orderid, detail, partid, qty)
    VALUES (6157, 3, 1001, 1);
INSERT INTO OrderItems (orderid, detail, partid, qty)
    VALUES (6157, 4, 1005, 3);
```

```
INSERT INTO Orders (orderid, empid, custid, salesdate)
    VALUES (6168, 107, 15, '1995-12-15');
INSERT INTO OrderItems (orderid, detail, partid, qty)
    VALUES (6168, 1, 1007, 1);
INSERT INTO OrderItems (orderid, detail, partid, qty)
    VALUES (6168, 2, 1008, 1);
INSERT INTO OrderItems (orderid, detail, partid, qty)
    VALUES (6168, 3, 1002, 3);
INSERT INTO OrderItems (orderid, detail, partid, qty)
    VALUES (6168, 4, 1003, 3);
INSERT INTO OrderItems (orderid, detail, partid, qty)
    VALUES (6168, 5, 1004, 2);
INSERT INTO OrderItems (orderid, detail, partid, qty)
    VALUES (6168, 6, 1006, 1);
```

```
INSERT INTO Orders (orderid, empid, custid, salesdate)
    VALUES (6170, 109, 15, '1995-11-15');
INSERT INTO OrderItems (orderid, detail, partid, qty)
    VALUES (6170, 1, 1008, 1);
INSERT INTO OrderItems (orderid, detail, partid, qty)
    VALUES (6170, 2, 1009, 1);
```

```
INSERT INTO OrderItems (orderid, detail, partid, qty)
    VALUES (6170, 3, 1010, 5);
INSERT INTO OrderItems (orderid, detail, partid, qty)
    VALUES (6170, 4, 1001, 2);
INSERT INTO OrderItems (orderid, detail, partid, qty)
    VALUES (6170, 5, 1002, 10);
INSERT INTO OrderItems (orderid, detail, partid, qty)
    VALUES (6170, 6, 1003, 1);
INSERT INTO OrderItems (orderid, detail, partid, qty)
    VALUES (6170, 7, 1004, 1);
INSERT INTO OrderItems (orderid, detail, partid, qty)
    VALUES (6170, 8, 1006, 2);
INSERT INTO OrderItems (orderid, detail, partid, qty)
    VALUES (6170, 9, 1007, 1);
```

```
INSERT INTO Orders (orderid, empid, custid, salesdate)
    VALUES (6174, 104, 16, '1995-12-12');
INSERT INTO OrderItems (orderid, detail, partid, qty)
    VALUES (6174, 1, 1009, 1);
INSERT INTO OrderItems (orderid, detail, partid, qty)
    VALUES (6174, 2, 1010, 1);
INSERT INTO OrderItems (orderid, detail, partid, qty)
    VALUES (6174, 3, 1001, 5);
INSERT INTO OrderItems (orderid, detail, partid, qty)
    VALUES (6174, 4, 1002, 5);
INSERT INTO OrderItems (orderid, detail, partid, qty)
    VALUES (6174, 5, 1004, 5);
INSERT INTO OrderItems (orderid, detail, partid, qty)
    VALUES (6174, 6, 1005, 5);
INSERT INTO OrderItems (orderid, detail, partid, qty)
    VALUES (6174, 7, 1006, 2);
INSERT INTO OrderItems (orderid, detail, partid, qty)
    VALUES (6174, 8, 1007, 2);
INSERT INTO OrderItems (orderid, detail, partid, qty)
    VALUES (6174, 9, 1008, 1);
```

```
INSERT INTO Orders (orderid, empid, custid, salesdate)
    VALUES (6175, 105, 16, '1995-12-12');
INSERT INTO OrderItems (orderid, detail, partid, qty)
    VALUES (6175, 1, 1010, 1);
INSERT INTO OrderItems (orderid, detail, partid, qty)
    VALUES (6175, 2, 1001, 1);
INSERT INTO OrderItems (orderid, detail, partid, qty)
    VALUES (6175, 3, 1002, 2);
INSERT INTO OrderItems (orderid, detail, partid, qty)
    VALUES (6175, 4, 1003, 1);
INSERT INTO OrderItems (orderid, detail, partid, qty)
    VALUES (6175, 5, 1004, 10);
INSERT INTO OrderItems (orderid, detail, partid, qty)
    VALUES (6175, 6, 1005, 1);
```

```
INSERT INTO OrderItems (orderid, detail, partid, qty)
     VALUES (6175, 7, 1007, 2);
INSERT INTO OrderItems (orderid, detail, partid, qty)
     VALUES (6175, 8, 1008, 1);
INSERT INTO OrderItems (orderid, detail, partid, qty)
     VALUES (6175, 9, 1009, 1);
```

```
INSERT INTO Orders (orderid, empid, custid, salesdate)
     VALUES (6196, 108, 18, '1995-12-15');
INSERT INTO OrderItems (orderid, detail, partid, qty)
     VALUES (6196, 1, 1001, 1);
INSERT INTO OrderItems (orderid, detail, partid, qty)
     VALUES (6196, 10, 1010, 10);
INSERT INTO OrderItems (orderid, detail, partid, qty)
     VALUES (6196, 2, 1002, 2);
INSERT INTO OrderItems (orderid, detail, partid, qty)
     VALUES (6196, 3, 1003, 1);
INSERT INTO OrderItems (orderid, detail, partid, qty)
     VALUES (6196, 4, 1004, 1);
INSERT INTO OrderItems (orderid, detail, partid, qty)
     VALUES (6196, 5, 1005, 10);
INSERT INTO OrderItems (orderid, detail, partid, qty)
     VALUES (6196, 6, 1006, 10);
INSERT INTO OrderItems (orderid, detail, partid, qty)
     VALUES (6196, 7, 1007, 10);
INSERT INTO OrderItems (orderid, detail, partid, qty)
     VALUES (6196, 8, 1008, 10);
INSERT INTO OrderItems (orderid, detail, partid, qty)
     VALUES (6196, 9, 1009, 10);
```

```
INSERT INTO Orders (orderid, empid, custid, salesdate)
     VALUES (6214, 108, 21, '1995-12-12');
INSERT INTO OrderItems (orderid, detail, partid, qty)
     VALUES (6214, 1, 1001, 10);
INSERT INTO OrderItems (orderid, detail, partid, qty)
     VALUES (6214, 2, 1002, 2);
INSERT INTO OrderItems (orderid, detail, partid, qty)
     VALUES (6214, 3, 1003, 1);
INSERT INTO OrderItems (orderid, detail, partid, qty)
     VALUES (6214, 4, 1004, 1);
INSERT INTO OrderItems (orderid, detail, partid, qty)
     VALUES (6214, 5, 1005, 10);
INSERT INTO OrderItems (orderid, detail, partid, qty)
     VALUES (6214, 6, 1006, 1);
INSERT INTO OrderItems (orderid, detail, partid, qty)
     VALUES (6214, 7, 1008, 2);
INSERT INTO OrderItems (orderid, detail, partid, qty)
     VALUES (6214, 8, 1009, 2);
INSERT INTO OrderItems (orderid, detail, partid, qty)
     VALUES (6214, 9, 1010, 5);
```

```
INSERT INTO Orders (orderid, empid, custid, salesdate)
    VALUES (6215, 109, 21, '1995-12-12');
INSERT INTO OrderItems (orderid, detail, partid, qty)
    VALUES (6215, 1, 1002, 1);
INSERT INTO OrderItems (orderid, detail, partid, qty)
    VALUES (6215, 10, 1001, 2);
INSERT INTO OrderItems (orderid, detail, partid, qty)
    VALUES (6215, 2, 1003, 1);
INSERT INTO OrderItems (orderid, detail, partid, qty)
    VALUES (6215, 3, 1004, 1);
INSERT INTO OrderItems (orderid, detail, partid, qty)
    VALUES (6215, 4, 1005, 1);
INSERT INTO OrderItems (orderid, detail, partid, qty)
    VALUES (6215, 5, 1006, 1);
INSERT INTO OrderItems (orderid, detail, partid, qty)
    VALUES (6215, 6, 1007, 1);
INSERT INTO OrderItems (orderid, detail, partid, qty)
    VALUES (6215, 7, 1008, 1);
INSERT INTO OrderItems (orderid, detail, partid, qty)
    VALUES (6215, 8, 1009, 1);
INSERT INTO OrderItems (orderid, detail, partid, qty)
    VALUES (6215, 9, 1010, 1);
```

```
INSERT INTO Orders (orderid, empid, custid, salesdate)
    VALUES (6216, 101, 22, '1995-12-12');
INSERT INTO OrderItems (orderid, detail, partid, qty)
    VALUES (6216, 1, 1003, 6);
INSERT INTO OrderItems (orderid, detail, partid, qty)
    VALUES (6216, 2, 1004, 6);
INSERT INTO OrderItems (orderid, detail, partid, qty)
    VALUES (6216, 3, 1005, 6);
INSERT INTO OrderItems (orderid, detail, partid, qty)
    VALUES (6216, 4, 1006, 10);
INSERT INTO OrderItems (orderid, detail, partid, qty)
    VALUES (6216, 5, 1007, 10);
INSERT INTO OrderItems (orderid, detail, partid, qty)
    VALUES (6216, 6, 1001, 1);
INSERT INTO OrderItems (orderid, detail, partid, qty)
    VALUES (6216, 7, 1002, 6);
```

```
INSERT INTO Orders (orderid, empid, custid, salesdate)
    VALUES (6217, 102, 22, '1995-12-15');
INSERT INTO OrderItems (orderid, detail, partid, qty)
    VALUES (6217, 1, 1004, 1);
INSERT INTO OrderItems (orderid, detail, partid, qty)
    VALUES (6217, 2, 1005, 2);
INSERT INTO OrderItems (orderid, detail, partid, qty)
    VALUES (6217, 3, 1006, 3);
INSERT INTO OrderItems (orderid, detail, partid, qty)
    VALUES (6217, 4, 1007, 3);
```

```
INSERT INTO OrderItems (orderid, detail, partid, qty)
    VALUES (6217, 5, 1008, 3);
INSERT INTO OrderItems (orderid, detail, partid, qty)
    VALUES (6217, 6, 1009, 3);
INSERT INTO OrderItems (orderid, detail, partid, qty)
    VALUES (6217, 7, 1010, 1);
INSERT INTO OrderItems (orderid, detail, partid, qty)
    VALUES (6217, 8, 1003, 1);
```

```
INSERT INTO Orders (orderid, empid, custid, salesdate)
    VALUES (6218, 103, 22, '1995-12-15');
INSERT INTO OrderItems (orderid, detail, partid, qty)
    VALUES (6218, 1, 1005, 1);
INSERT INTO OrderItems (orderid, detail, partid, qty)
    VALUES (6218, 10, 1004, 1);
INSERT INTO OrderItems (orderid, detail, partid, qty)
    VALUES (6218, 2, 1006, 1);
INSERT INTO OrderItems (orderid, detail, partid, qty)
    VALUES (6218, 3, 1007, 1);
INSERT INTO OrderItems (orderid, detail, partid, qty)
    VALUES (6218, 4, 1008, 1);
INSERT INTO OrderItems (orderid, detail, partid, qty)
    VALUES (6218, 5, 1009, 1);
INSERT INTO OrderItems (orderid, detail, partid, qty)
    VALUES (6218, 6, 1010, 1);
INSERT INTO OrderItems (orderid, detail, partid, qty)
    VALUES (6218, 7, 1001, 1);
INSERT INTO OrderItems (orderid, detail, partid, qty)
    VALUES (6218, 8, 1002, 1);
INSERT INTO OrderItems (orderid, detail, partid, qty)
    VALUES (6218, 9, 1003, 1);
```

```
INSERT INTO Orders (orderid, empid, custid, salesdate)
    VALUES (6219, 104, 22, '1995-10-15');
INSERT INTO OrderItems (orderid, detail, partid, qty)
    VALUES (6219, 1, 1006, 1);
INSERT INTO OrderItems (orderid, detail, partid, qty)
    VALUES (6219, 2, 1007, 1);
INSERT INTO OrderItems (orderid, detail, partid, qty)
    VALUES (6219, 3, 1008, 1);
INSERT INTO OrderItems (orderid, detail, partid, qty)
    VALUES (6219, 4, 1009, 1);
INSERT INTO OrderItems (orderid, detail, partid, qty)
    VALUES (6219, 5, 1010, 1);
INSERT INTO OrderItems (orderid, detail, partid, qty)
    VALUES (6219, 6, 1005, 1);
```

```
INSERT INTO Orders (orderid, empid, custid, salesdate)
    VALUES (6227, 103, 25, '1995-10-15');
INSERT INTO OrderItems (orderid, detail, partid, qty)
    VALUES (6227, 1, 1007, 1);
```

```
INSERT INTO OrderItems (orderid, detail, partid, qty)
    VALUES (6227, 10, 1006, 1);
INSERT INTO OrderItems (orderid, detail, partid, qty)
    (6227, 2, 1008, 1);
INSERT INTO OrderItems (orderid, detail, partid, qty)
    (6227, 3, 1009, 1);
INSERT INTO OrderItems (orderid, detail, partid, qty)
    VALUES (6227, 4, 1010, 1);
INSERT INTO OrderItems (orderid, detail, partid, qty)
    VALUES (6227, 5, 1001, 1);
INSERT INTO OrderItems (orderid, detail, partid, qty)
    VALUES (6227, 6, 1002, 1);
INSERT INTO OrderItems (orderid, detail, partid, qty)
    VALUES (6227, 7, 1003, 1);
INSERT INTO OrderItems (orderid, detail, partid, qty)
    VALUES (6227, 8, 1004, 1);
INSERT INTO OrderItems (orderid, detail, partid, qty)
    VALUES (6227, 9, 1005, 1);
```

```
INSERT INTO Orders (orderid, empid, custid, salesdate)
    VALUES (6228, 104, 25, '1995-10-15');
INSERT INTO OrderItems (orderid, detail, partid, qty)
    VALUES (6228, 1, 1008, 10);
INSERT INTO OrderItems (orderid, detail, partid, qty)
    VALUES (6228, 2, 1009, 1);
INSERT INTO OrderItems (orderid, detail, partid, qty)
    VALUES (6228, 3, 1010, 1);
INSERT INTO OrderItems (orderid, detail, partid, qty)
    VALUES (6228, 4, 1001, 1);
INSERT INTO OrderItems (orderid, detail, partid, qty)
    VALUES (6228, 5, 1002, 1);
INSERT INTO OrderItems (orderid, detail, partid, qty)
    VALUES (6228, 6, 1003, 1);
INSERT INTO OrderItems (orderid, detail, partid, qty)
    VALUES (6228, 7, 1004, 1);
INSERT INTO OrderItems (orderid, detail, partid, qty)
    VALUES (6228, 8, 1007, 10);
```

```
INSERT INTO Orders (orderid, empid, custid, salesdate)
    VALUES (6237, 104, 26, '1995-10-15');
INSERT INTO OrderItems (orderid, detail, partid, qty)
    VALUES (6237, 1, 1009, 1);
INSERT INTO OrderItems (orderid, detail, partid, qty)
    VALUES (6237, 10, 1008, 1);
INSERT INTO OrderItems (orderid, detail, partid, qty)
    VALUES (6237, 2, 1010, 1);
INSERT INTO OrderItems (orderid, detail, partid, qty)
    VALUES (6237, 3, 1001, 3);
INSERT INTO OrderItems (orderid, detail, partid, qty)
    VALUES (6237, 4, 1002, 3);
INSERT INTO OrderItems (orderid, detail, partid, qty)
    VALUES (6237, 5, 1003, 3);
```

```
INSERT INTO OrderItems (orderid, detail, partid, qty)
    VALUES (6237, 6, 1004, 3);
INSERT INTO OrderItems (orderid, detail, partid, qty)
    VALUES (6237, 7, 1005, 3);
INSERT INTO OrderItems (orderid, detail, partid, qty)
    VALUES (6237, 8, 1006, 1);
INSERT INTO OrderItems (orderid, detail, partid, qty)
    VALUES (6237, 9, 1007, 2);
```

```
INSERT INTO Orders (orderid, empid, custid, salesdate)
    VALUES (6238, 105, 26, '1995-10-15');
INSERT INTO OrderItems (orderid, detail, partid, qty)
    VALUES (6238, 1, 1010, 1);
INSERT INTO OrderItems (orderid, detail, partid, qty)
    VALUES (6238, 2, 1001, 1);
INSERT INTO OrderItems (orderid, detail, partid, qty)
    VALUES (6238, 3, 1002, 1);
INSERT INTO OrderItems (orderid, detail, partid, qty)
    VALUES (6238, 4, 1003, 1);
INSERT INTO OrderItems (orderid, detail, partid, qty)
    VALUES (6238, 5, 1004, 1);
INSERT INTO OrderItems (orderid, detail, partid, qty)
    VALUES (6238, 6, 1005, 1);
INSERT INTO OrderItems (orderid, detail, partid, qty)
    VALUES (6238, 7, 1006, 1);
INSERT INTO OrderItems (orderid, detail, partid, qty)
    VALUES (6238, 8, 1009, 1);
```

```
INSERT INTO Orders (orderid, empid, custid, salesdate)
    VALUES (6239, 106, 26, '1995-12-15');
INSERT INTO OrderItems (orderid, detail, partid, qty)
    VALUES (6239, 1, 1001, 1);
INSERT INTO OrderItems (orderid, detail, partid, qty)
    VALUES (6239, 10, 1010, 2);
INSERT INTO OrderItems (orderid, detail, partid, qty)
    VALUES (6239, 2, 1002, 1);
INSERT INTO OrderItems (orderid, detail, partid, qty)
    VALUES (6239, 3, 1003, 1);
INSERT INTO OrderItems (orderid, detail, partid, qty)
    VALUES (6239, 4, 1004, 1);
INSERT INTO OrderItems (orderid, detail, partid, qty)
    VALUES (6239, 5, 1005, 1);
INSERT INTO OrderItems (orderid, detail, partid, qty)
    VALUES (6239, 6, 1006, 1);
INSERT INTO OrderItems (orderid, detail, partid, qty)
    VALUES (6239, 7, 1007, 2);
INSERT INTO OrderItems (orderid, detail, partid, qty)
    VALUES (6239, 8, 1008, 2);
INSERT INTO OrderItems (orderid, detail, partid, qty)
    VALUES (6239, 9, 1009, 2);
```

```
INSERT INTO Orders (orderid, empid, custid, salesdate)
    VALUES (6249, 107, 27, '1995-12-15');
INSERT INTO OrderItems (orderid, detail, partid, qty)
    VALUES (6249, 1, 1001, 1);
INSERT INTO OrderItems (orderid, detail, partid, qty)
    VALUES (6249, 2, 1002, 1);
INSERT INTO OrderItems (orderid, detail, partid, qty)
    VALUES (6249, 3, 1003, 1);
INSERT INTO OrderItems (orderid, detail, partid, qty)
    VALUES (6249, 4, 1004, 1);
INSERT INTO OrderItems (orderid, detail, partid, qty)
    VALUES (6249, 5, 1005, 1);
INSERT INTO OrderItems (orderid, detail, partid, qty)
    VALUES (6249, 6, 1006, 1);
INSERT INTO OrderItems (orderid, detail, partid, qty)
    VALUES (6249, 7, 1007, 1);
INSERT INTO OrderItems (orderid, detail, partid, qty)
    VALUES (6249, 8, 1008, 1);
INSERT INTO OrderItems (orderid, detail, partid, qty)
    VALUES (6249, 9, 1010, 10);
```

```
INSERT INTO Orders (orderid, empid, custid, salesdate)
    VALUES (6251, 109, 27, '1995-11-15');
INSERT INTO OrderItems (orderid, detail, partid, qty)
    VALUES (6251, 1, 1002, 1);
INSERT INTO OrderItems (orderid, detail, partid, qty)
    VALUES (6251, 10, 1001, 1);
INSERT INTO OrderItems (orderid, detail, partid, qty)
    VALUES (6251, 2, 1003, 10);
INSERT INTO OrderItems (orderid, detail, partid, qty)
    VALUES (6251, 3, 1004, 1);
INSERT INTO OrderItems (orderid, detail, partid, qty)
    VALUES (6251, 4, 1005, 1);
INSERT INTO OrderItems (orderid, detail, partid, qty)
    VALUES (6251, 5, 1006, 1);
INSERT INTO OrderItems (orderid, detail, partid, qty)
    VALUES (6251, 6, 1007, 1);
INSERT INTO OrderItems (orderid, detail, partid, qty)
    VALUES (6251, 7, 1008, 1);
INSERT INTO OrderItems (orderid, detail, partid, qty)
    VALUES (6251, 8, 1009, 1);
INSERT INTO OrderItems (orderid, detail, partid, qty)
    VALUES (6251, 9, 1010, 2);
```

```
INSERT INTO Orders (orderid, empid, custid, salesdate)
    VALUES (6252, 101, 28, '1995-11-15');
INSERT INTO OrderItems (orderid, detail, partid, qty)
    VALUES (6252, 1, 1003, 1);
INSERT INTO OrderItems (orderid, detail, partid, qty)
    VALUES (6252, 2, 1004, 1);
```

```
INSERT INTO OrderItems (orderid, detail, partid, qty)
    VALUES (6252, 3, 1005, 1);
INSERT INTO OrderItems (orderid, detail, partid, qty)
    VALUES (6252, 4, 1006, 2);
INSERT INTO OrderItems (orderid, detail, partid, qty)
    VALUES (6252, 5, 1007, 10);
INSERT INTO OrderItems (orderid, detail, partid, qty)
    VALUES (6252, 6, 1008, 1);
INSERT INTO OrderItems (orderid, detail, partid, qty)
    VALUES (6252, 7, 1009, 1);
INSERT INTO OrderItems (orderid, detail, partid, qty)
    VALUES (6252, 8, 1001, 2);
INSERT INTO OrderItems (orderid, detail, partid, qty)
    VALUES (6252, 9, 1002, 10);
```

```
INSERT INTO Orders (orderid, empid, custid, salesdate)
    VALUES (6260, 109, 28, '1995-11-15');
INSERT INTO OrderItems (orderid, detail, partid, qty)
    VALUES (6260, 1, 1004, 1);
INSERT INTO OrderItems (orderid, detail, partid, qty)
    VALUES (6260, 2, 1005, 1);
INSERT INTO OrderItems (orderid, detail, partid, qty)
    VALUES (6260, 3, 1006, 1);
INSERT INTO OrderItems (orderid, detail, partid, qty)
    VALUES (6260, 4, 1007, 1);
INSERT INTO OrderItems (orderid, detail, partid, qty)
    VALUES (6260, 5, 1008, 1);
INSERT INTO OrderItems (orderid, detail, partid, qty)
    VALUES (6260, 6, 1009, 1);
INSERT INTO OrderItems (orderid, detail, partid, qty)
    VALUES (6260, 7, 1010, 1);
INSERT INTO OrderItems (orderid, detail, partid, qty)
    VALUES (6260, 8, 1003, 1);
```

```
INSERT INTO Orders (orderid, empid, custid, salesdate)
    VALUES (6269, 109, 29, '1995-12-15');
INSERT INTO OrderItems (orderid, detail, partid, qty)
    VALUES (6269, 1, 1005, 1);
INSERT INTO OrderItems (orderid, detail, partid, qty)
    VALUES (6269, 10, 1004, 1);
INSERT INTO OrderItems (orderid, detail, partid, qty)
    VALUES (6269, 2, 1006, 1);
INSERT INTO OrderItems (orderid, detail, partid, qty)
    VALUES (6269, 3, 1007, 1);
INSERT INTO OrderItems (orderid, detail, partid, qty)
    VALUES (6269, 4, 1008, 1);
INSERT INTO OrderItems (orderid, detail, partid, qty)
    VALUES (6269, 5, 1009, 1);
INSERT INTO OrderItems (orderid, detail, partid, qty)
    VALUES (6269, 6, 1010, 10);
```

```
INSERT INTO OrderItems (orderid, detail, partid, qty)
    VALUES (6269, 7, 1001, 1);
INSERT INTO OrderItems (orderid, detail, partid, qty)
    VALUES (6269, 8, 1002, 1);
INSERT INTO OrderItems (orderid, detail, partid, qty)
    VALUES (6269, 9, 1003, 1);
```

```
INSERT INTO Orders (orderid, empid, custid, salesdate)
    VALUES (6270, 101, 30, '1995-11-16');
INSERT INTO OrderItems (orderid, detail, partid, qty)
    VALUES (6270, 1, 1006, 1);
INSERT INTO OrderItems (orderid, detail, partid, qty)
    VALUES (6270, 2, 1008, 1);
INSERT INTO OrderItems (orderid, detail, partid, qty)
    VALUES (6270, 3, 1009, 1);
INSERT INTO OrderItems (orderid, detail, partid, qty)
    VALUES (6270, 4, 1010, 1);
INSERT INTO OrderItems (orderid, detail, partid, qty)
    VALUES (6270, 5, 1001, 10);
INSERT INTO OrderItems (orderid, detail, partid, qty)
    VALUES (6270, 6, 1003, 1);
INSERT INTO OrderItems (orderid, detail, partid, qty)
    VALUES (6270, 7, 1004, 1);
INSERT INTO OrderItems (orderid, detail, partid, qty)
    VALUES (6270, 8, 1005, 1);
```

```
INSERT INTO Orders (orderid, empid, custid, salesdate)
    VALUES (6279, 101, 33, '1995-12-15');
INSERT INTO OrderItems (orderid, detail, partid, qty)
    VALUES (6279, 1, 1007, 1);
INSERT INTO OrderItems (orderid, detail, partid, qty)
    VALUES (6279, 2, 1008, 1);
INSERT INTO OrderItems (orderid, detail, partid, qty)
    VALUES (6279, 3, 1009, 1);
INSERT INTO OrderItems (orderid, detail, partid, qty)
    VALUES (6279, 4, 1010, 1);
INSERT INTO OrderItems (orderid, detail, partid, qty)
    VALUES (6279, 5, 1002, 1);
INSERT INTO OrderItems (orderid, detail, partid, qty)
    VALUES (6279, 6, 1003, 1);
INSERT INTO OrderItems (orderid, detail, partid, qty)
    VALUES (6279, 7, 1006, 1);
```

```
INSERT INTO Orders (orderid, empid, custid, salesdate)
    VALUES (6292, 105, 43, '1995-11-12');
INSERT INTO OrderItems (orderid, detail, partid, qty)
    VALUES (6292, 1, 1008, 1);
INSERT INTO OrderItems (orderid, detail, partid, qty)
    VALUES (6292, 10, 1007, 1);
INSERT INTO OrderItems (orderid, detail, partid, qty)
    VALUES (6292, 2, 1009, 10);
```

```
INSERT INTO OrderItems (orderid, detail, partid, qty)
    VALUES (6292, 3, 1010, 1);
INSERT INTO OrderItems (orderid, detail, partid, qty)
    VALUES (6292, 4, 1001, 1);
INSERT INTO OrderItems (orderid, detail, partid, qty)
    VALUES (6292, 5, 1002, 1);
INSERT INTO OrderItems (orderid, detail, partid, qty)
    VALUES (6292, 6, 1003, 1);
INSERT INTO OrderItems (orderid, detail, partid, qty)
    VALUES (6292, 7, 1004, 1);
INSERT INTO OrderItems (orderid, detail, partid, qty)
    VALUES (6292, 8, 1005, 1);
INSERT INTO OrderItems (orderid, detail, partid, qty)
    VALUES (6292, 9, 1006, 1);
```

```
INSERT INTO Orders (orderid, empid, custid, salesdate)
    VALUES (6293, 106, 43, '1995-11-12');
INSERT INTO OrderItems (orderid, detail, partid, qty)
    VALUES (6293, 1, 1009, 1);
INSERT INTO OrderItems (orderid, detail, partid, qty)
    VALUES (6293, 10, 1008, 1);
INSERT INTO OrderItems (orderid, detail, partid, qty)
    VALUES (6293, 2, 1010, 1);
INSERT INTO OrderItems (orderid, detail, partid, qty)
    VALUES (6293, 3, 1001, 1);
INSERT INTO OrderItems (orderid, detail, partid, qty)
    VALUES (6293, 4, 1002, 1);
INSERT INTO OrderItems (orderid, detail, partid, qty)
    VALUES (6293, 5, 1003, 1);
INSERT INTO OrderItems (orderid, detail, partid, qty)
    VALUES (6293, 6, 1004, 1);
INSERT INTO OrderItems (orderid, detail, partid, qty)
    VALUES (6293, 7, 1005, 1);
INSERT INTO OrderItems (orderid, detail, partid, qty)
    VALUES (6293, 8, 1006, 1);
INSERT INTO OrderItems (orderid, detail, partid, qty)
    VALUES (6293, 9, 1007, 1);
```

```
INSERT INTO Orders (orderid, empid, custid, salesdate)
    VALUES (6303, 107, 53, '1995-11-12');
INSERT INTO OrderItems (orderid, detail, partid, qty)
    VALUES (6303, 1, 1010, 1);
INSERT INTO OrderItems (orderid, detail, partid, qty)
    VALUES (6303, 10, 1009, 1);
INSERT INTO OrderItems (orderid, detail, partid, qty)
    VALUES (6303, 2, 1001, 1);
INSERT INTO OrderItems (orderid, detail, partid, qty)
    VALUES (6303, 3, 1002, 1);
INSERT INTO OrderItems (orderid, detail, partid, qty)
    VALUES (6303, 4, 1003, 1);
INSERT INTO OrderItems (orderid, detail, partid, qty)
    VALUES (6303, 5, 1004, 1);
```

```
INSERT INTO OrderItems (orderid, detail, partid, qty)
     VALUES (6303, 6, 1005, 2);
INSERT INTO OrderItems (orderid, detail, partid, qty)
     VALUES (6303, 7, 1006, 1);
INSERT INTO OrderItems (orderid, detail, partid, qty)
     VALUES (6303, 8, 1007, 10);
INSERT INTO OrderItems (orderid, detail, partid, qty)
     VALUES (6303, 9, 1008, 1);
```

```
INSERT INTO Orders (orderid, empid, custid, salesdate)
     VALUES (6304, 108, 53, '1995-12-12');
INSERT INTO OrderItems (orderid, detail, partid, qty)
     VALUES (6304, 1, 1001, 1);
INSERT INTO OrderItems (orderid, detail, partid, qty)
     VALUES (6304, 2, 1002, 1);
INSERT INTO OrderItems (orderid, detail, partid, qty)
     VALUES (6304, 3, 1003, 1);
INSERT INTO OrderItems (orderid, detail, partid, qty)
     VALUES (6304, 4, 1006, 1);
INSERT INTO OrderItems (orderid, detail, partid, qty)
     VALUES (6304, 5, 1007, 1);
INSERT INTO OrderItems (orderid, detail, partid, qty)
     VALUES (6304, 6, 1008, 1);
INSERT INTO OrderItems (orderid, detail, partid, qty)
     VALUES (6304, 7, 1009, 1);
INSERT INTO OrderItems (orderid, detail, partid, qty)
     VALUES (6304, 8, 1010, 1);
```

```
INSERT INTO Orders (orderid, empid, custid, salesdate)
     VALUES (6313, 108, 79, '1995-11-12');
INSERT INTO OrderItems (orderid, detail, partid, qty)
     VALUES (6313, 1, 1001, 1);
INSERT INTO OrderItems (orderid, detail, partid, qty)
     VALUES (6313, 2, 1002, 1);
INSERT INTO OrderItems (orderid, detail, partid, qty)
     VALUES (6313, 3, 1003, 1);
INSERT INTO OrderItems (orderid, detail, partid, qty)
     VALUES (6313, 4, 1007, 1);
INSERT INTO OrderItems (orderid, detail, partid, qty)
     VALUES (6313, 5, 1008, 1);
INSERT INTO OrderItems (orderid, detail, partid, qty)
     VALUES (6313, 6, 1009, 1);
INSERT INTO OrderItems (orderid, detail, partid, qty)
     VALUES (6313, 7, 1010, 2);
```

```
INSERT INTO Orders (orderid, empid, custid, salesdate)
     VALUES (6314, 109, 79, '1995-12-12');
INSERT INTO OrderItems (orderid, detail, partid, qty)
     VALUES (6314, 1, 1002, 2);
```

```
INSERT INTO OrderItems (orderid, detail, partid, qty)
    VALUES (6314, 2, 1003, 2);
INSERT INTO OrderItems (orderid, detail, partid, qty)
    VALUES (6314, 3, 1009, 2);
INSERT INTO OrderItems (orderid, detail, partid, qty)
    VALUES (6314, 4, 1010, 2);
```

Chapter 6 Examples

In Chapter 6 we discussed the command for querying your SQL system, the **SELECT** statement. Several tables with corresponding data were used to illustrate this important command, and this where we show you how to create them.

The Foobar Table

Here we will be showing you how to create the **Foobar** table used to demonstrate the inner workings of the command. Everything you need for this example is provided on the enclosed disk, but for the sake of complementing the earlier chapter we will show you how to do it here.

> Remember that all tables and data listed in the Appendices are provided on the disk in the back of the book.

Creating the Table

Here is the general code to create the table structure:

```
CREATE TABLE Foobar
(a INTEGER NOT NULL,
 b INTEGER NOT NULL,
 c INTEGER);
```

The first statement creates the columns, then the statements insert the necessary data into the table. You need to avoid having a **NOT NULL** clause for column **c** because for this example you actually need to place a **NULL** value in it.

Inserting the Data

The following statements insert the data:

```
INSERT INTO Foobar VALUES (1,23,10);
INSERT INTO Foobar VALUES (1,23,10);
INSERT INTO Foobar VALUES (2,17,11);
INSERT INTO Foobar VALUES (3,32,12);
INSERT INTO Foobar VALUES (4,41,NULL);
```

The Foo Table

There are a couple of other tables in Chapter 6, the first is Foo:

```
CREATE TABLE Foo
(a INTEGER NOT NULL,
 x INTEGER);
```

The data can be inserted as follows:

```
INSERT INTO Foo (a,x) VALUES (1,10);
INSERT INTO Foo (a,x) VALUES (2,20);
INSERT INTO Foo (a,x) VALUES (3,30);
```

The Bar Table

The next table is Bar which can be created as followed:

```
CREATE TABLE Bar
(x INTEGER NOT NULL,
 b CHAR);
```

The data required for this table is initialized with:

```
INSERT INTO Bar (x,b) VALUES (10,'A');
INSERT INTO Bar (x,b) VALUES (20,'B');
INSERT INTO Bar (x,b) VALUES (40,'C');
```

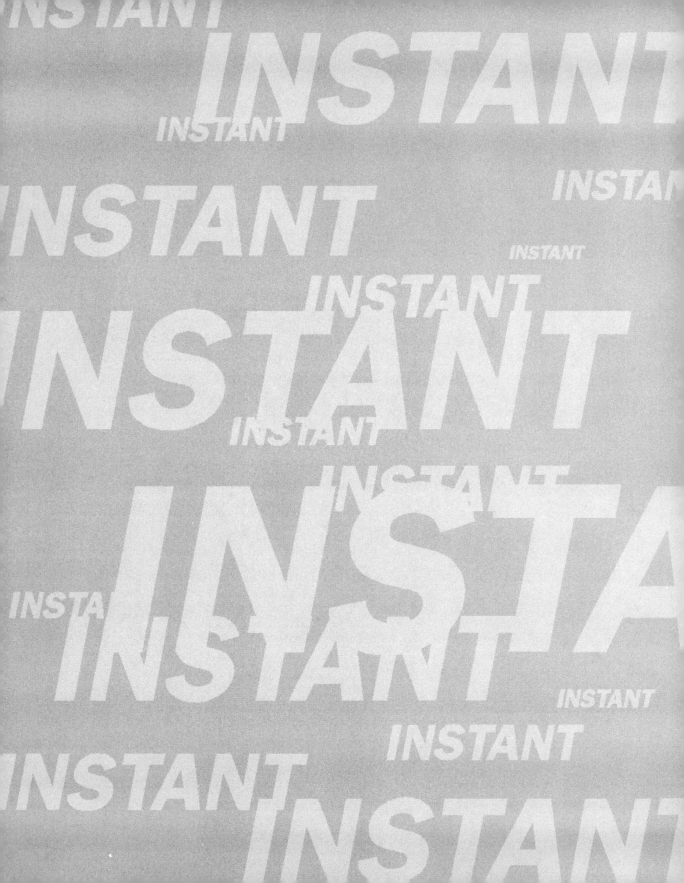

Appendix

Security and Control in Your Database

Privileges and Security

This appendix briefly considers the main aspects of the Data Control Language (DCL) in SQL. The function of DCL is to maintain security in a multi-user environment. We will be looking at the main commands that the DBA will need to know in the DCL. The security model that SQL uses is based on three major concepts:

 users

 schema objects

 privileges

We will look at each of these in turn. There are also two operations that SQL uses to maintain security:

 GRANT

 REVOKE

Frankly, SQL is weak where security is concerned. The conforming entry SQL-92, which effectively is SQL-89 with a few corrections, doesn't even have to have a **REVOKE** statement at all.

More serious security systems have several levels of security (confidential, secret, top secret and so forth), which are often arranged in rings. Other security systems have the ability to deny data access to particular users; in SQL, one grantor can pass privileges that another grantor wishes to deny. Some secure systems will even lie to the user based on his or her status, providing a 'cover story' for them.

SQL maintains security rules in a subset of the Information Schema tables and views in much the same way that the Information Schema tables maintain a description of the database. While SQL-92 defines a standard set of Information Schema tables, the truth is that each product is different. Since the **GRANT** and **REVOKE** statements are the only way to change these tables, the user doesn't really have to worry about the practical differences.

The GRANT Statement in Watcom SQL

Watcom's **GRANT** statement can be used to create a new user ID and to grant querying, creating and updating privileges to a user. We'll start by showing you can create to a new user.

Users

The mapping of names and passwords, or authorization identifiers as they are called in SQL, to operating system users is implementation dependent. This can be done as part of the **GRANT CONNECT TO** Watcom SQL statement and as part of the **CONNECT** statement in other SQLs, or it can be done separately and may or may not be linked to the operating system.

However we'll look at what happens in Watcom SQL. To specify a new user you need to **GRANT CONNECT TO** the new user name and identify them with a unique password. Typically, the DBA is the only one who can create new accounts. A normal query would run:

```
GRANT CONNECT TO Joe IDENTIFIED BY A1B2C3;
```

Granting Privileges

Once the new user id has been created, the next stage is to give the user certain privileges. This is done with the **GRANT** statement:

```
GRANT <privileges> ON <object name> TO { PUBLIC | <user
identifier> } [WITH GRANT OPTION]

<privileges> ::= ALL PRIVILEGES | <action list>

<action list> ::= <action> [{ , <action> }...]

<action> ::= SELECT | DELETE | INSERT | UPDATE | REFERENCES |
USAGE
```

In terms of the three concepts discussed earlier, the **GRANT** clause deals with the privileges, while the **ON** clause deals with the schema objects, and the **TO** clause deals with the users.

Grantors and Grantees

Users are subdivided into grantors and grantees. The grantor isn't explicitly shown in the statement, but it's assumed that they're the one issuing the command.

The grantor has to hold the privilege that they grant and must have a **WITH GRANT OPTION** to pass it to another user. If the grantor also passes those privileges via the **WITH GRANT OPTION** then the grantee can become a grantor of those same privileges.

In short this is a chain of authority, but the chain has to start somewhere. SQL has a fictional grantor of all things named **_SYSTEM** (note the single underscore) in the database at its creation, who has the rights to everything. The users can access the schema definition tables and the DBA can set up the initial configuration only because they have these privileges from **_SYSTEM**. When a user creates a new schema object, the fiction is that all of their privileges as the owner of the object come from **_SYSTEM**. In practice the DBA will gain control of the **_SYSTEM** password immediately and play this role.

If a grantor to tries to give the same privileges to a grantee twice then the duplicate privilege descriptors are redundant and won't appear in the Information Schema tables.

It is possible for two or more grantors to try and give the same privileges to the same grantee. If two privilege descriptors are identical except that one indicates that the privilege is grantable and the other indicates that the privilege isn't grantable then both privilege descriptors are set to indicate that the privilege is grantable. This is a point where SQL's security is particularly weak; other people can sabotage your attempts to restrict access to data and you have to get the other grantors to explicitly **REVOKE** privileges.

The PUBLIC Grantee

The fictional grantee **PUBLIC** means that all users, present and future, have privileges listed. **PUBLIC** is important because the DCL starts off by giving **PUBLIC** certain **USAGE** privileges to schema information tables, domains, character sets, collations, and translations. It then **SELECT**s privileges for the Information Schema views to **PUBLIC WITH GRANT OPTION** so they can be queried by any user, so that the **SELECT** privilege can be further granted on views that reference the Information Schema views. (No further privilege is granted on them, so they can only be updated by the **_SYSTEM** and *not* by users.)

Schema Objects

The schema objects that the DCL controls can be base tables, views, columns, domains, character sets, collations, and translations. The last four objects are new to SQL-92 and we won't be worrying about them. Obviously they've existed implicitly in SQL before now - it would be impossible to store data without character sets or to do a sort without a collation sequence, but SQL-92 has made them explicit for internationalization and ISO conformance.

Privileges

If a user tries to do something for which he or she doesn't have privileges then the system issues a warning - 'privilege not granted' or something similar and the transaction fails. If there aren't any security problems then the statement is passed along to the query processor where it will succeed or fail on its own merits.

Actions

The privileges action list tells the grantee what the grantor will let them do with the table or the updatable view. The possible actions are:

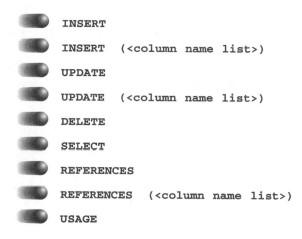

INSERT

INSERT (<column name list>)

UPDATE

UPDATE (<column name list>)

DELETE

SELECT

REFERENCES

REFERENCES (<column name list>)

USAGE

ALL PRIVILEGES is a shorthand which explains itself.

The actions **INSERT, UPDATE, DELETE, SELECT,** or **REFERENCES** are called table privilege descriptors. The actions **SELECT (<column name list>), INSERT (<column name list>), UPDATE (<column name list>),** and **REFERENCES (<column name list>)** are called column privilege descriptors. Most implementations today only have table privilege descriptors and they achieve the column privilege descriptors effect by using views.

The **INSERT, UPDATE, DELETE** and **SELECT** actions allow the grantee to use those statements on that schema object. When these privilege descriptors are specified without a column name, privilege descriptors are also automatically created for each column in the table or view.

The **USAGE** privilege allows the grantee to use a character set or other 'meta data' schema objects when constructing new schema objects. This action was defined in SQL-92 and isn't yet common place.

There is a difference between **USAGE** and **REFERENCES**. The **REFERENCES** privilege is the ability to refer to another table, but without being able to use **INSERT**, **UPDATE**, **DELETE** or **SELECT** on it. The schema object might be hidden in the layers of views or used in constraints on the table upon which we do have privileges. For example, imagine that a table of **Orders** has constraints based on the **Inventory** table - we might need to use a part number from **Inventory** in a query, but otherwise you never see the **Inventory** table. Again, this action was defined in SQL-92 and isn't yet common in most products.

Example Usage of the GRANT Statement

Now for an example of how to grant privileges. If we wished to give the user **Joe**, the ability to query the **Salespersons** table, but nothing else, then we would use the following statement:

```
GRANT SELECT
ON Salespersons
TO Joe;
```

The user **Joe**, once he'd logged would be able to query the **Salespersons** table. However, for the user **Joe**, it isn't quite as straightforward as simply typing in the query, as you might expect:

```
SELECT  *  FROM  Salespersons;
```

The user **Joe** has to specify who owns the table also, which in this case is DBA. This creates a secondary problem in Watcom SQL as DBA is a reserved keyword, and therefore has to be encased in quotation marks. To actually query the Salespersons table, **Joe** has to use the following query:

```
SELECT  *  FROM  "DBA".Salespersons;
```

If you wished to pass on all privileges to **Joe** on the **Inventory** table and allow him to pass on these privileges to other users, then the following statement would apply:

```
GRANT ALL PRIVILEGES
ON Inventory
TO Joe
WITH GRANT OPTION;
```

Joe would then in turn be able to pass on those privileges to other users, providing that the other users had been created by the **GRANT CONNECT TO** statement.

The REVOKE Statement

It is also possible to remove these privileges just as easily. This statement destroys privileges. The syntax of the **REVOKE** command is:

REVOKE [GRANT OPTION FOR] <privileges> ON <object name> FROM PUBLIC | <grantee> [{, <grantee> }...] { CASCADE | RESTRICT }

The **REVOKE** statement has to be done by the grantor who granted the privileges to the grantee. Once the grantee has lost those privileges, the effect can cascade down to the users to whom the grantee granted privileges. If two different grantors have given the same privileges to a grantee, then only one set of privileges is revoked. If a schema object is completely cut off from any grantor, so that nobody can get privileges on it, then the object is supposed to be dropped from the schema. Likewise, if an object is dropped, then all privileges granted on it are automatically revoked.

GRANT OPTION FOR removes the ability to grant that privilege, but not the privilege itself.

INSERT, **UPDATE**, **DELETE**, **SELECT** and **REFERENCES** are equivalent to specifying both the table privilege and **UPDATE (<privilege column list>)** options.

The **RESTRICT** clause says that if this privilege would also remove the ability to access a schema object from another user, then give a warning message and not to perform the revocation. The **CASCADE** clause says revoke the privileges for the named users and keep following the chain until you've cleared out all derived privileges.

The SQL-92 standard requires that one of these options be used, but most implementations don't have them yet. Right now, each SQL implementation has a default behavior which might be a **CASCADE**, a **RESTRICT** or something else. You will also see other special fictional users in Sybase, groups of privileges and objects put together as **ROLE**s in Oracle 7.0 and so forth.

Example Usage of the REVOKE Statement

If we wished to reverse the privileges we had granted earlier for the user **Joe**, then we use the following statements. The first is to revoke the **SELECT** privilege:

```
REVOKE SELECT ON Salespersons FROM Joe;
```

The second statement revokes all privileges, on the **Inventory** table:

```
REVOKE ALL PRIVILEGES ON Inventory FROM Joe;
```

Summary

We have looked very briefly at the main concepts of the DCL. It revolves around 3 main concepts: users, schema objects and privileges. As SQL is weak on security, a lot of the emphasis in keeping tight security must revolve around good security practices. This means giving **GRANT OPTIONS** only to those who can be trusted not to freely dish them out. We've looked at the main commands used in assigning and revoking privileges, but basically it's up to the administrators of the system to ensure that security isn't violated or compromised.

Standards and Quasi-standards Groups Involved with SQL

In the USA they are as follows:

American National Standards Institute
X3H2 Database Standards Committee
11 West 42nd Street
New York, NY 10035
ph: (212) 642-4900; fx: (212) 302-1286

Open Systems Foundation
11 Cambridge Center
Cambridge, MA 02142
ph: (617) 621-8763

SQL Access Group
4699 Old Ironsides Drive #450
Santa Clara, CA 95054
ph: (408) 988-3545; fx: (408) 988-6712

Transaction Processing Council
Shanley Public Relations
777 North First Street #600
San Jose, CA 95112

X/Open Foundation
c/o Blanc & Otis Public Relations
100 Spear Street #425
San Francisco, CA 94105
Att: Steven Curry
ph: (415) 546-8080; ph: (415) 546-8090

National Technical Information Service
5285 Port Royal Road
Springfield, VA 22161
ph: (703) 487-4650

Global Engineering Inc.
2805 McGaw Avenue
Irvine, CA   92714
ph: (800) 854-7179

National Institute for Standards & Technology
Technology A-266
Gaithersberg, MD 20899

In the UK:

British Standards Institution
389 Chiswick High Road
London W4 4AL
ph: (0181)-996-9000 fx: (0181)-996-7001

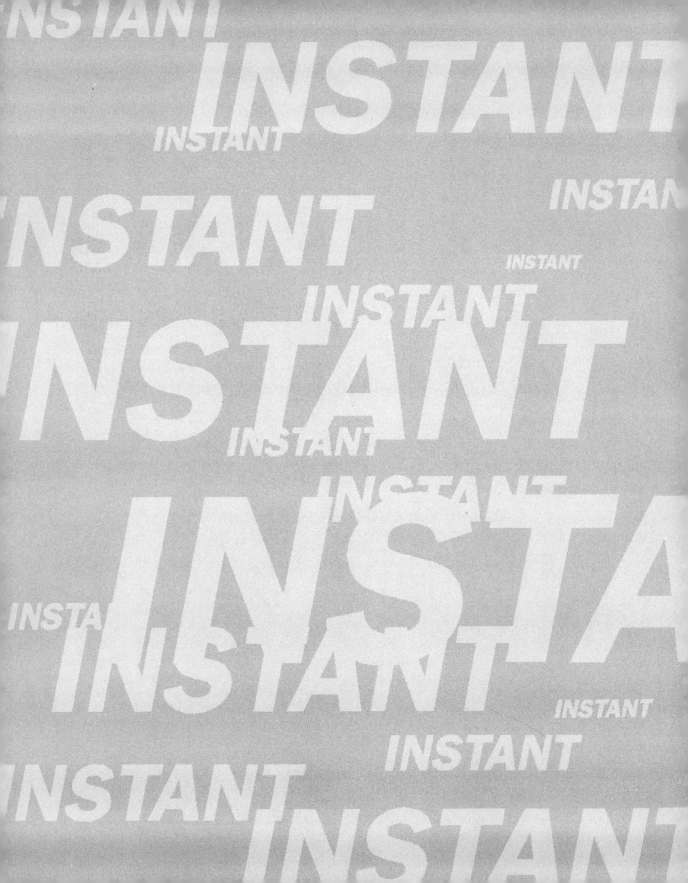

Table of Legal Conversions

Over the page is a table of the valid combinations of source and target data types in SQL-92. This is often referred to as the 'table of legal conversions'.

The key is as follows:

 Y means that the combination is syntactically valid without restriction.

 M indicates that the combination is valid, subject to other syntax rules.

 N indicates that the combination isn't valid.

<value expr> \ <cast target>	Exact Num	Approx Num	Variable Length Char	Fixed Length Char	Variable Length Bit String	Fixed Length Bit String	Date	Time	Time Stamp	Year Month Interval	Day Time Interval
Exact Numeric	Y	Y	Y	Y	N	N	N	N	N	M	M
Approximate Numeric	Y	Y	Y	Y	N	N	N	N	N	N	N
Character (Fixed or Variable)	Y	Y	M	M	Y	Y	Y	Y	Y	Y	Y
Bit String (Fixed or Variable)	N	N	Y	Y	Y	Y	N	N	N	N	N
Date	N	N	Y	Y	N	N	Y	N	Y	N	N
Time	N	N	Y	Y	N	N	N	Y	Y	N	N
TimeStamp	N	N	Y	Y	N	N	Y	Y	Y	N	N
Year Month Interval	M	N	Y	Y	N	N	N	N	N	Y	N
Day Time Interval	M	N	Y	Y	N	N	N	N	N	N	Y

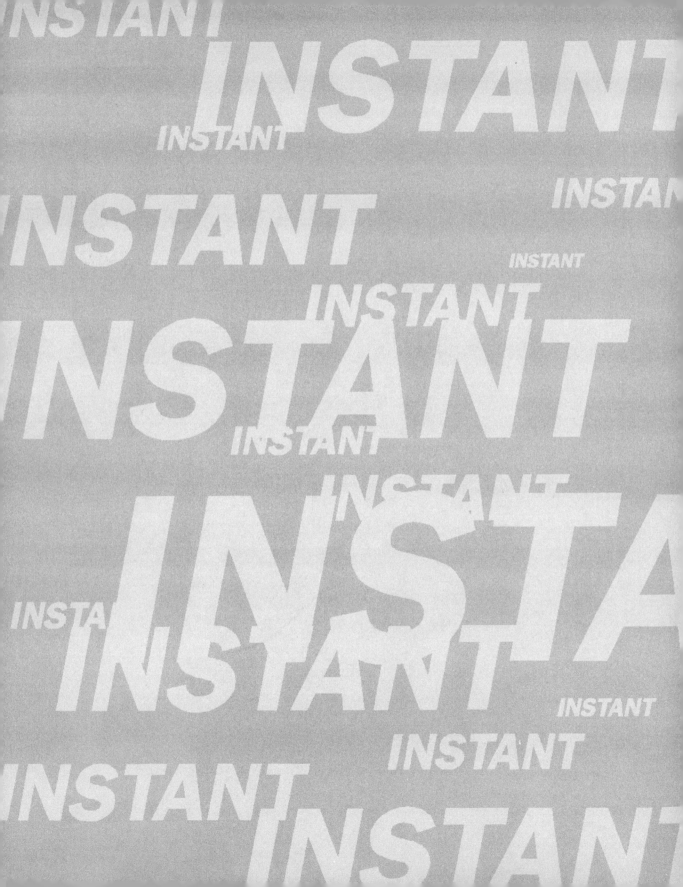

INSTANT
SQL

Index

syntax 63

privileges

GRANT in Watcom SQL

See Appendix C

procedural versus declarative languages
12

READ and WRITE statements 14

projection 160

PUBLIC

privileges in DCL

See Appendix C

Q

quantified predicates

ALL 239, 242 - 243

and subqueries 239

ANY 239 - 242

queries 158 - 178

BETWEEN 174 - 176

hints on how to write 299 - 308

the HAVING clause 303

table names and FROM 301

joining tables 302

test and repair 307

IN 172 - 173

IS NULL 176

IS TRUE 176

IS FALSE 176

IS UNKNOWN 176

LIKE 170 - 171

NULLs and empty strings 172

ORDER BY 177 - 178

WHERE 166 - 169

query insertion 146

R

radix

precision P 55

references 64

referential integrity 66, 113

syntax 65

referential actions 134

SQL-89 vs SQL-92 134

table events 134

referential integrity 27, 113, 126

constraints 27

FOREIGN KEY 130

PRIMARY KEY 130

UNIQUE 128

drop behavior 132

keys 113

referential actions 134

relational databases

SQL 15

RESTRICT 132

restriction 166

result table 45

REVERSE() function 90

REVOKE

security in a multi-user environment

See Appendix C

rolling back 26

ROUND() function 86

row

definition 21

spreadsheet analogy 22

union compatibility 49

row comparisons 107 - 109

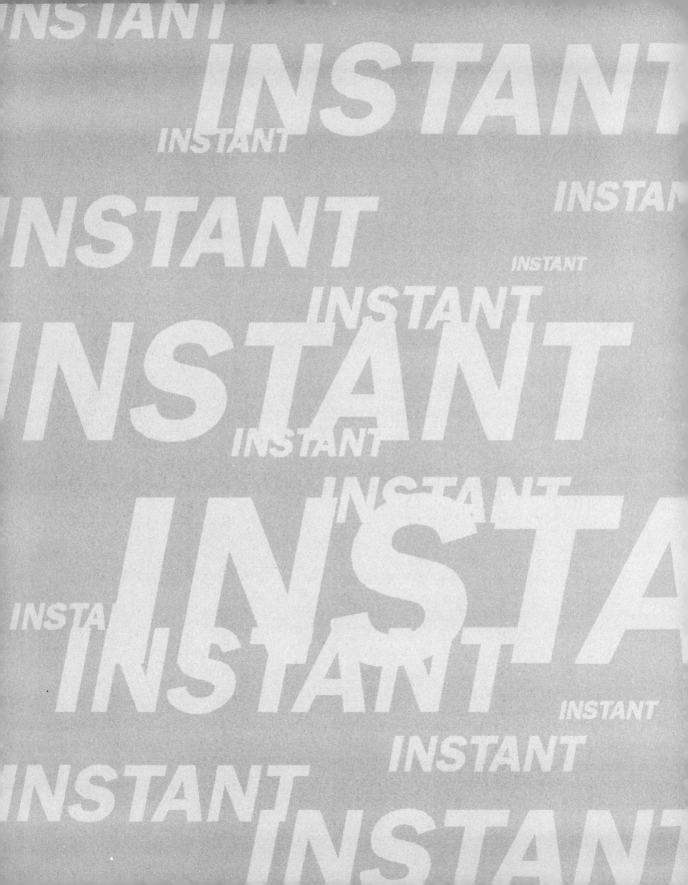

INSTANT DELPHI PROGRAMMING

This book provides a fast guide to the essentials of Borland's new development tool. Borland have put together fast executable Pascal code with a truly intuitive event-driven environment. The result is a powerful, yet easy to use program, and this book caters for programmers who want to master its fundamental advantages. Taking developers through the strengths of the innovative Object Pascal code, its access to a database engine, as well as advanced features such as using VBX controls, this book will help programmers from many different backgrounds move successfully into Borland's strong new package.

AUTHOR: Dave Jewell   ISBN: 1-874416-57-5   PRICE: $24.95 C$34.95 £22.99

THE REVOLUTIONARY GUIDE TO ACCESS - PROFESSIONAL DEVELOPER'S EDITION

Microsoft Access isn't restricted to a single user system. According to the market, Client/Server is the place to be, and Access has many powerful assets to lever you into the new database age. Written for developers, the book covers all the advanced features and explains the more interesting features that other books gloss over. By the end, the reader will be able to use Access to develop applications which integrate seamlessly with other office packages. Written by a leading commercial developer of Access based solutions, this book comes complete with a CD-ROM containing all source code, shareware tools and a hypertext version of the book.

AUTHOR: Stephen Wynkoop ISBN: 1-874416-39-7 PRICE: $44.95 C$62.95 £41.99

THE REVOLUTIONARY GUIDE TO WIN 32 PROGRAMMING WITH VISUAL C++

This book is the definitive guide to programming the 32 bit editions of Windows with Visual C++ 2.1. Comprehensive coverage of the MFC 3.1 provides the programmer with all the tools required to take advantage of the 32bit architectures of Win32s, Windows NT 3.51 and the forthcoming Windows'95 (aka Chicago). Written by one of the leading members of Microsoft's Visual C++ team, it is a must for Visual C++ developers. The book assumes that the reader is familiar with the concepts of object-oriented programming and comes complete with a CD-ROM containing all source code, a full hypertext version of the book and various third party tools and samples.

AUTHOR: Mike Blaszczak   ISBN: 1-874416-47-8   PRICE: $44.95 C$62.95 £41.99

Watcom SQL 4.0 Runtime Version

Throughout this book, we have referenced an example database. The example database was created exclusively on Watcom SQL 4.0 and the underlying base table structures are provided with the runtime version of Watcom SQL 4.0. With the runtime version you can run all of the examples provided in Chapters 5 to 11, unless expressly stated within the text.

The runtime version doesn't allow **ALTER**, **CALL**, **COMMENT**, **CREATE**, **DROP**, user-defined trigger commands or stored procedures to be performed. **GRANT** and **REVOKE** allow you to add new users and change passwords, but the runtime database engine prevents a user from changing the permissions on the tables. In addition, to simplify database administration, the runtime system has an integrated transaction log.

The Watcom SQL Server product has networking features which are beyond the scope of the stand-alone version of Watcom SQL. As a result, features such as **DBWATCH, DBCLIENW** and **DBSERVEW** are only available on the Watcom SQL Server product line and aren't included in Watcom SQL or Watcom SQL runtime.

Once you have used runtime version you may decide that you wish to upgrade to the full version of the Watcom SQL engine. You can contact Watcom at the following addresses:

In the USA:	Internationally:	In the UK:
Watcom, Inc. 561 Virginia Road, Concord, MA 01742	Watcom International Corp. 415 Phillip Street, Waterloo, Ontario, Canada N2L 3X2	Powersoft UK. Windsor Court, Kingsmead Business Centre, High Wycombe, Bucks, HP11 1JU
Ph: 1800 395 3525 Fx:	519 886 3700 519 747 4971	0800 444455

Your Free SQL Software

Wrox Press in conjunction with Watcom International Corporation have brought you a convenient way to test your SQL-92 code contained within the book. As stated in the introduction, this is not a complete version of the Watcom SQL 4.0 product, however certain license restrictions must be adhered to. You are obliged to read and conform to the following agreement.

WIN FREE BOOKS

TELL US WHAT YOU THINK!

Complete and return the bounce back card and you will:

- Help us create the books you want.
- Receive an update on all Wrox titles.
- Enter the draw for 5 Wrox titles of your choice.

FILL THIS OUT to enter the draw for free Wrox titles

Name _____

Address _____

_____

_____

_____ Postcode/Zip _____

Occupation _____

How did you hear about this book?

☐ Book review (name) _____

☐ Advertisement (name) _____

☐ Recommendation

☐ Catalogue

☐ Other _____

Where did you buy this book?

☐ Bookstore (name) _____

☐ Computer Store (name) _____

☐ Mail Order

☐ Other _____

I would be interested in receiving information about Wrox Press titles by email in future. My email/Internet address is:

_____

What influenced you in the purchase of this book?

☐ Cover Design

☐ Contents

☐ Other (please specify) _____

How did you rate the overall contents of this book?

☐ Excellent ☐ Good

☐ Average ☐ Poor

What did you find most useful about this book? _____

What did you find least useful about this book? _____

Please add any additional comments. _____

What other subjects will you buy a computer book on soon? _____

What is the best computer book you have used this year? _____

Note: This information will only be used to keep you updated about new Wrox Press titles and will not be used for any other purpose or passed to any other third party.

Please do not put me on your mailing list ☐

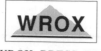

WROX

WROX PRESS INC.

Wrox writes books for you. Any suggestions, or ideas about how you want information given in your ideal book will be studied by our team. Your comments are always valued at WROX.

Free phone in USA 800 814 4527
Fax (312) 465 4063

Compuserve 100063,2152.
UK Tel. (44121) 706 6826 Fax (44121) 706 2967

Computer Book Publishers

NB. If you post the bounce back card below in the UK, please send it to:
Wrox Press Ltd. Unit 16, Sapcote Industrial Estate, 20 James Road, Birmingham, B11 2BA

NO POSTAGE
NECESSARY
IF MAILED
IN THE
UNITED STATES

BUSINESS REPLY MAIL
FIRST CLASS MAIL   PERMIT#64   LA VERGNE, TN

POSTAGE WILL BE PAID BY ADDRESSEE

WROX PRESS
2710 WEST TOUHY AVE
CHICAGO IL 60645-9911